JEAN RHYS

GARLAND REFERENCE LIBRARY
OF THE HUMANITIES
(VOL. 435)

JEAN RHYS
A Descriptive and Annotated
Bibliography of Works and Criticism

Elgin W. Mellown

GARLAND PUBLISHING, INC. • NEW YORK & LONDON
1984

Library of Congress Cataloging in Publication Data

Mellown, Elgin W.
Jean Rhys : a descriptive and annotated bibliography
of works and criticism.

(Garland reference library of the humanities ;
v. 435)
Includes index.
1. Rhys, Jean—Bibliography. I. Title. II. Series.
Z8741.7.M44 1984 [PR6035.H96] 016.823′912 83-48267
ISBN 0-8240-9079-9 (alk. paper)

Printed on acid-free, 250-year-life paper
Manufactured in the United States of America

CONTENTS

INTRODUCTION

Biographical Sketch of Jean Rhys

For many years the accounts of the life of Jean Rhys, like her own novels, presented a mixture of fact and fiction. Most authorities gave her date of birth as 24 August 1894, while her actual name was said to have been Jean Williams or Ella Gwen Rhys Williams. But the posthumous autobiography *Smile Please* (1979) gives a Foreword by her editor and long-time friend Diana Athill with biographical details that have more claim to accuracy than those in other sources.

Jean Rhys was born in 1890 in Roseau, Dominica, in the West Indies. She was named Ella Gwendolen Rees Williams and was the daughter of Minna Lockhart Williams, whose originally Scottish family dated back to the slave-owning days of Dominica, and of William Rees Williams, a doctor who had trained in London after leaving his Welsh home (his father, another William Rees Williams, was rector of the parish of Gyfylliog, Denbighshire, from 1874 to 1900). As a youth he had run away from home to become a sailor, had trained as a doctor and served as a ship's doctor, and had taken a government post in Dominica. Here he fell ill and was nursed back to health by his future wife. There were five children of this union—two older brothers, an older sister who went to live with a maternal aunt, Ella Gwendolen, and a younger sister. As a young girl Jean Rhys attended the Convent School run by the local order of Roman Catholic nuns in which the white girls were very much in the minority.

The family was visited by their English relatives, and in 1907 Dr. Williams' sister, Clarice Rees Williams, took her niece back to England and enrolled her in the Perse School, Cambridge. After one term she decided that she wanted a theatrical career, and the seventeen-year-old girl went to London to study at Beerbohm

Tree's recently founded school of dramatic art (in 1920 it became the Royal Academy of Dramatic Art). But in 1908 Dr. Williams died and there was no money for his daughter's support. She went to a theatrical agency and got a job as a chorus girl in a touring company.

For the period 1908–1919 there is very little published information about Jean Rhys. Certain facts are known: she worked as a chorus girl in touring companies; she had a love affair with an older man who continued to support her long after the affair was over; she had an illegal abortion; she worked as a model for various painters and as an extra in the films; and during the First World War she was employed in a railway canteen in London. During this period she began calling herself by different names—at one point she used the name "Gray" as a surname. While the facts of Jean Rhys's life in this period cannot be absolutely established, one thing is clear: a young girl from a respectable colonial family came to England and lived a life that brought her into the demi-mondaine society of pre-War England.

In late 1917 the future novelist met Jean Langlet. A Dutchman with French connections, he had worked in some capacity with the Foreign Office while holding a diplomatic passport. He proposed, and in 1919 she went to Holland where they were married. Again it is difficult to ascertain the facts, for the newly married couple lived in several different European countries and in widely differing circumstances—at one moment they were in a luxury hotel, and the next, literally on the streets. It is definite, however, that in 1920 Mme Langlet gave birth to a son, who was named William and who died shortly after birth, and in 1922, to a daughter, Maryvonne, who is her only surviving child (Maryvonne Langlet was raised by her father's family in Holland, visiting her mother in England from time to time during her childhood; she stayed in Holland during the Second World War and was active in the Resistance, actually being imprisoned by the Gestapo for a few weeks—her father was sent to a concentration camp but survived and wrote several books after the war; in 1945 she married Job Moermann, one of her fellow Underground fighters, and is the mother of a daughter, Ellen Ruth). In 1923 the Langlets found themselves in Paris where Langlet was arrested by the French authorities and spent some time in prison for offenses against currency regulations. While he was in prison his wife tried to support herself in various jobs, and she met Ford Madox Ford, the expatriate English writer and editor, and his common-law wife, Stella Bowen, the Australian painter. Again one is hard-pressed to separate fact from fiction, for the resulting relationship between these three is the basis for the novels *Quartet* and *After Leaving Mr Mackenzie* and colors many of the other novels and stories. The liaison with Ford lasted for several years, during which time Langlet was extradited to Holland and ceased to have much direct contact with his wife; but it ended in 1926 or 1927, when Ford fell in love with another woman. For the next several years Jean Rhys (for she had so named herself in 1927 with the publication of her first book) lived in London and Paris, visiting her daughter in Holland from time to time. She had met Leslie Tilden Smith in London where he was a publisher's reader for Hamish Hamilton, and in 1932 after her marriage with Langlet was legally ended, she married him. In the 1930s, Smith inherited a considerable sum of money and they made a voyage to Dominica, the only time that Rhys returned to her homeland. During the war years they moved about a great deal, and in 1945 Smith died very suddenly of a heart attack. Jean Rhys stayed for a time with her brother, Col. William Rees Williams, in Devon, with whom she had had little contact since her childhood. Some two years later she married Smith's cousin, George V. Max Hamer; they lived in London where Hamer worked in a business office. In late 1949 he was charged with illegal financial dealings, and after serving six months in prison, he and his wife moved to Cornwall and then to Devonshire. It was here in the provincial village of Cheriton FitzPaine that she continued to live after Hamer's death, with periodic visits to London during the winter months, until her death on 14 May 1979, following a fall in which she broke her hip. Her body was cremated in Exeter.

The Writings of Jean Rhys

In 1927 Jean Rhys published her first book, *The Left Bank and Other Stories* in both London and New York. It included a long preface by Ford Madox Ford, who had been instrumental in getting it published, and a total of twenty-two pieces ranging from only a page or so to full-length stories. While most of them reflected the author's life in post-war Europe and particularly in Paris, several were based on her childhood in the Caribbean. Following this publication she translated the novel *Perversité* by Francis Carco. Ford had arranged for her to make this translation and indeed was so involved in the negotiations for its publication in the United States (Carco was another of his literary friends) that his name was given as that of translator when it was published in Chicago in 1928 as *Perversity*. At the same time Ford arranged for her to work as a "ghost-writer" for Mme Huenot, the mother of Natoma Valentino, Rudolph Valentino's wife. The break-up with Ford occasioned the writing of *Quartet* (entitled *Postures* by the publisher when it was published in London in 1928) in which the story of two couples easily identified as the Langlets and the Fords is told. The same story is used—in a less direct manner—by Ford in his novel *When the Wicked Man* (New York: 1931) in which Rhys is given the name Lola Porter, and by Jean Langlet writing under his pen-name of Édouard de Nève, in *Barred* (London: 1932).

Gradually Rhys's life became centered in London with Leslie Tilden Smith, although she continued to make periodic trips to Paris. She wrote *After Leaving Mr Mackenzie* and it was published in London in February 1931. In some ways a sequel to *Quartet*, it tells the story of an aging woman in Paris whose latest lover has rejected her; she seeks assistance from former friends and family in London; and after various unhappy experiences returns to Paris, presumably to continue her aimless, drifting life.

Jean Rhys continued to write short stories, but the only one which appears to have been published is "The Christmas Presents of Mynheer van Rooz" in 1931. She also returned to the work which had first attracted Ford's attention to her. This was an account which she had written long before the First World War of her traumatic first love affair; she had kept the notebooks with her during all of her travels about Europe, and in 1922 Mrs. George Adam had transcribed the notebooks and edited the story which the young woman had written. When Ford was shown the typescript he was immediately interested in the young writer (he had a reputation for his ability to discover new talent, D. H.Lawrence being one of his discoveries); and he encouraged her to continue work: *The Left Bank* stories were the result. The original notebooks may lie behind one or two of these stories, but by and large she had not yet tapped them. By 1931 Rhys was emotionally prepared to return to this difficult period of her life and to recast the notebooks in a fictional form. The story she told was that of a young girl coming from the Caribbean and experiencing life in London. The work is based on the girl's simultaneous memory of her childhood life and realization of her present situation. The title which Rhys used for the novel as she was working on it—indeed it was even used for pre-publication advertising—was "Two Tunes," a reference to the "Past" and "Present" of the heroine. At the last moment before publication Rhys changed the title to *Voyage in the Dark*, and it was so published in November 1934 in London, and in 1935 in New York. It was the only one of Rhys's pre-World War II novels to enjoy a commercial success, going into a cheap edition in May 1936.

It was five years before Rhys published her next novel, *Good Morning, Midnight*, in London in April 1939. This work carries forward the technical innovations which Rhys had experimented with in *Voyage in the Dark*, for the account of the aging heroine who goes from London to Paris to revisit the scenes of her former life is treated through all the devices associated with modernist literature, particularly the use of stream-of-consciousness technique. Published on the eve of World War II, *Good Morning, Midnight* was sold in various bindings as publishers' supplies grew scarce, but it was not reprinted. The difficulties of the war years and the death of Smith kept the novelist from trying to publish any of her work, although she tried to dramatize her earlier novels and she continued to write short stories.

In 1949 Rhys received her first public recognition in almost a decade when the Dutch-English actress Selma Vaz Dias gave a one-woman reading of *Good Morning, Midnight* in London; and in the next several years she and Vaz Dias discussed Rhys's literary future and the novelist's current and future writings. Rhys was anxious to continue publishing and, hoping to earn money from her earlier novels, she entered into an arrangement whereby Vaz Dias was to have dramatic rights to the earlier novels. Gradually the two women drifted apart; Rhys dropped out of London life after Hamer's legal difficulties and subsequently retired to the country; and when Vaz Dias managed to persuade the BBC to broadcast her version of *Good Morning, Midnight* on the Third Programme in May 1957, it was necessary first to advertise for the missing author, as Vaz Dias had earlier done in 1949. The much publicized "discovery" of Jean Rhys actually happened twice—once in 1949 and again in 1956.

While the "romance" of the long-lost writer has an immediate appeal, there is a less attractive story that remains to be told, the story of an aging woman whose talent and helplessness invited the unscrupulous—and sometimes even the well-meaning and good-intentioned—to prey upon her. Many of Rhys's difficulties in her later years were certainly due to her own actions, but by then her difficult life and her physical failings kept her from being altogether responsible for those actions. For example, acting sometimes on her own, sometimes on the advice of friends, she assigned her writings to different agents so arbitrarily that no one was quite sure who was responsible for which titles, and she irresponsibly signed away rights in her own work. Since all of the evidence is not available—and presenting that which is would be an embarrassment to persons still alive—the story of the lawsuits and the unhappinesses of Jean Rhys's last years cannot yet be fully detailed.

Meanwhile the London writer, editor, and critic Francis Wyndham who had long been a devoted reader of Rhys's novels, wrote appreciatively of her work as early as 1949; in 1956 he wrote another essay about her, presuming that she was dead. When she was "found," he got in touch with her, and since he was associated with André Deutsch he introduced her work to Diana Athill. Athill and Wyndham enthusiastically encouraged her to continue writing, and in 1960, through the influence of Wyndham, various London magazines began publishing her short stories while she continued to work on the novel which she had begun in the 1950s, acting perhaps on a suggestion by, or at least following a discussion with, Selma Vaz Dias. It is the story of "the madwoman in the attic"—the first Mrs. Rochester of Charlotte Brontë's *Jane Eyre*. By 1957 Rhys had decided on the form of the work—the use of personal monologues—and had realized that she could use some material she had already written. This novel was finally published as *Wide Sargasso Sea* in

November 1966 and marked her return to the literary scene as an acknowledged master of the twentieth-century novel. She followed it with *Tigers Are Better-Looking*, a gathering of eight of her post-World War II stories, along with nine pieces from *The Left Bank*. She was almost seventy-eight years old when this volume appeared in March 1968, yet she was still to write (or, in some cases, revise) those essays and stories that appeared in the limited edition of *My Day* (New York: 1975) and *Sleep It Off Lady*, a collection of sixteen stories that was issued in 1976. Her last years were spent in trying to write her autobiography. Her practice had always been to write each sentence over and over again in her attempt to find the perfect expression. She frequently wrote on scraps of paper which she would then arrange in the correct order (Ford satirized this practice in his 1931 novel). But by the time she reached her eighties she was suffering from all the problems of old age; and she found that she could no longer organize her work. She had to be assisted by a number of persons, chief among whom was the American novelist David Plante. His hand is very evident in the posthumous autobiography *Smile Please* which was published in the autumn of 1979.

Although there are no doubt a few stories by Jean Rhys yet to be located (since she never mentioned the story "The Christmas Presents of Mynheer van Rooz" here listed for the first time I presume she forgot about it—and conclude that there may be other such forgotten titles), the last work by her which readers can look forward to will be the "Collected Letters" which Francis Wyndham began editing in 1981.

The Literary Reception of Jean Rhys

Probably the most important influence upon the reception of Jean Rhys's first book was its "Preface"—for the name of Ford Madox Ford attracted the attention of all reviewers. It was immaterial that the "Preface" is actually a long essay about Ford's feelings for Paris and that Jean Rhys and her writings are mentioned only in the last few paragraphs. Ford's name, not the content of the essay, was all that mattered. He had of course recommended the book to its publishers, Jonathan Cape, and six months after its London publication Harper & Brothers issued it in New York.

The collection of stories was reviewed by the major newspapers and journals in the United States and England. The *New York Times Book Review* declared that "the spirit these stories show of undisciplined and unconventional youth, of hardship, of disillusion, of loose and nervous and artificial existences, is expressively brought out by the term 'left bank.' " The attitude which characterizes the stories was seen by the *Times Literary Supplement* as "a rather self-conscious antagonism towards the Anglo-American invaders of Paris," and all reviewers commented on the terse style—the "clarity of . . . vision and the exquisite economy of . . . style," as the *Spectator* called it. D. B. Wyndham Lewis, writing for the *Saturday Review*, appreciated the fact that "there is no gush. Some of [the sketches], coming after Mr. Ford Madox Ford's slightly mellifluous preface, are like a blow in the eye. . . . The form of Miss Rhys's studies is purely French, both in balance and in strict economy of the descriptive. . . . They are French in their poise, directness, and clarity." The reviewer of the *Nation and Athenaeum* and "L.S.M." of the *New Republic* commented on the author's subject matter: "Miss Rhys understands the heroism of the underdog and the hysteria or apathy of the down-and-out," was the comment of the former, while the latter wrote: "Her sympathy goes to the down-and-outers, who are crippled by fear of starvation and the law. . . . [We] see the triviality and complacency of all stupid people who have been lucky toward those who have been unlucky." And while some reviewers acknowledged that this volume was apprentice work, all agreed that, as the *New York Times* put it, "Miss Rhys is worth keeping an eye on."

Yet when the next book appeared, it was noticed by only a few reviewers in London. There may have been very good reasons for their silence. The novel had been offered to Jonathan Cape and had been refused because the publisher immediately saw the danger of a libel suit. Chatto & Windus agreed to publish it but required that the title be changed to *Postures* (while this title might be considered marginally less provocative than *Quartet*, a book with the title *Quartet* had actually been published by Scribner's). Review editors could recognize libels as well as publishers could, but in any event their reviewers uniformly disapproved of the subject matter of the novel. "A peculiarly sordid" story, the *Times Literary Supplement* reviewer sniffed, recounting the plot in such a way as to emphasize its melodrama and concluding: "The method of the book is that of the 'films'; a series of clearly cut impressions . . . and the characters, also, have something of the effect of those that gesticulate before us on the screen." The *New Statesman* saw the "clarity and truthfulness" in the writing but was disappointed that Miss Rhys "has no perception as yet of a beauty in life capable of dazzling her." Such attitudes were typical of the reception of much modern or avant-garde literature: *Ulysses* had been condemned in very similar terms, as had several of Lawrence's novels.

Unlike the British critics, the American reviewers of the late 'twenties were much more in sympathy with new types of writing and were less demanding that writers conform to establishment attitudes. They were able to take the subject of *Quartet* in their stride, and their reviews were consistently favorable. Robert Morss Lovett, writing for the *Bookman*, felt that "We shall have to go far to find another novel so powerfully wrought out of weakness, futility, betrayal, lust, and fear." The reviewers of the *New York Times Book Review* and the *Saturday Review of Literature* were equally strong in their praise, while T. S. Matthews (in the *New Republic*) and Herbert Gorman (in the *Herald-Tribune*) compared *Quartet* to *The Sun Also Rises*. They saw that while the book was not as good as Hemingway's "Miss Rhys scores another for the school of simplicity" (Matthews), and that her work was "quite as ruthless" as Hemingway's (Gorman). Only a year earlier Gorman had written "A Portrait in Impressions" of Ford Madox Ford for the *Bookman* in which he had described Ford's acquaintances in Paris, including "Stella and Olga and Jean and Ernest and Bill"; and so it was with a clear familiarity with the models that he wrote:

> There is no doubt about the power of Miss Rhys's characterizations. She knows these characters with that peculiar intimacy that always suggests prototypes, and, because of this surprising verisimilitude, the painful reality of the situation is raised to a higher plane than that of mere story telling. Her prose is staccato and purposeful and calculated to bring out clearly the essential note of her theme.

By 1929, then, Jean Rhys was well launched on her literary career, and these various reviews show the respect which her work earned from important critics of the period.

A similar difference can be seen in the English and American reviews of *After Leaving Mr Mackenzie.* The English reviewers were uncomfortable with the subject matter, even though they immediately recognized the literary merit of the novel itself. Rebecca West reminded readers of the *Daily Telegraph* that "Miss Jean Rhys has already in 'The Left Bank' shown herself to be one of the finest writers of fiction under middle age," and she declared that "This book is superb." Gerald Gould was less enthusiastic when he reviewed the book for the *Observer,* and the *Times Literary Supplement* was typical in recognizing "the admirable clarity and economy of language" and yet being unhappy with the subject matter: the novel "leaves one dissatisfied. It is a waste of talent."

American reviewers, who had less rigid ideas of what a novel should be about, were willing to accept the fact that the protagonist ends as no more than a common streetwalker. The reviewer of the *New York Times Book Review* declared:

> Miss Rhys's novel is the latest addition to the vast body of fiction which hails Flaubert as master. It offers no new note in treatment. Because no human particle is deemed unworthy to be celebrated, the school, as its master claimed for it, takes on a significance as large as life. If one, wearied of the method and tempted by the allusion, were inclined to add "and twice as natural," that the technique of "Madame Bovary" and "Pierre et Jean" made for over-simplification to the point of naïveté when used by more ordinary mortals, the fact remains that out of this method have come masterpieces and much excellent secondary work. Miss Rhys's study, slight and certainly over-simplified as it is, contains many of the merits of its species. It succeeds in bringing to the reader a small fragment of a life which is in turn an infinitesimal fragment of all life.

Other writers were equally sure that they were looking at a masterpiece, minor, perhaps, but still a masterpiece, of both realism and the clear style associated with such a school. And such reviewers as Gladys Graham (for the *Saturday Review of Literature*) and Margaret Cheney Dawson (for the *New York Her-*

ald-Tribune) were able to see the feminist element in the novel, the quality that has so endeared Jean Rhys to a later generation of women readers.

While Rhys was from the first a meticulous polisher of her language, *Voyage in the Dark* actually went through more revision than any of her other works to this date. She had written it as an account of her first affair; it had then received the editing of Mrs. George Adam and become the "unpublishably sordid novel" that so affronted Stella Bowen in Paris in 1924; and now it received the editing of Michael Sadleir at Constable's—who insisted that Anna Morgan could not die at the end of the novel: at his insistence Rhys added the last four sentences. The novelist's efforts were repaid by the praise of her critics, for on both sides of the Atlantic *Voyage in the Dark* was recognized as the realization of the earlier promise. In London, where Constable published the book in October 1934, Frank Swinnerton chose it as one of the Book Society's recommended titles; Sylvia Lynd praised it in the *News Chronicle*; and the *Times Literary Supplement* finally found in Miss Rhys's work "a sense of beauty [that] lights a lamp that redeems much of the gloom and tragedy." William Morrow was the New York publisher in the Spring of 1935; and again reviewers hailed Rhys as a master of her art. Florence Haxton Britten, writing for the *New York Herald-Tribune*, saw that her technique was the same as that of the Imagist poets:

> Put into words the thing itself. Just that. No metaphors, no phrases that fall into familiar poetical cliches, no allusions, no echoes. Just the thing itself, stated with precision. Out of that will come new, original beauty of a high order. . . . So also it is, when the method is instinctively adhered to by a novelist of fresh, sensitive vision and rare artistry.

Jane Spence Southron (in the *New York Times Book Review*) praised the "undeniable artistic excellence" of the book but concentrated on the subject matter, woman as a victim of society. Hazel Hawthorne, in the *New Republic*, stated directly: "Jean Rhys . . . is one of the finest writers of this time."

Five years passed before Rhys's next book was ready for the public. *Good Morning, Midnight* was published in London in April 1939 by Constable, and the *Times Literary Supplement* immediately selected it as its "Recommended . . . First Choice" in fiction for its issue of 22 April. The reviewer noted that "Miss Rhys has built a story, doggedly tough in a feminine way, that is always clear and is sometimes poignant. There is not a lot of it, but what there is goes a little in advance of, say, Mr. Hemingway, the father of all such as wear a hardboiled heart on their sleeve." The reviewer was particularly struck by the honesty of the writing which, "time and again . . . comes to the rescue and enables Miss Rhys to escape sentimentality by the skin of her teeth. There is, indeed, an air of almost desperate urgency about the whole thing that claims and rewards sympathy."

Frank Swinnerton, the regular reviewer of novels for the *Observer*—and one of the most influential of the London critics—reviewed *Good Morning, Midnight* along with Margery Sharp's *Harlequin House*, to which it afforded a sharp contrast. As Swinnerton noted, "Miss Jean Rhys's new story, 'Good Morning, Midnight,' is as different from 'Harlequin House' as la tristesse from la joie. It is not at all 'nice.' " He went ahead to describe the women of Rhys's earlier novels and to summarize (somewhat inaccurately) the contents of this one, concluding:

> Miss Rhys's impressionist gift enables her instantly to picture a room or a street; and in catching at association or some weary, innocent thought in the victim's mind she never falters. Her work is not for optimists, readers of Miss Sharp, or those who shrink from squalor; but its quality as black-and-white craftsmanship is quite exceptional.

Swinnerton's counterpart at the *Sunday Times* was Ralph Straus, and he was equally impressed by the novel, writing that "It is not a book to be lightly recommended" although, "if one finds Miss Rhys's technique at times irritating, one can understand why it has been used, and must admire the considerable effect which it produces." Kate O'Brien, in the *Spectator*, saw that the novel was "of a kind so very modish as almost in its moment of appearance to be already out of date." Yet while she complained of some of the "technical tricks," she appreciated the sensibility which underlay the writing: "The whole effect is femininely acute and painful, and the end very pitiful, very bitter."

The unrelenting realism of *Good Morning, Midnight* caused John Mair to write in the *New Statesman* that "Miss Rhys has drawn a portrait that is very near perfection, and the result is as

profoundly depressing as it is possible for a work of art to be."
But the Spring of 1939 was the wrong time to achieve perfection
of this type, for the harsh realities of the oncoming war made
readers long for fiction that would allow them to escape into a
world of fantasy. Rachel Field's *All This and Heaven Too*, published
about the same time, provided such an escape for readers (and
later for movie-goers), and so did Daphne Du Maurier's *Rebecca*
(1938). In view of the world crises of the time, one is not surprised that in spite of these excellent reviews, *Good Morning,
Midnight* did not find many readers and did not achieve a second
printing. It was not published in the United States until 1970.

Although Jean Rhys's first five books received good reviews,
her work was not taken up by the literary critics who specialized
in contemporary literature. Cyril Connolly, in his 1936 essay
"The Novel-Addict's Cupboard," listed the women writers
whom he collected—Compton-Burnett, Woolf, Elizabeth
Bowen, and Rosamund Lehmann, as well as others—and included "*Voyage in the Dark* (Constable) by Jean Rhys, a short and
tragic book." Ten years later, John Hampson wrote a lengthy and
valuable essay on "Movements in the Underground," a study of
the literature of the proletariat, for John Lehmann's *Penguin New
Writing*. In it he gave two paragraphs to the Rhys novels as
telling "the lives of prostitutes," and he suggested the unique
quality to be found in them: "These novels are unusual, they
have a vivid clarity and oddness which recall sharply the sinister
and menacing figures encountered in dreams."

But during the 1939–1945 war Jean Rhys's books went out of
print, and the novel-reading public forgot her. There were a few
enthusiasts, such as John Hampson, and foremost among these
was Francis Wyndham. In 1950 he wrote a lengthy appreciation
of her novels for the Labour Party's independent weekly, the
Tribune, in a series on "Neglected Books." He entitled his essay
"An Inconvenient Novelist" and tried to explain why she had
"not yet received the wider recognition that is her due."

> She is, perhaps, too uncompromising to be a best-seller, or
> even moderately popular at the lending-libraries. Most sub-
> scribers like to be able to place a novelist's characters in
> convenient categories, but Miss Rhys's heroines have an
> equivocal position for which there is no accurate descriptive
> word. "Prostitute" or "tart" over-simplify; "courtesan" is too

exalted, "kept woman" too vague. All these terms have become literary clichés, suggesting either Sadie Thomson with her books and parasol or Marguérite Gautier with her camellias. Miss Rhys writes about women who are often found in life but seldom in books, and she describes their experiences from the inside. Her treatment of the subject is unconventional, her understanding of it unique, but an utter lack of vulgarity in her writing robs it of the shock-value, the cheap sensationalism that it might easily have had. Were she either cruder or more sentimental her novels might be more successful commercially if in no other way; they might have either enjoyed a steady sale near Leicester Square or else have been Books of the Month, and later films, instead of being now (the price paid for subtle restraint and artistic integrity) almost extinct.

Wyndham went ahead to summarize the novels, omitting *The Left Bank* and *Postures* ("so rare that it is almost impossible to find copies of these"), and to express his hope that "Jean Rhys's books will be reprinted." Rhys probably did not read this essay (the *Tribune* was not widely distributed and Wyndham himself had no personal knowledge of the author). She remained out of the public eye and even forgotten by her former publishers until 1956 when Selma Vaz Dias dramatized *Good Morning, Midnight* for the BBC. Needing to secure copyright permissions for the broadcast the BBC advertised in the *New Statesman* and the author herself responded to this advertisement; through Selma Vaz Dias, Francis Wyndham learned that Rhys was living in Devon and was indeed writing again. He began corresponding with her and when he learned that she was working on a new novel, he recommended the as-yet-unwritten novel to André Deutsch Publishers, to whom he was then literary advisor. According to Diana Athill, a director of André Deutsch, "we bought an option on it at once, and agreed to follow it by republishing *Good Morning, Midnight* and *Voyage in the Dark*." Penguin Books subsequently bought the paperback rights for the United Kingdom.

When *Wide Sargasso Sea* was published in 1966 it was prefaced by Wyndham's essay, an expansion of the piece he had originally written in 1950. Its critical stance was taken over by many of the reviewers of the novel. One should perhaps note the extensive publicity given the novel by André Deutsch—but the novel won its public on its own merits. Reviewer after reviewer, in the "quality" weeklies and Sunday papers, as well as in the more popular newspapers, praised the novel. Certainly the circumstances of the publication and the situation of the author helped to capture public attention, but after pointing to these matters critics focussed on the novel itself, "an inspired piece of literary research and a superb creation in its own right," as Neville Braybrooke wrote in the *Spectator.* The romantic evocation of the Caribbean scene won the praise of all reviewers, while the psychological justification provided for the actions of Charlotte Brontë's characters caused the *Times Literary Supplement* reviewer to observe that "Antoinette becomes mad because she is dispossessed" and to compare her to Virginia Woolf's Clarissa Dalloway:

> Like Mrs. Dalloway, her alienation is to a large extent aesthetic. A Creole narcissus, she sees the world in terms of its beauty, but the only beauty she understands derives from the experiences and fantasies of her own childhood; and above all from the exotic landscape. It is that which gives her a sense of herself and of her own beauty; and with it belongs safety and happiness.

The form of the novel—the extended personal monologue—reminded some critics of Faulkner: Francis Hope, writing for the *New Statesman,* saw that "As in *The Sound and the Fury,* [Miss Rhys's] scatterbrained narrative is a commentary on itself." And the general style ("a rare synthesis of the baroque and the precise, the coolly empirical and the lushly pretty," in the words of the *Times Literary Supplement*) caused John Knowler to write in *Books and Bookmen,* "It is a measure of [Miss Rhys's] stature that as an old woman she has written a novel of the past in a language of lyrical matter-of-factness that seems immediately present."

The reception accorded *Wide Sargasso Sea* confirmed the critical judgment of Francis Wyndham and of the publishers that the novel was a significant piece of fiction; and the renewed interest in the novelist was further strengthened in June 1967, when Deutsch reissued *Good Morning, Midnight* and *Voyage in the Dark.* The Royal Society of Literature recognized Rhys's literary accomplishments by electing her a Fellow and by awarding the Heinemann prize for fiction to *Wide Sargasso Sea*. The novel also won the £1000 W. H. Smith Award, and the Arts Council awarded Rhys a £1200 Bursary. In March 1969 Deutsch issued a collection of Rhys's new short stories entitled *Tigers Are Better-Looking*, including in it a selection of stories from *The Left Bank*. Reprints of *After Leaving Mr Mackenzie* and *Quartet* were published in May 1969.

While the English public rediscovered Jean Rhys in 1966–1967, the American public was slower in appreciating her qualities, even though her works had initially received a more welcome reception in America than in Great Britain. *Wide Sargasso Sea* was published in New York in 1967, but while it was praised by such critics as Walter Allen in the *New York Times Book Review* (18 June 1967), it was not widely read. (One could reasonably speculate that American readers were not familiar enough with *Jane Eyre* to be interested in a novel about one of its characters.) The American "discovery" did not come about until March 1974 when A. Alvarez, the well-known English critic and novelist who had earlier "discovered" Sylvia Plath, wrote an essay for the *New York Times Book Review* in which he called Rhys "the best living English novelist." This essay, along with the re-issue of paperback editions of the novels, made Rhys into one of the best-selling novelists of the year, for the growing woman's movement took her as one of their writers and many thousands of her books were sold.

Although Jean Rhys said that the W. H. Smith Award for *Wide Sargasso Sea* had come too late, she actually had thirteen more years before her, and during them she saw her books re-issued in edition after edition in both the United States and England and translated into almost all of the European languages. She continued to write in these last years, and while she did not compose another novel, she wrote a number of stories which any writer would be proud of, no matter what his or her age. Most of them were collected in *Sleep It Off Lady* (1976). In addition she composed or revised the brief sketches of her earlier years which form her autobiography, *Smile Please* (1979). While her name did not appear in the popular press in the 'seventies with the frequency that it had in the late 'sixties, she was being read by literary students and her reputation was growing. In 1968 Wally Look Lai published the first academic study of *Wide Sargasso Sea*; noting her birth in Dominica and the Caribbean setting of this novel, he suggested that Rhys might be considered a Third World writer. Then in 1972 the first study for an academic journal of all of her work was made by the present writer who, working with the novels and stories available and with the published biographical information, attempted to understand the relationship between the life of the novelist and that of the fictional heroine whom he recognized as a composite figure related to the novelist herself. This point of view—shared by such authorities as Francis Wyndham and Walter Allen and encouraged by the novelist in different interviews—was taken by some later critics as unsympathetic and even, in some way, insulting to the novelist, although none of them brought forward a better way of seeing the central figures of the novels in relationship to their author. During the 'seventies other academic critics studied and wrote about Rhys; a new generation of readers grew up who approached her without any of the preconceptions that had influenced earlier critics; and when her autobiography was posthumously published, it occasioned many reviews and essays on both sides of the Atlantic. These reviews and other contemporary studies show that by the early 'eighties criticism of Jean Rhys falls into several distinct areas.

A continuing problem for many critics is the experiential: should or can the novels and stories be examined as works of fiction, or must they be considered autobiographical projections? If they embody Rhys's view of the world, then the novelist obviously had a very low opinion of women in general and of her put-upon characters in particular and cannot be considered to any extent a feminist. If, on the other hand, the novels give thinly disguised self-portraits, then they have a historical significance as the record of the brutality of men to women; they are a *cri de coeur* for all oppressed women; and Jean Rhys should be viewed as a rallying figure for feminists. Perhaps the most sensible answer to this question was given by the writer of the "TLS Commentary" in 1974 after viewing a televised interview with Rhys. This critic suggested that the novelist took "the unhappy parts of her life, invented girls like the girl she was to live them, and found to her pleasure and excitement that they [had] gone their own way."

Certainly Rhys's fiction has been read by many because of its feminist appeal. Some readers find depths of outrage and bitterness such as few writers have presented; others are able to perceive subtleties of humor and awarenesses of personal relationships such as they find in few other writers. In this connection it is indeed instructive to read Rhys (1890–1979) alongside Katherine Mansfield (1888–1923), Virginia Woolf (1882–1941), and Rebecca West (1892–1983), three near-contemporaries with whom she can be compared and to note the particular qualities of each, as well as the similarities and differences of the four writers.

Academic studies which push beyond the issue of feminism offer yet further approaches to the novelist. One of the most rewarding of these is that pioneered by Thomas Staley: understanding the novels within the context of the literary movement we know as modernism. Obviously in terms of chronology Rhys is a younger member of the modernist group, and certainly the technique of her novels is closely linked to the experiments made by these writers. Yet another approach is to consider her in terms of her origin, and more and more detailed claims are being made for her expression of a "Caribbean temperament" or "outlook." Whatever credit is given to these claims, those critics who have traced the Caribbean references in the novels back to their origins have helped to establish the novels as truthful representations of the actual world. That *Wide Sargasso Sea* not only amplifies Charlotte Brontë's *Jane Eyre* but also tells the story of Jean Rhys's grandmother facing a riot on her plantation in Dominica offers another dimension to this imaginative work.

Obviously there are many areas yet to be explored by critics: the publication of the collected letters will surely provide more accurate biographical information than is presently available and will no doubt help to give a more balanced picture of the novelist in her relations to other people. One hopes, too, that it will help to show what many already know: that Jean Rhys was an extremely well-read person who frequently used a literary allusion to focus the meaning of a scene or even a story. Thus there is no ending to "The Day They Burned the Books" unless one knows the stories of *Kim* and *Fort Comme la Mort*, the two books which the children save from the fire—and then one realizes that Rhys has told us the future lives of the children.

This bibliography shows that Jean Rhys has begun to receive the critical attention which is so clearly her due, and it will enable students of her work to see where they need to direct their attention. There is no need to make extravagant claims for the novelist: her limited output and the circumstances of her publication kept her from being an influence upon other writers in her lifetime, and her technique, so carefully crafted to express the sensibilities of the women of her time, may not be of great value to writers of a later generation. But the unconquerable human spirit which informs all of her work cannot date, and one knows that readers and writers of the future, whether male or female, will continue to appreciate her expression of the feelings and longings of the isolated individual. Jean Rhys may be a minor figure in relation to the literary giants of the twentieth century, but within her own area she is an artist without a peer.

Acknowledgments

I began compiling this bibliography in the late 1960's and continued to work on it while I was in England in 1972. Then and later Jean Rhys answered my questions and filled in my questionnaires, as did Diana Athill and Francis Wyndham. I am very grateful to them for their help. In December 1976 Professor Robert E. McDowell, editor of *World Literature Written in English,* asked me if I had a bibliography of Rhys at hand, and he published the first version of this work in April 1977. While I continued to make additions in the following years, it was not until January 1982, when Dr. David Farmer, Director, Rare Books and Special Collections, McFarlin Library, University of Tulsa, invited me to examine the Jean Rhys Collection in the McFarlin Library that I realized that I should bring my ongoing work to some conclusion. After spending a week in Tulsa in July 1982, I decided to publish the work in its present form, the terminal date being 1981, although there are a few entries of a later date. This bibliography would probably not have been published had Professor McDowell and Dr. Farmer not shown an interest in it, and I thank them both for their encouragement.

During these years I have worked in many libraries and have

always been given the most generous assistance. I am grateful to the librarians and their staffs at the British Library, London; at the University of London Library; at the University of Tulsa Library; and of course at the Perkins Library, Duke University, where the reference librarians at both Perkins and the East Campus Library have been unfailing sources of help. At the Perkins Library I made use of the DIALOG Information Retrieval Service to search the files of Newsearch, National Newspaper, and Magazine Index. I owe special thanks to Peter Hoy, Merton College Oxford, with whom I have worked on previous bibliographical projects and who has, through the years, sent me Rhys items as he found them. His generosity is a model for all scholars.

The Duke University Research Council gave me travel funds for my trip to Tulsa, and I gratefully acknowledge the assistance of the Council.

Various research chores have been undertaken by Muriel J. Mellown, Thomas J. Mellown, and Mary Ruth Mellown, to whom the gratitude of a husband and a father is once more given. For their assistance with the Index I thank my daughter and John M. Houston.

In organizing the material in this volume I have tried to keep in mind the needs of students, whatever their discipline, of general readers, and of book collectors. Since the details of Rhys's long career, broken as it was by her silence from 1939 to 1960, are not generally known, I have deliberately gone beyond the usual boundaries of bibliography to give as much information about Rhys as I am able. I have placed all reviews of a particular volume in chronological order after the description of it so that the nature of its reception is immediately obvious. Section E, Adaptations, presents information not always found in the strictly literary bibliography and acknowledges the fact that Rhys's stories and novels are proving a rich source for, among others, writers for television and the cinema. There will certainly be additions to this section, as indeed there will be to Section A, Books, and elsewhere; and I have provided space after each section for listing future Rhys publications.

A Note on Certain Rhys Titles

Since Jean Rhys's title for her first novel was *Quartet* I have used it everywhere except when the title *Postures*—given to the novel by the British publisher—had to be used. On the other hand, since Rhys was in close contact with her publisher when *Tigers Are Better-Looking* and *Sleep It Off Lady* were published, I have consistently used these British titles, hyphenating the last two words of the former and not adding a comma to the latter. The practice of the American publishers has varied with these two titles. Again, the original title of *After Leaving Mr Mackenzie* does not have a period after *Mr*, and I have generally followed this form. And finally, the story "Pioneers, Oh, Pioneers" was first published as "My Dear, Darling Mr Ramage," not as "Dear, Darling Mr Ramage."

Section A
Books

A. Books

A1a. First English Edition, 1927

THE LEFT BANK | & OTHER STORIES BY | JEAN RHYS | * | WITH A
PREFACE BY | FORD MADOX FORD | JONATHAN CAPE | THIRTY BEDFORD
SQUARE | LONDON

Format: [A]$_8$-I$_8$, K$_8$-Q$_8$. Each signature page includes the
initials "L. B."

Pagination: [1] half title; [2] blank; [3] title page; [4]
FIRST PUBLISHED IN MCMXXVII | MADE & PRINTED IN GREAT BRITAIN
| BY BUTLER & TANNER LTD | FROME AND | LONDON | *; 5, Contents;
[6] blank; 7-27, text of PREFACE: RIVE GAUCHE, signed F.M.F.
on p. 27; [28] blank; 29-47, text; [48] blank; 49-81, text;
[82] blank; 83-85, text; [86] blank; 87-97, text; [98] blank;
99-103, text; [104] blank; 105-121,text; [122] blank; 123-129,
text; [130] blank; 131-143, text; [144] blank; 145-153, text;
[154] blank; 155-191, text; [192] blank; 193-256, text. [Each
story begins on a recto; if it ends on a recto, the verso is
blank and unnumbered.]

Contents: Preface: Rive Gauche, by Ford Madox Ford. Illusion.
A Spiritualist. From a French Prison. In a Café. Tout Mont-
parnasse and a Lady. Mannequin. In the Luxemburg Gardens.
Tea with an Artist. Trio. Mixing Cocktails. Again the An-
tilles. Hunger. Discourse of a Lady Standing a Dinner to a
Down-and-Out Friend. A Night. In the Rue de l'Arrivée.
Learning to be a Mother. The Blue Bird. The Grey Day. The
Sidi. At the Villa d'Or. La Grosse Fifi. Vienne.

Binding: Chrome-yellow linen weave cloth boards; on spine a
white paper label with lettering in black and an ornamental
rule in yellow: * | THE | LEFT BANK | BY | JEAN RHYS | * .
Top and fore edges trimmed. White end-papers. 7 6/10 x 5
inches.

Publication: March 1927 at seven shillings and sixpence.

Copies examined: British Library deposit copy, pressmark
NN 13587, received 12 October 1927.

Notes: Although I have not seen a dust-jacket for this volume,
Neville Braybrooke in his review of *Voyage in the Dark* wrote:
"The dust-jacket of *The Left Bank* describes its contents as
'Studies and Sketches of Present-Day Bohemian Paris' ..." (see
below, A4d: Reviews).
    In 1970 the Books for Libraries Press issued a photograph-
ic reprint priced at $8.00 of pp. 5-256 of *The Left Bank* with
new pages [1]-[4] as follows: [1] half-title; [2] blank; [3]
title page: THE LEFT BANK | & OTHER STORIES BY | JEAN RHYS |
WITH A PREFACE BY | FORD MADOX FORD | SHORT STORY INDEX REPRINT
SERIES | * [to the left of these last three lines:] BOOKS FOR
LIBRARIES PRESS | A DIVISION OF ARNO PRESS, INC. | NEW YORK,
NEW YORK: [4] FIRST PUBLISHED 1927 | REPRINTED 1970 | INTER-
NATIONAL STANDARD BOOK NUMBER: | 0-8369-3698-1 | LIBRARY OF
CONGRESS CATALOG CARD NUMBER: | 79-134976 | PRINTED IN THE
UNITED STATES OF AMERICA. The signatures are of course identical with those in the first edition, but the volume actually
consists of eight gatherings of sixteen leaves. *Binding*: purple imitation leather boards, lettered on the spine in gilt
from head to tail: RHYS LEFT BANK AND OTHER STORIES *; all
edges trimmed; white end-papers; 8 x 5 1/4 inches (Perkins
Library copy).
    Nine stories from *The Left Bank* are included in *Tigers Are
Better-Looking*: see below, A7a.

Reviews:

Spectator, 138 (30 April 1927), 772.

    The reviewer praises the "clarity of ... vision and exquis-
    ite economy of ... style."

D. B. Wyndham-Lewis, "Hinterland of Bohemia." *Saturday Review*
(London), 143 (23 April 1927), 637.

    Wyndham-Lewis's discursive essay (not unlike Ford's Pref-
    ace) is primarily concerned with the expatriate Anglo-Amer-
    icans in Paris, but there is ample appreciation for the

stories: "The form of Miss Rhys's studies is purely French,
both in balance and in strict economy of the descriptive.
They begin ... where they should, and end exactly when
their job is done. They are French in their poise, directness, and clarity."

New Statesman, 29 (30 April 1927), 90.

The reviewer describes the contents of the volume, remarking that "if Mr. Ford's admiration [in the Preface], like
too many of his admirations, is a little exaggerated, it
is certainly not misplaced."

Times Literary Supplement, No. 1318 (5 May 1927), p. 320.

The critic gives only qualified approval to the collection
and singles out "La Grosse Fifi" as "the most sustained
piece of writing in the book and ... the best."

Nation and Athenæum, 41 (25 June 1929), 424.

Certain passages in the collection "are distinguished by
a sympathy which gives promise of some future achievement
of a sense of universal values, provided that the writer
chastens her emotionalism."

H.A. Law. *Irish Statesman*, 22 October 1927.

Alb. First American Edition, 1927

THE LEFT BANK │ & OTHER STORIES BY │ JEAN RHYS │ WITH A PREF-
ACE BY │ FORD MADOX FORD │ * │ HARPER & BROTHERS │ NEW YORK
AND LONDON

Format: Identical to that of Ala, with the exception of the
title page, leaf [A]$_2$, which is tipped in.

Pagination: Identical to that of Ala, with the following exceptions: [3] title page; [4] MADE & PRINTED IN GREAT BRITAIN
│ BY BUTLER & TANNER LTD │ FROME AND │ LONDON │ *.

Contents: Identical to Ala.

Binding: Blue, smooth cloth boards; on spine a light blue paper label printed in dark blue and black: * │ THE │ LEFT BANK
│ & │ OTHER STORIES │ BY │ JEAN RHYS │ * │ HARPER & BROTHERS │

*. All edges trimmed; white end-papers. 7 3/8 x 5 inches.

Publication: Autumn 1927 at $2.00.

Copies examined: Perkins Library copy.

Reviews:

Conrad Aiken. *New York Evening Post*, 1 October 1927, p. 10
(Not seen)

Saturday Review of Literature, 4 (5 November 1927), 287.

"[T]he book as a whole indicates that Miss Rhys's vision
of things has not yet clarified, though the tricks of
her trade are already mastered."

"A Mistress of the *Conte*." *New York Herald Tribune Books*,
4 (6 November 1927), 16.

(Not seen)

Boston Evening Transcript, 9 November 1927, p. 7.

(Not seen)

L.S.M. [?Lucy Sprague Mitchell]. *New Republic*, 52 (16 November 1927), 345.

The reviewer writes appreciatively, stressing the theme of
"the triviality and complacency of all stupid people who
have been lucky toward those who have been unlucky."

"Miss Rhys's Short Stories." *New York Times Book Review*,
11 December 1927, pp. 28, 30.

The critic analyzes the technique (Rhys "gains her effects
as much by what she omits as by what she includes") and
compares Rhys to Katherine Mansfield. "Miss Rhys is
worth keeping an eye on."

Translation. 1. French, 1981 (Not seen)

Rive Gauche: Nouvelles, translated by Jacques Tournier.
Paris: Mercure de France (Domaine Anglais). Pp. 198.

"Reunit les nouvelles 'Tigers are Better Looking' non
recueillies dans 'Les Tigres Sont plus Beaux,' et 'Ma

journée,' 'My Day,' extrait de 'Vogue' 1975." (*Les Livres Disponibles, 1982*)

A2   POSTURES   1928

[preferred title:] QUARTET

A2a. First English Edition

POSTURES | BY | JEAN RHYS | [quotation] ... Beware | Of good Samaritans--walk to the right | Or hide thee by the roadside out of sight | Or greet them with the smile that villains wear. | R.C. Dunning. | CHATTO & WINDUS | LONDON

Format: [*]$_2$, A$_8$-I$_8$, K$_8$-Q$_8$, [*]$_2$. The gatherings marked [*] are tipped in, not sewn.

Pagination: [i] half title; [ii] BY THE SAME AUTHOR:-- | THE LEFT BANK (STORIES); [iii] title page; [iv] FIRST PUBLISHED 1928 | PRINTED IN GREAT BRITAIN: ALL RIGHTS RESERVED; 1-[254] text; [255-256] blank; [257-260] Chatto and Windus Catalogue.

Contents: Twenty-three chapters without titles and numbered in arabic numerals; chapter subdivisions have roman numerals.

Binding: Light blue, linen weave cloth boards. Front and back covers have a double blind rule around extreme edges to form a panel. On the spine in gilt: * | POSTURES | BY | JEAN RHYS | CHATTO & WINDUS | * . Top and fore edges trimmed; top edges stained blue (?). White end-papers. 7 4/10 x 4 9/10 inches.

Publication: September 1928 at seven shillings and sixpence.

Copies examined: British Library deposit copy, pressmark NN 14614, received 25 September 1928. The description above is of the British Library copy. The University of Tulsa Rhys Collection contains a copy with the signatures of "G.Fruzelier" and "Diana Athill" on the front free end-paper, and of "Jean Rhys" and "Selma Vaz Dias" on the title page. There is no Catalogue in this copy, which is bound in tan (now fading to pink) linen weave cloth boards. The front cover has a single black rule at the extreme edges to form a panel, and the spine is lettered in black, rather than in gilt. The top and fore edges are trimmed but not stained. Since the author's signature clearly dates from her late years, it offers no help in dating this binding. However, the absence of the publisher's catalogue, the general appearance of the volume, and the presence of the blue binding in the copyright library suggest that the tan binding was later than the blue.

Reviews:

Times Literary Supplement, No. 1392 (4 October 1928), p. 706.

The reviewer recounts the plot and emphasizes the melodramatic qualities: "The method of the book is that of the 'films' ... and the characters, also, have something of the effect of those that gesticulate before us on the screen."

"Books in Brief." *Nation and Athenæum*, 44 (6 October 1928), 26.

"Shorter Notices." *New Statesman*, 31 (6 October 1928), 806.

Comparing the novel to the stories in *The Left Bank*, the reviewer points out that "The tales were short but satisfying; one had no more than time to admire the deftness with which a character or a situation was sketched in than the scene changed and one's admiration began anew. It is less entertaining to follow the same set of individuals upon the futile repetition ... of their dreary round." After a summary of the plot he concludes: "All that Miss Rhys writes has clarity and truthfulness; her satiric vision blinks at nothing. But she has no perception as yet of a beauty in life capable of dazzling her."

"Books of the Month." *Bookman* (London), 75 (November 1928), 144.

Postures is included in this list for the period 15 September to 10 October 1928. This issue of the *Bookman* also includes a full-page advertisement (p. 129) from Chatto and Windus in which *Postures* is featured, along with Lytton Strachey's *Elizabeth and Essex* and Aldous Huxley's *Point Counter Point*.

A2b. First American Edition, 1929

QUARTET | A NOVEL | BY | JEAN RHYS | 1929 | SIMON & SCHUSTER
| INC | NEW YORK [title page enclosed with four rectangles]

Format: Information not available.

Pagination: [i-ii] blank; [iii] Simon and Schuster publish-
ing device; [iv] BY THE SAME AUTHOR: | THE LEFT BANK (STORIES);
[v] title page; [vi] ALL RIGHTS RESERVED | COPYRIGHT, 1929, BY
SIMON AND SCHUSTER, INC. | 37 WEST 57 STREET NEW YORK | PRINTED
IN U..S. A. BY VAIL-BALLOU PRESS, BINGHAMTON | BOUND BY H.
WOLFF EST., N.Y. | DESIGNED BY ANDOR BRAUN ; [vii] half title;
[viii] blank; 1-228, text; [229-232] blank.

Contents: Identical with A2a.

Binding: Grey cloth boards, printed in white and grey; on
front cover a line drawing of two couples seated at a side-
walk cafe table; QUARTET BY JEAN RHYS incorporated in design
which is continued on spine with QUARTET | JEAN RHYS at head
and SIMON & SCHUSTER at tail. All edges trimmed and top edges
stained. 7 1/2 x 5 1/4 inches.

Publication: Early winter, 1929, at $2.50.

Copy examined: Library of Congress copy: PZ.3.R3494.Qu.

Reviews:

F. Van de Water. *New York Evening Post,* 2 February 1929,p. 9.

(Not seen)

Herbert Gorman, "The Unholy Four." *New York Herald Tribune
Books,* 10 February 1929, p. 7.

Gorman, James Joyce's first biographer, was an intimate of
the Anglo-American expatriates in Paris; and while avoid-
ing any libellous identifications, he conveys his awareness
that *Quartet* is a *roman à clef,* while noting that "It is not
as good as [*The Sun Also Rises*], but it is quite as ruthless." Knowing the originals, he analyzes in detail the
characters in terms both of Rhys's realization of them and
of their standing as representative figures. "There is no
doubt about the power of Miss Rhys's characterizations....
[B]ecause of this surprising verisimilitude, the painful

reality of the situation is raised to a higher plane than
that of mere story telling. Her prose is staccato and pur-
poseful and calculated to bring out clearly the essential
note of her theme." This highly important review is accompanied by a reproduction of the cover design of the book.

"Poignant Tragedy." *New York Times Book Review,* 10 February
1929, p. 8.

The reviewer provides a lengthy study of the novel in completely positive terms, noticing particularly the characters. "Not only does [Rhys] deal with the most complex
personalities, exploring the most intimate recesses of
their psychology, but she does so with the directness and
certitude of the fine artist. The style, especially of the
dialogue, belongs to the new tradition in prose, which shuns
elaboration for sharpness and intensity of effect. Whatever
extension of range in character or setting that Miss Rhys
may bring to her future work, it seems scarcely possible
that she will be able to surpass the strength and
poignancy of 'Quartet.'"

"Latin Quarter Rotters Characters of this Yarn." *New York
World,* 69 (10 February 1929), 11.

(Not seen)

Boston Evening Transcript, 20 March 1929, p. 2.

(Not seen)

Springfield Republican, 24 March 1929, p. 7.

(Not seen)

Robert Morss Lovett. *Bookman* (New York), 69 (April 1929), 193.

Lovett succinctly summarizes the plot and the psychological
explorations: "The tense, literal narration, almost ironic
in its monotone, is a further enforcement ... [of the]
harsh relief [provided by] the background of Paris. Manner
is perfectly adapted to matter. We shall have to go far
to find another novel so powerfully wrought out of weakness,
futility, betrayal, lust, and fear."

T. S. Matthews, "The Cocktail Hour." *New Republic,* 58 (17
April 1929), 258-259.

Matthews reviews four novels, beginning with *Quartet* and
ending with Evelyn Waugh's *Decline and Fall.* Having summarized the plot, he praises the style: " ... Miss Rhys
scores another for the school of simplicity. Though the
writing is not a bit like Hemingway's, its negative qual-

ities are the same--it leaves out everything irrelevant.
Though Miss Rhys does not often achieve Hemingway's harsh
silences, by her restraint and economy she manages often
to get the same effect of inevitability ... ; her people
are quiet even in their violence, under a sky that is like
the ceiling of a prison."

Saturday Review of Literature, 5 (20 April 1929), 936.

The reviewer points out similarities and differences of
characters and settings to those of Hemingway's *The Sun
Also Rises*. This "beautifully articulated anatomy of disintegration" is a "close-knit study of mordant personality
.... The quartet move to their fates with inevitability
beating time as relentlessly as in any Greek drama...."
The writer gives unqualified praise to both content and
style: "The brittle objectivity of the very modern style
which Miss Rhys employs scrupulously throughout only adds
by its impersonality to her indictment of emotional egotism."

A2c. Second English Edition, 1969

QUARTET | JEAN RHYS | [four-line quotation] ... Beware | Of
good Samaritans--walk to the right | Or hide thee by the road-
side out of sight | Or greet them with the smile that villains
wear. | R.C. Dunning | * | ANDRE DEUTSCH

Format: [ ]$_{16}$, Q.B$_{16}$ - Q.F$_{16}$. The fifth leaf of each gathering bears the signature: Q-[letter of the gathering] ★.

Pagination: Unnumbered blank leaf; [1] half title with twelve-
line description of the novel; [2] BY THE SAME AUTHOR | WIDE
SARGASSO SEA | GOOD MORNING, MIDNIGHT | VOYAGE IN THE DARK |
AFTER LEAVING MR MACKENZIE | TIGERS ARE BETTER LOOKING (STOR-
IES); [3] title page; [4] THIS EDITION FIRST PUBLISHED 1969
BY | ANDRE DEUTSCH LIMITED | 105 GREAT RUSSELL STREET | LONDON
WC1 | FIRST PUBLISHED 1928 BY | CHATTO AND WINDUS | UNDER THE
TITLE POSTURES | ALL RIGHTS RESERVED | PRINTED IN GREAT BRIT-
AIN BY | EBENEZER BAYLIS AND SON LTD | THE TRINITY PRESS |
WORCESTER AND LONDON | SBN 233 96050 3; 5-[186] text; two
unnumbered blank leaves.

Contents: Twenty-three chapters without titles and numbered
in arabic numerals; chapter subdivisions are marked by a
single asterisk.

Binding: Rose-colored, textured paper on boards. On the
spine in gilt: * | QUARTET | * | JEAN | RHYS | * | * |
ANDRE | DEUTSCH. All edges trimmed. White end-papers.
7 3/4 x 5 inches.

Publication: May 1969 at twenty-five shillings.

Copies examined: University of London Library; Perkins
Library (two copies).

Reviews:

Vernon Scannell, "The Destruction of Innocence." *Sunday
Times*, No. 7615 (11 May 1969), p. 57.

In this review of *Quartet, After Leaving Mr Mackenzie,* and
three other novels, Scannell gives the first third to the
Rhys novels, noting that "all of her books are in print."
He tells the story of *Quartet* and suggests that "its main
theme is the way in which innocence is irresistible to and
defenceless against the corruption of self-seeking cynicism." *After Leaving Mr Mackenzie* is summarized in more
general terms; in it "Rhys tells the truth about a certain
kind of woman in a certain historical and social context,
and her truth is not comfortable; yet ... through the al-
chemy of her art, it has the power, paradoxically, to
console."

Robert Nye, "Women in a Man's World." *Guardian*, 15 May 1969,
p. 9 (reprinted in the *Manchester Guardian Weekly*, 100 [22
May 1969], 15).

Nye reviews *Quartet, After Leaving Mr Mackenzie,* and three
other novels, giving three-fifths of the essay to summaries
of the stories of the Rhys novels. He declares that "Rhys's
achievement in these astonishing books is to distil and make
lucid certain aspects of woman's experience of the male--
her injured pride in giving herself, her sorry dependence
when love is dead, her loneliness in love or out--which
are not often admitted, or if admitted, so clearly seen.
The clarity comes from dry-eyed understanding. These are
plausible, sometimes profound studies of important human
relationships. I rate her higher than Colette."

Margaret Lane, "Life and Hard Times." *Spectator*, 222
(16 May 1969), 649-650.

In this lengthy, appreciative review Lane retells the
stories of *Quartet* and *After Leaving Mr Mackenzie*, con-
centrating on Rhys's depiction of women who "are the vic-
times of circumstance, or ... of life" and on the "economy"
and "wit" with which Rhys writes. Lane notes the "tone of
immediacy" which makes the novels so contemporary in spite
of their age. She considers the "heroines, whatever their
names, [to be] the same person: a fading young woman without a sou, a sophisticated innocent, a drifter ... [who is]
as alien as possible to the pull-yourself-together school
of thought;" and she praises "the haunting quality of
[Rhys's] light-toned voice, the integrity of its style,
its uncomfortable truth."

Paul Bailey, "Bedrooms in Hell." *Observer*, No. 9279 (18 May
1969), p. 30.

Bailey tells the stories of *Quartet* and *After Leaving Mr
Mackenzie* as he colorfully gives his impressions of Rhys's
"doomed heroines." He points out "how little these books
have dated since they first came out--the works of 'bigger'
writers have not fared so well." There are no negative
comments in this enthusiastic review.

A2d. Second American Edition, 1971

QUARTET | JEAN RHYS | * [publisher's device incorporating
the date 1817] HARPER & ROW, PUBLISHERS | NEW YORK, EVANSTON,
SAN FRANCISCO, LONDON

Format: Six gatherings of sixteen leaves. No signatures.

Pagination: [i-ii] blank; [iii] half title; [iv] BY THE SAME
AUTHOR | WIDE SARGASSO SEA | GOOD MORNING, MIDNIGHT | VOYAGE
IN THE DARK | AFTER LEAVING MR MACKENZIE | TIGERS ARE BETTER
LOOKING (STORIES); [1] title page; [2] QUARTET. COPYRIGHT ©
1929, 1957 BY JEAN RHYS. ALL RIGHTS RESERVED. | PRINTED IN
THE UNITED STATES OF AMERICA. NO PART OF THIS BOOK MAY BE |
USED OR REPRODUCED IN ANY MANNER WHATSOEVER WITHOUT WRITTEN
PERMIS- | SION EXCEPT IN THE CASE OF BRIEF QUOTATIONS EMBOD-
IED IN CRITICAL ARTICLES | AND REVIEWS. FOR INFORMATION AD-
DRESS HARPER & ROW, PUBLISHERS, INC., | 49 EAST 33RD STREET,
NEW YORK, N.Y. 10016. PUBLISHED SIMULTANEOUSLY | IN CANADA
BY FITZHENRY & WHITESIDE LIMITED, TORONTO. | FIRST U.S. EDI-

TION | LIBRARY OF CONGRESS CATALOG CARD NUMBER: 77-138795;
[3] [four-line quotation] ... Beware | Of good Samaritans--
walk to the right | Or hide thee by the roadside out of sight
| Or greet them with the smile that villains wear. | --R.C.
Dunning; [4] blank; 5-[186] text; [187] blank; [188] blank
except for code numbers at bottom: 71 72 73 10 9 8 7 6 5 4 3
2 1.

Contents: Identical with A2c.

Binding: Olive-green, paper-covered boards, the spine and one-
half of the front and back bound with bright orange cloth. On
the front cover in the bottom right-hand corner, the publisher's device blind-stamped. On the spine printed in black from
head to tail: JEAN RHYS QUARTET; and horizontally at the
tail: HARPER | & ROW. Top edges trimmed. End-papers of
bright orange. 8 x 5 1/2 inches.

Publication: Spring 1971 at $4.95.

Copy examined: Library of Congress copy (marked "gift publisher copy"), call number PZ3. R3494. Qu. 8.

Notes: The statement on the copyright page that this is the
"First American Edition" is of course incorrect. This description has been supplied by Mary Ruth Mellown.

Reviews:

Shirley Hazzard, *New York Times Book Review*, 11 April 1971,
p. 6.

The reviewer perceptively outlines the history of Rhys's
literary career, noting that while the novels "cannot be
said to deal with an identical character, [they] are pro-
gressively concerned with the incapacity of an intelligent
woman to defend her affections" and show "an imaginative,
susceptible nature destroyed by the assertive, unyielding
world." Hazzard stresses that "irony is never absent, even
when the author is most deeply in sympathy." Two-thirds of
the full-page review is given over to an analysis of the
characters and story in which Hazzard obliquely points to
the actual models used by Rhys. Printed with the review
is an early photograph of Rhys.

Diana Loercher, "'When a gel must cut loose.'" *Christian
Science Monitor*, 63 (20 May 1971), 4.

Writing from the point of view of the feminist, Loercher
provides a brief sketch of the main action of the novel,
judging that "This is hardly a great novel, and its language is often irritatingly stilted, but it does have value
as a relentless dissection of the dangerously submissive
woman, still disturbingly recognizable today.... One sym-
pathizes with the implied conditions of femininity that
have ossified [Marya's] capacity to act, and is relieved
by her final outburst of rage which, though it leads in-
evitably to her destruction, is the only honest expression
of a lost self."

Vivien Raynor, "Woman as Victim." *Book World* [*Chicago Tribune* and *Washington Post*], 5 (23 May 1971), 9.

Encountering Rhys for the first time, the reviewer provides
an inaccurate account of her career and a skeleton outline
of the story of the novel. Raynor has difficulty with the
style: "It takes a while to get with the jerky rhythm--
caused by bald narrative departing unexpectedly into flash-
backs or unspoken thoughts. At times it reads like notes
for a novel...." She considers the main character to be
"a papery personality who exists only through what others
do to her." The reviewer is uncertain of the period and
location of the novel, but feels that the characters "have
stepped out of art deco illustrations."

"A Selection of Recent Titles." *New York Times Book Review*,
6 June 1971, p. 3

In this listing of titles published in the past six
months *Quartet* is described as "a fine first novel ...
by a newly rediscovered British writer." This entry is
repeated in a listing of 1971 titles in the same newspaper, 5 December 1971, p. 84.

Agnes Ringer. *Library Journal*, 96 (August 1971), 2547.

Stressing the "fresh and new" qualities of the novel,
Ringer summarizes its plot. Mindful that the review
will be read by professional librarians who must decide
which books to buy, she recommends *Quartet* for both public
and academic libraries.

A2e. First English Paperback, 1973 (Not seen)

(2nd impression, 1977; 3rd impression, 1981;
4th impression, 1982, described below:)

JEAN RHYS | QUARTET | PENGUIN BOOKS

Format: [   ]$_8$, $Q \cdot 2_8$ - $Q \cdot 9_8$.

Pagination: [1] PENGUIN BOOKS | QUARTET | [three-paragraph
description of Jean Rhys's literary career and life]; [2]
blank; [3] title page; [4] PENGUIN BOOKS LTD, HARMONDSWORTH, |
MIDDLESEX, ENGLAND | PENGUIN BOOKS, 625 MADISON AVENUE, |
NEW YORK, NEW YORK 10022, U.S.A. | PENGUIN BOOKS AUSTRALIA
LTD, RINGWOOD, | VICTORIA, AUSTRALIA | PENGUIN BOOKS CAN-
ADA LTD, 2801 JOHN STREET, | MARKHAM, ONTARIO, CANADA L3R
1B4 | PENGUIN BOOKS (N.Z.) LTD, 182-190 WAIRAU ROAD, | AUCK-
LAND 10, NEW ZEALAND | FIRST PUBLISHED BY CHATTO & WINDUS
1928 | UNDER THE TITLE POSTURES | THIS EDITION FIRST PUB-
LISHED BY ANDRE DEUTSCH 1969 | PUBLISHED IN PENGUIN BOOKS
1973 | REPRINTED 1977, 1981, 1982 | COPYRIGHT 1928 BY JEAN
RHYS | ALL RIGHTS RESERVED | MADE AND PRINTED IN GREAT BRIT-
AIN BY | HUNT BARNARD PRINTING, AYLESBURY, BUCKS. | SET IN
MONOTYPE BASKERVILLE | EXCEPT IN THE UNITED STATES OF AMERICA,
| THIS BOOK IS SOLD SUBJECT TO THE CONDITION THAT | IT SHALL
NOT, BY WAY OF TRADE OR OTHERWISE, BE LENT, | RE-SOLD, HIRED
OUT, OR OTHERWISE CIRCULATED WITHOUT | THE PUBLISHER'S PRIOR
CONSENT IN ANY FORM OF | BINDING OR COVER OTHER THAN THAT IN
WHICH IT IS | PUBLISHED AND WITHOUT A SIMILAR CONDITION | IN-
CLUDING THIS CONDITION BEING IMPOSED ON THE | SUBSEQUENT PUR-
CHASER; [5] [verse quotation:] ... Beware | Of good Samar-
itans--walk to the right | Or hide thee by the roadside out
of sight | Or greet them with the smile that villains wear. |
R.C. Dunning; [6] blank; 7-[144] text.

Contents: Identical with A2c.

Binding: Glossy yellow paper covers. On the front a montage
of photographs in color of the actors in the film of *Quartet*
and, in red and black letters: JEAN RHYS | QUARTET | NOW A
HAUNTING FILM | *. Orange spine lettered in black and white
from head to tail: JEAN RHYS QUARTET ISBN 0 14 | 00.3610 5 *.
On the back cover, two-line quotation from the *Daily Telegraph*
and a three-paragraph description of the novel, followed by a
three-line statement about the film. At the bottom: U.K.
£1.25 | AUST. $3.50 | (RECOMMENDED) | CAN. $2.50. All edges
trimmed. 7 1/8 x 4 3/8 inches.

Publication: First impression of this edition: April 1973.

Copy examined: Personal copy.

Reviews:

"Paperback Short List." *Sunday Times*, No. 7820 (29 April 1973), p. 40.

A notice of the publication of *Quartet* and *Tigers Are Better-Looking* by Penguin Books.

"Paperbacks: Fiction." *Books and Bookmen*, 18 (August 1973), 137.

A brief summary of the plot of *Quartet*.

"A Choice of Paperbacks." *British Book News*, October 1981, p. 581.

A brief summary of the plot of *Quartet* in which the reviewer identifies Heidler as "based on Ford Madox Ford" and Marya as "the Rhys figure."

"Paperback Choice." *Observer*, No. 9920 (11 October 1981), p. 32.

A brief notice in which *Quartet* is identified as having been "written in the aftermath of a marital disaster and a tortured affair with Ford Madox Ford who discovered [Rhys] as a writer."

A2f. First American Paperback, 1974

QUARTET | JEAN RHYS | [four-line quotation] ... Beware | Of good Samaritans--walk to the right | Or hide thee by the roadside out of sight | Or greet them with the smile that villains wear. | R.C. Dunning | * | VINTAGE BOOKS | A DIVISION OF RANDOM HOUSE / NEW YORK

Format: Perfect binding.

Pagination: [1] half title; [2] blank; [3] title page; [4] FIRST VINTAGE BOOKS EDITION, SEPTEMBER 1974 | ALL RIGHTS RESERVED. PUBLISHED IN THE UNITED STATES BY RAN- | DOM HOUSE,

INC., NEW YORK. PUBLISHED BY ARRANGEMENT | WITH HARPER & ROW,
PUBLISHERS, INC. FIRST PUBLISHED IN | 1928 IN GREAT BRITAIN
BY CHATTO AND WINDUS UNDER THE | TITLE POSTURES. | LIBRARY OF
CONGRESS CATALOGUING IN PUBLICATION DATA | RHYS, JEAN. | QUAR-
TET. | FIRST PUBLISHED IN LONDON IN 1928 UNDER TITLE:| POS-
TURES. | REPRINT OF THE 1969 ED. PUBLISHED BY DEUTSCH, | LON-
DON. | I. TITLE. | PZ3R3494QU10 [PR6035.H96] 823'.9'12 78-
8114 | ISBN 0-394-71319-2 | MANUFACTURED IN THE UNITED STATES
OF AMERICA; 5-[186] text; [187] eight-line description of Jean
Rhys's life and career including six titles by Rhys; [188]
blank; [189]-[192] publisher's advertisement for Vintage books.

Contents: Identical with A2c.

Binding: Glossy paper covers. On the front, a photograph of
a girl's face; printed at the top in black: " ... QUITE SIM-
PLY, THE BEST LIVING ENGLISH NOVELIST."| --A. ALVAREZ, THE NEW
YORK TIMES BOOK REVIEW; and at the bottom in white: QUARTET
| BY JEAN RHYS | [in black] 394-71319-2 * $1.65 V-319. On the
spine, from head to tail: QUARTET * JEAN RHYS; and horizontal-
ly at the tail: * | V-319 | VINTAGE. On the back cover a nine-
line description of the novel; at the bottom: COVER PHOTOGRAPH:
BY ANTONI ALBA. All edges trimmed. 7 1/4 x 4 1/4 inches.

Publication: September 1974 at $1.65.

Copy examined: Personal copy.

Notes: According to Alice K. Turner, *Publishers Weekly*, 206
(1 July 1974), 56, the first printing of this edition consisted of 15,000 copies.

Reviews:

Publishers Weekly, 206 (1 July 1974), 85.

   Quotation of parts of the *Publishers Weekly* review of 15
   February 1971 of A2d (see above, A2d: Reviews).

New York Times Book Review, 13 October 1974, p. 44.

   The anonymous reviewer recalls Alvarez's describing Rhys
   as "the best living English novelist" (see below, F.3:
   1974) and points out that the first four novels "share the
   same heroine (although she goes by different names)˙ and
   the same seedy background...." Now *After Leaving Mr. Mackenzie, Good Morning, Midnight* and *Quartet* are available
   in Vintage editions.

A2g. Third English (Large Print) Edition, 1981

QUARTET │ JEAN RHYS │ [four-line quotation] ... Beware │ Of
good Samaritans--walk to the right │ Or hide thee by the road-
side out of sight │ Or greet them with the smile that villains
wear. │ R.C. Dunning │ * │ A NEW PORTWAY LARGE PRINT BOOK │
* │ CHIVERS PRESS │ BATH

Pagination: [i] half title with a one-paragraph summary of the
novel; [ii] blank; [iii] title page; [iv] FIRST PUBLISHED 1928
UNDER THE TITLE POSTURES │ BY │ CHATTO AND WINDUS │ THIS LARGE
PRINT EDITION PUBLISHED BY │ CHIVERS PRESS │ BY ARRANGEMENT
WITH ANDRE DEUTSCH LIMITED │ AND IN THE U.S.A. WITH HARPER &
ROW │ PUBLISHERS, INC. │ AT THE REQUEST OF │ THE LONDON & HOME
COUNTIES BRANCH │ OF │ THE LIBRARY ASSOCIATION │ 1981 │ ISBN
0 85119 102 9 │ ALL RIGHTS RESERVED │ BRITISH LIBRARY CATALOG-
UING IN PUBLICATION DATA │ RHYS, JEAN │ QUARTET. │ I. TITLE │
823'.9'1F PR6035. H96Q │ ISBN 0-85119-102-9 │ PHOTOSET, PRINT-
ED AND BOUND │ IN GREAT BRITAIN BY │ REDWOOD BURN LIMITED │
TROWBRIDGE & ESHER; [v] half title; [vi] blank; 1-233, text;
[234] blank.

Contents: Twenty-three numbered chapters with numbers written
out, and asterisks to indicate divisions within chapters.

Binding: Blue cloth boards lettered in gilt on spine. At head
in circular rule: LARGE │ PRINT. From head to tail within an
oval rule: QUARTET JEAN RHYS. At tail within a circular rule:
NEW │ PORTWAY.

Publication: January 1981 at five pounds and twenty-five pence.

Copy examined: University of Tulsa Library.

A2h. Second American Paperback, 1981

QUARTET │ JEAN RHYS │ * │ PERENNIAL LIBRARY │ HARPER & ROW,
PUBLISHERS │ NEW YORK, CAMBRIDGE, PHILADELPHIA, SAN FRANCISCO
│ LONDON, MEXICO CITY, SÃO PAULO, SYDNEY

Format: Perfect binding.

Pagination: [i] half title with three-line quotation from
Ford's "Preface" to *The Left Bank*; [ii] blank; [iii] BOOKS BY
JEAN RHYS │ QUARTET │ AFTER LEAVING MR MACKENZIE │ VOYAGE IN

THE DARK | GOOD MORNING, MIDNIGHT | WIDE SARGASSO SEA | TIGERS
ARE BETTER LOOKING (STORIES) | SLEEP IT OFF, LADY | SMILE PLEASE
(AUTOBIOGRAPHY); [iv] blank; [1] title page; [2] A HARDCOVER
EDITION OF THIS BOOK WAS ORIGINALLY PUBLISHED IN THE UNITED |
STATES BY HARPER & ROW, PUBLISHERS. | QUARTET. COPYRIGHT ©
1929, 1957 BY JEAN RHYS. ALL RIGHTS RESERVED. | PRINTED IN
THE UNITED STATES OF AMERICA. NO PART OF THIS BOOK MAY BE
USED OR | REPRODUCED IN ANY MANNER WHATSOEVER WITHOUT WRIT-
TEN PERMISSION EXCEPT | IN THE CASE OF BRIEF QUOTATIONS EMBOD-
IED IN CRITICAL ARTICLES AND REVIEWS. FOR | INFORMATION AD-
DRESS HARPER & ROW, PUBLISHERS, INC., 10 EAST 53RD STREET, |
NEW YORK, N.Y. 10022. | ISBN: 0-06-080568-4 | FIRST PERENNIAL
LIBRARY EDITION PUBLISHED 1981. | 81 82 83 84 85 10 9 8 7 6 5
4 3 2 1; [3] [four-line quotation] ... Beware | Of good Samar-
itans--walk to the right | Or hide thee by the roadside out of
sight | Or greet them with the smile that villains wear. |
--R.C. Dunning; [4] blank; 5-186, text; one blank leaf.

Contents: Identical with A2c.

Binding: Glossy, plastic-treated, light-blue paper covers. On
the front in red letters: QUARTET | JEAN RHYS | P568 * PEREN-
NIAL LIBRARY $2.50, in a framed design including color photo-
graphs of the four principal actors in the film of *Quartet*.
On the spine in red letters, horizontally at the head: P568 |
*, and from head to tail: QUARTET JEAN RHYS. On the back cov-
er, a white panel printed in red and black giving one paragraph
of description of the novel, one paragraph of advertisement for
the film *Quartet*, and a two-line quotation from the *Daily Telegraph*: COVER DESIGN BY DEBORAH SCHEIN. All edges trimmed.
7 x 4 1/8 inches.

Publication: 1981 at $2.50.

Copy examined: Personal copy.

Translation.   1.   French, 1973

JEAN | RHYS | QUATUOR | ROMAN | TRADUIT DE L'ANGLAIS | PAR
VIVIANE FORRESTER | LES LETTRES NOUVELLES | 26, RUE DE CONDÉ,
PARIS, 6E

Pagination: [1] Les Lettres Nouvelles | publication | dirigée
par Maurice Nadeau; [2] DU MÊME AUTEUR | DANS LA COLLECTION
"LES LETTRES NOUVELLES" | BONJOUR MINUIT | LA PRISONNIÈRE DES

SARGASSES; [3] title page; [4] TITRE EN ANGLAIS: QUARTET | ©
1969, BY A. DEUTSCH, LONDRES | © 1973, BY EDITIONS DENOËL, PAR-
IS 7E; [5] [quotation] Prends garde | Aux bons Samaritains--
marche sur la droite, | Ou cache-toi près du bord de la route
hors de vue, | Ou reçois-les avec le sourire du traître. | R.C.
Dunning.; [6] blank; [7]-223, text. Each chapter begins on a
recto; if the preceding chapter ends on a recto, then the verso
is blank and unnumbered (pp. [36], [68], [78], [128], [150],
[158], [174], [198], [208]). Bottom of [223]: * IMP. CARLO
DESCAMPS, CONDE-SUR-L'ESCAUT. D.L. 1ER TRIM. 1973 NO ÉDITION:
3746; [224] blank.

Contents: Twenty-three chapters numbered in Arabic without chapter subdivisions.

Binding: Perfect binding in white paper covers printed in red
and black on the front: JEAN | RHYS | QUATUOR | ROMAN | TRADUIT
DE L'ANGLAIS PAR | VIVIANE FORRESTER | LES LETTRES NOUVELLES |
DENOËL. From tail to head on spine: DENOËL LN QUATUOR JEAN
RHYS. On the back: five-paragraph description of the novel and
the author; at the bottom: IMP. PRIESTER, PARIS 2-73.

Copies examined: University of Tulsa Library; Perkins Library.

Notes: Second edition: Paris: Denoël (Arc-en-ciel), 1981.
Pp. 222. (Not seen)

Reviews:

Angelo Rinaldi, "Étranger. La Vieille Dame du Devonshire."
L'Express (Paris), 12-18 February 1973, pp. 77-78.

Emphasizing the "romance" of the forgotten writer who at
the age of eighty is at last recognized as "une des plus
grandes romancières de l'époque," Rinaldi notes the Rhys
titles available in French and examines the stories which
have French settings. While there are many details that
evoke the Paris of the 'twenties, Rhys's stories are not
dated. The great strength of the writer is her style, and
she has been well translated by Forrester. Rhys belongs
to the age of Joyce, Hemingway, and Fitzgerald and began
writing when Colette was at the peak of her career. *Quat-
our* shows that Rhys was much more advanced than either Colette or Fitzgerald. Her understanding of life and her attitude as expressed in her novels will keep her work alive.

Anne Fabre-Luce, "Incandescences." *Critique* (Paris), 29
(July 1973), 674-675.

The reviewer retells the story of the novel, stressing the
psychological relationships between the characters and the

intensity of Rhys's portrayals. The novel has been
"si admirablement traduit par Viviane Forrester."

Translation. 2. Dutch and Belgian, 1975 (Not seen)

Kwartet, translated by W.A. Dorsman-Vos. Utrecht: Bruna &
Zoon. Pp. 159.

Translation. 3. German, 1978 (Not seen)

Quartett, translated by Michaela Missen. Munich: Rogner und
Bernhard. Pp. 233. Second edition: Frankfurt am Main:
Fischer Taschenbuch Verlag, 1980. Pp. 158.

Translation. 4. Swedish, 1980. (Not seen)

Kvartett, translated by Britt Arenander. Stockholm: Tiden.
Pp. 224.

Review:

Immi Lundin, "Kvinnoliv på männens villkor." *Bonniers Litter-
ära Magasin*, 49 (October 1980), 327-328.

Translation. 5. Italian, 1981 (Not seen)

Quartetto, translated by M. G. Prestini. Milan: Sperling &
Kupfer. Pp. 200.

A3   AFTER LEAVING MR MACKENZIE   1931

A3a. First English Edition, 1931

AFTER LEAVING │ MR MACKENZIE │ BY │ JEAN RHYS │ * │ JONATHAN
CAPE │ THIRTY BEDFORD SQUARE │ LONDON

Format: [A]$_8$ - I$_8$, K$_8$ - P$_8$, Q$_6$. The title page, leaf [A]$_3$,
is a cancel, tipped on to a stub.

Pagination: [1-2] blank; [3] half title; [4] BY THE SAME AU-
THOR │ THE LEFT BANK--STORIES │ POSTURES--A NOVEL; [5] title
page; [6] FIRST PUBLISHED 1931 │ JONATHAN CAPE LTD., 30 BED-
FORD SQUARE, LONDON │ AND 91 WELLINGTON STREET WEST, TORONTO
│ JONATHAN CAPE & HARRISON SMITH INC. │ 139 EAST 46TH STREET,
NEW YORK │ PRINTED IN GREAT BRITAIN BY J. AND J. GRAY, EDIN-
BURGH │ PAPER MADE BY JOHN DICKINSON AND CO. LTD. │ BOUND BY
A.W. BAIN AND CO. LTD.; 7-[8] Contents; [9] half title; [10]
blank; [11] PART I; [12] blank; 13-82, text; [83] PART II;[84]
blank; 85-232, text; [233] PART III; [234] blank; 235-[252]
text. All chapters begin on a recto; if the preceding chapter
ends on a recto, then the verso is blank and unnumbered.

Contents: Three parts divided into numbered and titled chap-
ters, each chapter further subdivided into numbered sections
(Part One, four chapters; Part Two, fourteen chapters; Part
Three, three chapters).

Binding: Apple-green linen weave cloth boards; on spine a
dark green, rectangular label lettered in gold: AFTER LEAVING
│ MR MACKENZIE │ * │ JEAN RHYS. On back cover, blind-stamped
publisher's device (the same device appears on the title page).
Top and fore edges trimmed. White end-papers. 7 6/10 x 5
inches.

Publication: February 1931 at seven shillings and sixpence.

Copies examined: British Library deposit copy, pressmark NN
17886, dated 21 January 1931; Library of Congress copy, call
number PZ3. R3494. Af; and copy in Jean Rhys Collection, University of Tulsa Library.

Notes: On p. 14 the boxed advertisement for the "Hotel St Raph-
ael" contains the phrase "CHAUFFAGE CENTRALE." The error is

corrected in the American and all later editions so that the
phrase reads "CHAUFFAGE CENTRAL."
   The University of Tulsa copy was given to Selma Vaz Dias
by Jean Rhys and is inscribed by Rhys. This copy was originally owned by the Times Book Club; the first date stamped in it
is 1.31.

Reviews:

Gerald Gould, "New Novels. All Sorts of Societies." *Observer*, No. 7289 (8 February 1931), p. 6.

   Reviewing six new novels, Gould refers to *After Leaving Mr
Mackenzie* as "a hard, dry, desperate book, so rigid in its
economy that its impressiveness seems almost contemptuous,"
and points out that while it is not a "pleasant" work, "it
has more important merits." He summarizes the plot, quotes
the conclusion of the novel, and states that "Of its kind,
and within its limits, this book is a flawless work of art."

Rebecca West, *Daily Telegraph*. (Not seen)

   Selections from this review are quoted in the publisher's
advertisement in the *Sunday Times*, No. 5626 (8 February
1931), p. 10: "'Miss Jean Rhys has already in "The Left
Bank" shown herself to be one of the finest writers of fiction under middle age.... This book is superb.'"

Frank Swinnerton, *Evening News*. (Not seen)

   Selections from this review are quoted in the publisher's
advertisement in the *Observer*, No. 7291 (22 February 1931),
p. 4: "'[After Leaving Mr Mackenzie] is a terribly sharp
picture drawn by an artist whose ruthlessness is as great
as her understanding.... The book has this quality, that
although the theme is disagreeable, one continues to read
as eagerly as if it were a romance.'"

Times Literary Supplement, No. 1518 (5 March 1931), p. 180.

   On a page given over to brief notices of generally undis-
tinguished contemporary fiction, *After Leaving Mr Mackenzie*
receives a brief paragraph beginning "This book is an epi-
sode in the life of a prostitute." The anonymous reviewer
incompletely summarizes the story, concluding: "The sordid
little story is written with admirable clarity and economy
of language. But it leaves one dissatisfied. It is a
waste of talent."

A3b. First American Edition, 1931

[Title page divided into nine rectangular areas by two horizontal and two perpendicular rules. In top center area:]
BY JEAN RHYS   [in central rectangle:] * | AFTER LEAVING |
MR. MACKENZIE | * [in bottom center area:] ALFRED. A.
KNOPF. NEW YORK | MCMXXXI

Format: Fifteen gatherings of eight leaves. No signatures.

Pagination: [i-ii] blank; [iii] half title; [iv] [two horizontal and two perpendicular rules dividing the page into nine
areas, as on the title page. In the central rectangle:] SOME
NEW | ENGLISH NOVELS | [seven titles with names of authors] |
THESE ARE BORZOI BOOKS PUBLISHED BY | ALFRED A KNOPF; [v] title
page; [vi] COPYRIGHT 1931 BY JEAN RHYS | ALL RIGHTS RESERVED |
NO PART OF THIS BOOK MAY BE REPRINTED IN ANY FORM | WITHOUT
PERMISSION IN WRITING FROM THE PUBLISHER | FIRST EDITION |
MANUFACTURED IN THE UNITED STATES OF AMERICA; [vii] Contents;
[viii] blank; [1] PART ONE; [2] blank; 3-68, text; [69] PART
II; [70] blank; 71-209, text; [210] blank; [211] PART III;
[212] blank; 213-[228] text; [229] blank; [230] A NOTE ON THE
TYPE IN WHICH | THIS BOOK IS SET | * | [eleven lines of de-
scription of the type] | * | SET UP, ELECTROTYPED, PRINTED |
AND BOUND BY | VAIL-BALLOU PRESS, INC., | BINGHAMTON, N.Y. |
PAPER MANUFACTURED BY | S.D. WARREN CO., | BOSTON; one
blank leaf.

Contents: Identical with A3a.

Binding: Steel or slate-blue cloth boards with maroon lettering. The front cover duplicates the title page minus the publisher's device and the bottom two lines, thus: BY JEAN RHYS
| AFTER LEAVING | MR. MACKENZIE. On the spine there are twelve
horizontal maroon rules of varying widths; overprinted in black
on the third from the top is JEAN RHYS; on the eighth, AFTER
LEAVING | MR. MACKENZIE; and on the tenth, ALFRED A. KNOPF.
On the back cover, blind-stamped publisher's device. Top edges
trimmed and stained maroon. White end-papers. 7 1/2 x 5
inches.

Publication: Early summer 1931 at $2.00.

Copies examined: Library of Congress copy, call number PZ3.
R3494. Af2, stamped with the date "Jun 30 1931;" copy in Jean
Rhys Collection, University of Tulsa Library.

Notes: The descriptions of the Library of Congress copy were provided by Arthur A. Guthrie and Mary Ruth Mellown.

Reviews:

Margaret Cheney Dawson, "Unbearable Justice." *New York Herald Tribune Books,* 28 June 1931, p. 7.

Without overt reference to the issue of feminism, Dawson sympathetically points to the socio-economic causes of Julia's problems and comments that "It is surely true art that makes this long-eyed, alcoholic woman of consequence to us." The novelist "writes with a miraculous balance between cold, dry realism and the tender, introspective vein," never making "the mistake of supposing, as so many authors have done, that a segment of consciousness is fascinating no matter to whom it belongs or in what manner it is exposed." Dawson provides a succinct but complete summary of the novel and concludes: "Miss Rhys has managed to give an artist's definition of life and a rebel's criticism of it. She has also created out of it a novel with the magnetic attraction of a thriller."

"Twice-as-Naturalism," *New York Times Book Review*, 28 June 1931, p. 6.

The reviewer provides a detailed account of the story of the novel, giving particular attention to the analysis of Julia's character. He points out that while Miss Rhys consistently attempts "to make you understand [Julia], ... she never intrudes on the narrative or touches it up with sentimentality or bitterness;" she intends "no moral judgment ... either on Julia, or men in their relations with women, on society or on humanity." This detachment shows that "Miss Rhys's novel is the latest addition to the vast body of fiction which hails Flaubert as master." Even though one may feel that "the technique of 'Madame Bovary' and 'Pierre et Jean' made for over-simplification to the point of naïveté when used by more ordinary mortals, the fact remains that out of this method have come masterpieces and much excellent secondary work. Miss Rhys's study, slight and certainly over-simplified as it is, contains many of the merits of its species. It succeeds in bringing to the reader a small fragment of a life which is in turn an infinitesimal fragment of all life."

R.M.C., "Books, Books, Books." *New Yorker*, (4 July 1931), 53.

In the regular weekly review of new books the reviewer
identifies *After Leaving Mr Mackenzie* as being "on a theme
you may be getting a little tired of, to be sure--woman's
inability to emulate the amorous nomadism of a bachelor--
but it is told with more insight and more power than you'll
usually find; also, for the matter of that, with more restraint and less of *parti pris* than most lady novelists
seem capable of when they get on that subject." The critic
summarizes the plot in general terms, concluding, "It is
a very good book."

Edith Weigle, "Books." *Chicago Daily Tribune*, 90 (11 July
1931), 11.

Gladys Graham, "A Bedraggled Career." *Saturday Review of Literature*, 8 (25 July 1931), 6.

Graham provides an intense, appreciative study of Julia's
character type, pointing out that "There have been enough
bad women, weak women, and victimized women in novels since
novels began, yet where will one turn to find so bedraggled
and impotent a creature as this Julia Martin of Miss Rhys?"
Graham stresses Julia's addiction to alcohol. She is "The
quintessentially supine [who] has the devastating stubborn-
ness of the will-less.... The book is written with something
of the balance and beauty of verse. The shifting of a
phrase would be a threat against the whole.... Slight in
scope, minor in key, it perfects itself within its spher-
ical intent. It is a book that does not invite comparisons
.... Its excellence is individual, intrinsic; it measures
itself against itself."

Geoffrey Stone. *Bookman* (New York), 74 (September 1931), 84.

Stone stresses that the "sordid" nature of the story results
from Julia's character, for "it seems that under any conditions Julia's life would have been sordid." He is impressed
by the brilliance and "economy" of the novelist's style and
aware of the paradox that "Julia's existence and the existence of those with whom she came in contact are somehow made
meaningful by these very meaningless odds and ends of observation. In spite of the "hopeless course" of Julia's
life, "one is surprised to find that the meaning of the
book as a whole appears just as clearly, and is much
the same, as in any tale with a moral. It is no defect
in the work."

Boston Evening Transcript, 29 August 1931, p. 1.

(Not seen)

New Republic, 68 (16 September 1931), 134.

This rather pretentiously worded appreciation draws attention to Julia's predicament: her "subtlety of temperament
and simplicity of intention were inexpressible in the code
language of organized society, especially of middle-class
society." The reviewer recounts the events of the novel
and decides that "this faithful book, with its spare, sug-
gestive method, is more profoundly destructive of hypoc-
risies--social and esthetic subterfuges--than would be
volumes of diatribe less beautiful in complete restraint."

                    A3c. Second English Edition, 1969

AFTER │ LEAVING │ MR MACKENZIE │ JEAN RHYS │ * │ ANDRE DEUTSCH

Format: [ ]$_{16}$, B$_{16}$ - F$_{16}$.

Pagination: [1] [two-paragraph description of the story of the
novel]; [2] BY THE SAME AUTHOR │ WIDE SARGASSO SEA │ GOOD MORN-
ING, MIDNIGHT │ VOYAGE IN THE DARK │ QUARTET │ TIGERS ARE BET-
TER LOOKING (STORIES); [3] title page; [4] THIS EDITION FIRST
PUBLISHED 1969 BY │ ANDRE DEUTSCH LIMITED │ 105 GREAT RUSSELL
STREET │ LONDON WC1 │ FIRST PUBLISHED 1930 BY │ JONATHAN CAPE
│ ALL RIGHTS RESERVED │ PRINTED IN GREAT BRITAIN BY │ EBENEZER
BAYLIS AND SON LTD │ THE TRINITY PRESS │ WORCESTER AND LONDON
│ SBN 233 96051 1; [5-6] Contents; [7] PART I; [8] blank; [9]-
61, text; [62] blank; [63] PART II; [64] blank; [65]-175, text;
[176] blank; [177] PART III; [178] blank; [179]-191, text;
[192] blank.

Contents: Identical with A3a.

Binding: Dark red, paper-covered boards. On the spine, in
gilt: * │ AFTER │ LEAVING │ MR │ MACKENZIE │ * │ JEAN │ RHYS
│ * │ * │ ANDRE │ DEUTSCH. All edges trimmed. White end-papers. 7 3/4 x 5 inches.

Publication: May 1969 at twenty-five shillings.

Copies examined: British Library deposit copy, pressmark
X. 908/17976; University of London Library copy; and Perkins

Library copy.

Reviews:

Vernon Scannell, "The Destruction of Innocence." *Sunday Times,* No. 7615 (11 May 1969), p. 57.

See above, A2c: Reviews.

Robert Nye, "Women in a Man's World." *Guardian,* 15 May 1969, p. 9.

See above, A2c: Reviews.

Margaret Lane, "Life and Hard Times." *Spectator,* 222 (16 May 1969), 649-650.

See above, A2c: Reviews.

Paul Bailey, "Bedrooms in Hell." *Observer,* No. 9279 (18 May 1969), p. 30.

See above, A2c: Reviews.

A3d. First English Paperback, 1971

JEAN RHYS | AFTER LEAVING MR MACKENZIE | PENGUIN BOOKS

Format: [   ]$_8$, LMM·2$_8$ - LMM·9$_8$.

Pagination: [1] PENGUIN BOOKS | AFTER LEAVING MR MACKENZIE [nineteen-line description of Jean Rhys's literary career]; [2] blank; [3] title page; [4] PENGUIN BOOKS LTD, HARMONDS-WORTH | MIDDLESEX, ENGLAND | PENGUIN BOOKS AUSTRALIA LTD, RING-WOOD, | VICTORIA, AUSTRALIA | FIRST PUBLISHED BY JONATHAN CAPE 1930 | PUBLISHED BY ANDRÉ DEUTSCH 1969 | PUBLISHED IN PENGUIN BOOKS 1971 | MADE AND PRINTED IN GREAT BRITAIN BY | HUNT BAR-NARD PRINTING LTD, AYLESBURY | SET IN MONOTYPE BASKERVILLE | THIS BOOK IS SOLD SUBJECT TO THE CONDITION THAT | IT SHALL NOT, BY WAY OF TRADE OR OTHERWISE, BE LENT, | RE-SOLD, HIRED OUT, OR OTHERWISE CIRCULATED WITHOUT | THE PUBLISHER'S PRIOR CONSENT IN ANY FORM OF | BINDING OR COVER OTHER THAN THAT IN WHICH IT IS | PUBLISHED AND WITHOUT A SIMILAR CONDITION | INCLUDING THIS CONDITION BEING IMPOSED ON THE | SUBSEQUENT PURCHASER; [5] Contents; [6] blank; 7-[127] text [no page number on p. 46, the last page of Part One]; [128] blank; 129-[138] text; [139] MORE ABOUT PENGUINS [four-paragraph publisher's advertisement];

[140] blank; [141] [advertisement for Penguin Editions of
Jane Eyre and *Wuthering Heights*]; [142] [advertisement for
Wide Sargasso Sea]; [143] advertisement for *Voyage in the
Dark*]; [144] [advertisement for *Good Morning, Midnight*; the
three Rhys titles have the note, "Not for sale in the U.S.A."].

Contents: Identical with A3a.

Binding: Off-white paper covers printed in black and orange.
On the front cover a drawing of a girl's head and shoulders;
at the top: BY THE AUTHOR OF WIDE SARGASSO SEA * | JEAN RHYS
| AFTER LEAVING | MR MACKENZIE. On the spine, from head to
tail: JEAN RHYS   AFTER LEAVING MR MACKENZIE   ISBN 0 14 | 00.
3256 8 *.   On the back cover, a three-paragraph description
of the novel; at the bottom: COVER ILLUSTRATION BY FAITH
JAQUES | FOR COPYRIGHT REASONS THIS EDITION IS NOT FOR SALE
IN THE U.S.A. | UNITED KINGDOM 25P | AUSTRALIA $0.85 | NEW
ZEALAND $0.85 | SOUTH AFRICA R.0.60 | CANADA $1.15 [to the
right of the price list:] FICTION | ISBN 0 14 | 00.3256 8 .
All edges trimmed. 7 x 4 3/8 inches.

Publication: December 1971 at twenty-five pence.

Copy examined: Personal copy.

Notes: A second impression was issued in 1981.

Reviews:

Judith Bull, "Briefing: Paperbacks." *Observer*, No. 9421 (20
February 1972), p. 23.

An enthusiastic if brief notice of this "knock-out story."

A3e.   Second American Edition, 1972

AFTER | LEAVING | MR MACKENZIE | JEAN RHYS | * | HARPER & ROW,
PUBLISHERS | NEW YORK, EVANSTON, SAN FRANCISCO, LONDON

Format: Six gatherings of sixteen leaves.   No signatures.

Pagination: [1] half title; [2] BY THE SAME AUTHOR | WIDE
SARGASSO SEA | GOOD MORNING, MIDNIGHT | VOYAGE IN THE DARK |
QUARTET | TIGERS ARE BETTER LOOKING (STORIES); [3] title page;
[4] AFTER LEAVING MR MACKENZIE.   COPYRIGHT 1931 BY JEAN RHYS.

ALL RIGHTS │ RESERVED. PRINTED IN THE UNITED STATES OF AMER-
ICA. NO PART OF THIS BOOK MAY │ BE USED OR REPRODUCED IN ANY
MANNER WHATSOEVER WITHOUT WRITTEN PERMISSION │ EXCEPT IN THE
CASE OF BRIEF QUOTATIONS EMBODIED IN CRITICAL ARTICLES AND │
REVIEWS. FOR INFORMATION ADDRESS HARPER & ROW, PUBLISHERS,
INC., 49 EAST │ 33RD STREET, NEW YORK, N.Y. 10016. │ STANDARD
BOOK NUMBER: 06-013534-4 │ LIBRARY OF CONGRESS CATALOG CARD
NUMBER: 79-160658; [5-6] Contents; [7] PART I; [8] blank; [9]-
61, text; [62] blank; [63] PART II; [64] blank; [65]-175, text;
[176] blank; [177] PART III; [178] blank; [179]-191, text; [192]
blank except for code numbers at bottom: 72 73 10 9 8 7 6 5 4 3
2 1.

Contents: Identical with A3a.

Binding: Brown, paper-covered boards, the spine and one-half
of the front and back bound with light-blue cloth. On the
front cover in the bottom right-hand corner, the publisher's
device blind-stamped. On the spine printed in black from head
to tail: AFTER LEAVING MR MACKENZIE; and horizontally at the
head: RHYS; and horizontally at the tail: HARPER │ & ROW. Top
edges trimmed. End-papers of the same cream-colored paper
used for the pages. 8 1/8 x 5 inches.

Publication: Janury 1972 at $5.95.

Copy examined: Perkins Library copy.

Reviews:

Publishers Weekly, 200 (20 December 1971), 39.

> After a brief summary of the plot, the writer describes
> "this slim novel" as "the second of the author's post-
> World War II novels. The first was 'Wide Sargasso Sea'
> (1966); she published three other novels before 1939."
> For corrections of these errors, see above and below.

Lelde Gilman. *Library Journal*, 97 (1 February 1972), 517.

> Gilman provides a synopsis of the novel, preferring *Wide Sar-
> gasso Sea* to *After Leaving Mr Mackenzie* and pointing out that
> Rhys is "adept at the psychological novel, and masterful in
> her portrayal of isolation."

Paul Theroux, "Novels." *Book World [Chicago Tribune* and
Washington Post], 6 (13 February 1972), 6.

After recounting Rhys's literary history, Theroux wonders
if "her placelessness" held up her public recognition:
Joyce and Hemingway had nationalities, but is Rhys Welsh?
West Indian? English? Her problem is shared by Julia, and
the reviewer summarizes the story of the novel, remarking
at the end that "This is all the action; it is slight, but
it encloses a story of haunting despair, beautifully written and deftly fitting the dimensions of art."

Martin Levin, "New & Novel." *New York Times Book Review*, 27
February 1972, p. 52.

Levin summarizes the principal events of the novel as he
shows that Rhys "is an artist at capturing the let-down
and the defeated. Her heroines are innocents abroad in
cities that evoke T.S. Eliot's sleazy urban landscapes."
He concludes by asserting that the "pity" which Rhys com-
pels "for her impossible heroine is part of the measure of
her delicate art."

J. Thomas Gilboy. *Best Sellers*, 31 (1 March 1972), 532.

The reviewer analytically presents the events of the novel
in some detail and then turns to the writing itself in
which the dialogue is "too overdone for the sincerity of
the situations, the situations shadowy." The novel "might
provide an interesting case study for a social psychologist,
but it has most value as a sociological commentary...."

Walter Clemons. *Newsweek*, 79 (6 March 1972), 77.

Clemons provides a brief summary of "this short, lethally
quiet novel," noticing that Rhys's "special subject is the
longevity of fecklessness. We read her with apprehension--
fascinated, embarrassed. She is an extraordinary artist."

Pearl K. Bell, "Writers & Writing: Women Cast Adrift." *New
Leader*, 55 (20 March 1972), 14-15.

Bell gives a succinct account of Rhys's literary and personal history before turning to a summary of the novel. She
views it as a description of "Julia Martin's slow descent
into the lonely hell of madness." Rhys's accomplishment is
to transform "this exasperating bauble of a woman into a
poignant victim" while the "exquisitely precise and respon-
sive prose consistently maintains its uncanny balance between abhorrence and pity. In the last part of the review
Bell considers Helen Yglesia's *How She Died*.

New Yorker, 48 (8 April 1972), 130.

This anonymous paragraph in the "Briefly Noted" column
provides a short account of the plot and the statement that
Julia is a victim of her own vanity and of "the frivolous
role assigned to her by society, and in these respects her
story ... is more apposite now than ever."

V.S. Naipaul, "Without a Dog's Chance." *New York Review of
Books*, 18 (18 May 1972), 29-31.

In this highly important essay Naipaul studies the five
Rhys novels in terms of their relation to the novelist's
life and as they express certain themes. Noticing first
her West Indian background, he sees that the "heroine of
the first four books is a woman of mystery, inexplicably
bohemian, in the toughest sense of that word, appearing to
come from no society, having roots in no society, having
memories only of places, a woman who has 'lost the way to
England' and is adrift in the metropolis." The other women
in the novels are similar, while the men, who alone possess
money, are both "predators and prey." The main character
is isolated from temporal events; and "The mysterious jour-
ney from an unknown island, the break in a life: concrete
experience turns into the purest of symbols." Naipaul discusses *Wide Sargasso Sea* and *Voyage in the Dark* at length,
stressing always the delineation of the central figure. The
novels "modify one another and make a whole. They record a
total experience, with varying emphasis." Of them *After
Leaving Mr Mackenzie* "is the most brutal," and the reviewer gives an in-depth summary of it in which judicious interpretations accompany a close reading of the text. The passive attitudes are later modified by the more aggressive
stance of the woman in *Good Morning, Midnight*. In her first
four novels Rhys "identified many of the themes that engage
us today: isolation, an absence of society or community, the
sense of things falling apart, dependence, loss. Her
achievement is very grand. Her books may serve current
causes, but she is above causes."

Michael Cooke, "Recent Fiction." *Yale Review*, 61 (June 1972),
607-609.

A peripheral treatment of the novel within a general survey
of recent fiction: Cooke views it as "a proleptic document
for women's liberation, passionate without polemics, plain
without immodesty, a cameo of helpless female dignity in a
world where it does not amount to much to be a man."

A3f.   First American Paperback, 1974

AFTER │ LEAVING │ MR MACKENZIE │ JEAN RHYS │ * │ VINTAGE BOOKS
│ A DIVISION OF RANDOM HOUSE │ NEW YORK

Format: Perfect binding.

Pagination: [1] half title; [2] blank; [3] title page; [4]
VINTAGE BOOKS EDITION, MARCH 1974 │ COPYRIGHT 1931 BY JEAN RHYS
│ ALL RIGHTS RESERVED UNDER INTERNATIONAL AND PAN-AMER- │ ICAN
COPYRIGHT CONVENTIONS. PUBLISHED IN THE UNITED │ STATES BY
RANDOM HOUSE, INC., NEW YORK, AND SIMUL- │ TANEOUSLY IN CANADA
BY RANDOM HOUSE OF CANADA │ LIMITED, TORONTO. THIS EDITION
PUBLISHED BY ARRANGEMENT │ WITH HARPER & ROW, PUBLISHERS, INC.
│ LIBRARY OF CONGRESS CATALOGING IN PUBLICATION DATA │ RHYS,
JEAN. │ AFTER LEAVING MR. MACKENZIE. │ REPRINT OF THE ED. PUB-
LISHED BY HARPER & ROW, │ NEW YORK │ I. TITLE │ [PZ3.R3494Afl0]
[PR6035.H96] 823'.9'12 │ ISBN 0-394-71024-X 73-13785 │ MANUFAC-
TURED IN THE UNITED STATES OF AMERICA; [5-6] Contents; [7] PART
I; [8] blank; [9]-61, text; [62] blank; [63] PART II; [64]
blank; [65]-175, text;]176] blank; [177] PART III; [178] blank;
[179]-191, text; [192] [eight-line description of Rhys's lit-
erary career].

Contents: Identical with A3a.

Binding: Glossy, plastic-treated paper covers. On the front
a photograph of a woman's face and shoulders in tones of yellow
and brown; imposed in letters of white or black: AFTER LEAVING
│ MR MACKENZIE │ BY JEAN RHYS │ 394-71024-X * $1.65 V-24.
Spine and back cover have a light tan ground printed in rose
and black. Printed on the spine from head to tail: AFTER LEAV-
ING MR MACKENZIE * JEAN RHYS; and horizontally at the tail:
* │ V-24 │ VINTAGE. On the back cover, a two-line quotation
from A. Alvarez's essay (see below, F.3: 1974) and a three-
paragraph description of the novel.

Publication: March 1974 at $1.65.

Copy examined: Personal copy.

Notes: The description on the back cover contains a statement
by the novelist Marge Piercy, solicited by the publisher: "[The
novel] is about the sinking of a woman who didn't want to set-
le for things, who wanted to live a little, and who found the
only adventures open to her repetitive affairs with a series
of men. For a woman reading it, it is as stark, as ominous

as a skeleton." Rebecca West is also quoted as calling the
novel "terrible and superb."
   According to Alice K. Turner, *Publishers Weekly*, 206 (1 July
1974), 56, there had been, by July 1974, three printings of
this edition, each of 10,000 copies.

A3g. Second American Paperback, 1982

AFTER | LEAVING | MR MACKENZIE | JEAN RHYS | * | PERENNIAL
LIBRARY | HARPER & ROW, PUBLISHERS | NEW YORK, CAMBRIDGE,
PHILADELPHIA, SAN FRANCISCO | LONDON, MEXICO CITY, SÃO PAULO,
SYDNEY

Format: Perfect binding.

Pagination: [1] half title; [2] BOOKS BY JEAN RHYS | QUARTET
AFTER LEAVING MR MACKENZIE | VOYAGE IN THE DARK | GOOD MORNING,
MIDNIGHT | WIDE SARGASSO SEA | TIGERS ARE BETTER LOOKING (STOR-
IES) | SLEEP IT OFF, LADY | SMILE PLEASE (AUTOBIOGRAPHY); [3]
title page; [4] A HARDCOVER EDITION OF THIS BOOK WAS ORIGINALLY
PUBLISHED BY HARPER & ROW, | PUBLISHERS. | AFTER LEAVING MR
MACKENZIE. COPYRIGHT 1931 BY JEAN RHYS. ALL RIGHTS | RE-
SERVED. PRINTED IN THE UNITED STATES OF AMERICA. NO PART OF
THIS BOOK MAY BE | USED OR REPRODUCED IN ANY MANNER WHATSOEVER
WITHOUT WRITTEN PERMISSION EXCEPT | IN THE CASE OF BRIEF QUO-
TATIONS EMBODIED IN CRITICAL ARTICLES AND REVIEWS. FOR | IN-
FORMATION ADDRESS HARPER & ROW, PUBLISHERS, INC., 10 EAST 53RD
STREET, NEW | YORK, N.Y. 10022. | FIRST PERENNIAL LIBRARY ED-
ITION PUBLISHED 1982. | ISBN: 0-06-080579-X | 82 83 84 85 86
10 9 8 7 6 5 4 3 2 1; [5-6] Contents; [7] PART I; [8] blank;
[9]-61, text; [62] blank; [63] PART II; [64] blank; [65]-175,
text; [176] blank; [177] PART III; [178] blank; [179]-191,
text; [192] blank.

Contents: Identical with A3a.

Binding: Glossy, plastic-treated, white paper covers. On the
front a design including a woman's head and shoulders seen in
profile against a blue background with imposed white letters:
AFTER | LEAVING | MR MACKENZIE | JEAN RHYS; and at the bottom
in black print: P579 * PERENNIAL LIBRARY $2.95. On the
spine in black letters, horizontally at the head: P579 | * ,
and from the head to the tail: AFTER LEAVING MR MACKENZIE
JEAN RHYS. On the back cover a panel outlined in red giving
a one-paragraph quotation from the novel and quotations from

four critics (Marge Piercy [see above, A3f], A. Alvarez [see
below, F.3: 1974], Gladys Graham [see above, A3b: Reviews],
and Rebecca West [see above, A3f]) concerning the novel. At
the bottom left: COVER DESIGN | © BY FRED MARCELLINO; and at
the bottom right: >>$2.95 | ISBN 0-06-080579-X | 0128482.
All edges trimmed. 7 x 4 1/8 inches.

Publication: 1982 at $2.95.

Copy examined: Personal copy.

Translation. 1. Italian, 1975 (Not seen)

Dopo l'addio, translated by Luisa Theodoli.   Milan: Bompiani.
Pp. 190.

Translation. 2. Dutch and Belgian, 1977 (Not seen)

Na Meneer Mackenzie, translated by W. A. Dorsman-Vos.   Utrecht:
Bruna. Pp. 188.

Translation. 3. Swedish, 1977 (Not seen)

Efter Mr. Mackenzie, translated by Annika Preis.   Göteborg:
Stegeland. Pp. 164.

Translation. 4. Spanish, 1978 (Not seen)

Después de dejar al Señor Mac Kenzie, translated by Andrés
Bosch.   Barcelona: Noguer (Libros de Bolsillo Noguer No. 62).
Pp. 198.

Translation. 5. French, 1979 (Not seen)

Quai des Grands-Augustins, translated by Jacques Tournier.
Paris: Denoël (Arc-en-ciel). Pp. 188.

A4   VOYAGE IN THE DARK   1934

A4a. First English Edition, 1934

VOYAGE IN THE DARK | BY | JEAN RHYS | AUTHOR OF | AFTER LEAV-
ING MR. MACKENZIE | THE LEFT BANK | POSTURES | CONSTABLE & CO
LTD | LONDON

Format: [A]$_8$ - I$_8$, K$_8$ - O$_8$. Each signature page includes the
code "V.D."

Pagination: [i] half title; [ii] RECENT CONSTABLE FICTION |
[four titles--not by Rhys--with press quotations]; [iii] title
page; [iv] PUBLISHED BY | CONSTABLE AND COMPANY LTD. | LONDON
| * | OXFORD UNIVERSITY PRESS | BOMBAY CALCUTTA MADRAS | * |
THE MACMILLAN COMPANY | OF CANADA, LIMITED | TORONTO | * |
FIRST PUBLISHED 1934 | PRINTED IN GREAT BRITAIN BY THE WHITE-
FRIARS PRESS LTD. | LONDON AND TONBRIDGE; [1] PART I; [2] blank;
3-118, text; [119] PART II; [120] blank; 121-160, text; [161]
PART III; [162] blank; 163-210, text; [211] PART IV; [212]
blank; 213-[219] text; [220] blank. Bound in (on different
paper), Constable's Catalogue, pp. 1-24.

Contents: Four parts numbered I, II, III, and IV, and divided
into chapters without titles but numbered with Roman numerals.

Binding: Slate blue, linen-weave cloth boards, lettered on
the spine in dark blue: VOYAGE | IN THE | DARK * | BY JEAN |
RHYS * | CONSTABLE. All edges trimmed and top edge stained
blue. White end-papers. 7 3/10 x 4 7/10 inches.

Publication: October 1934 at five shillings.

Copies examined: British Library deposit copy, pressmark NN
23087, dated 18 October 1934; and copy in the Jean Rhys Collection, University of Tulsa. The description above agrees
in all respects with these copies. The Tulsa copy has the
following holograph inscription on the front free end-paper:
FOR SELMA | WITH LOVE | FROM | JEAN | [rule]. The inside
front cover is marked in pencil with the price (2/6) and the
hand-writing is that of Jean Rhys's old age. In her letters
to Selma Vaz Dias the novelist mentions buying copies of her
works to give to her new friend, and this copy is obviously
one which she bought in a second-hand bookshop.

The Cyril Connolly Collection at the University of Tulsa
also includes a copy of *Voyage in the Dark*; it is identical
with the other two copies except that it does not have the Constable Catalogue bound in and that the book is bound in light
red, textured cloth boards with lettering in black. There are
several broken pieces of type and irregularities of inking in
the text. It seems probable that the red binding was later
than the blue and that this volume may be the "cheap edition"
(see below, A4c).

Notes: The bound-in Catalogue described above contains an
entry for Jean Rhys, *Two Tunes*, along with a three-sentence
description of a novel which is obviously *Voyage in the Dark*.
Unlike the other titles in the Catalogue, there is no price
given for the Rhys novel.

Reviews:

Nieuwe Rotterdamsche Courant, 20 October 1934, p. 2.

Times Literary Supplement, No. 1709 (1 November 1934), p. 752.

Unlike most other contemporary reviewers, this anonymous
critic finds such qualities of "understanding" and "compas-
sion" in the novel that its "impact, ... with all its pity
and sordidness, is that of serenity and hope." Having outlined the details of the plot, he declares that "through the
whole pitiful story Miss Rhys's sense of beauty lights a
lamp that redeems much of the gloom and tragedy."

[Constable advertisement], *Observer*, No. 7484 (4 November
1934), p. 12.

The novel is advertised as "Recommended by the Book Society"
and Frank Swinnerton is quoted: "The book is quite masterly.
I do not know of any other man or woman who could have written it.... It has perfect and painful verisimilitude, poignant brevity, mercy, ruthlessness. It fascinates me." A
second advertisement appears in the *Observer*, No. 7486 (18
November 1934), p. 5, in which Swinnerton and Sylvia Lynd
(*News Chronicle* [see below]) are quoted; a third advertisement in the *Observer*, No. 7490 (16 December 1934), p. 4,
lists Constable's new titles; *Voyage in the Dark* is included
under "Fiction for Women."

Sylvia Lynd, *Harper's Bazaar*. (Not seen)

Selections from this review are quoted in the publisher's
advertisement in the *Sunday Times*, No. 5822 (11 November

1934), p. 8: "A brilliantly clever novel. The truth about the grotesque and ugly and wretched and contemptible side of life could scarcely be told better than it is told here."

Lady. (Not seen)

This unsigned review is quoted in the publisher's advertisement in the *Sunday Times*, No. 5822 (11 November 1934), p. 8: "Miss Rhys is not a scribbler leaning desperately on a shocking subject, but a really fine writer of fiction."

Norah Hoult, *Yorkshire Evening Post.* (Not seen)

A quotation from this review is given in the publisher's advertisement in the *Sunday Times*, No. 5822 (11 November 1934), p. 8: "Jean Rhys, the author of that extraordinarily fine novel, *After Leaving Mr. Mackenzie,* has now published another equally remarkable book."

Ralph Straus, "New Fiction: Some Feminine Portraits." *Sunday Times*, No. 5822 (11 November 1934), p. 9.

Discussing five novels "which do their best to uncover the feminine veil," Straus gives the first half of his review to "Elizabeth's" *The Jasmine Farm* which is obviously more to his taste than the "pitiless and pitiful picture" provided by Rhys in her "cameo in drab." He succinctly outlines the plot, noting that while "there have been such pictures before, ... few [were] so stark and ruthless and at the same time so clean and clear-cut." This issue of the newspaper includes Constable's advertisement for *Voyage in the Dark,* described as "A new 'Esther Waters,'" in which the comments by Lynd (*Harper's Bazaar*), Lady, and Norah Hoult (*Yorkshire Evening Post*) are quoted; Swinnerton and the *Times Literary Supplement* are also quoted. A second advertisement appeared in the *Sunday Times*, No. 5826 (9 December 1934), p. 12, with a quotation from Sylvia Lynd (*News Chronicle*); a third advertisement appeared on 16 December 1934; it is identical with that in the *Observer* for the same date. This advertisement also appeared in the *New Statesman*, 8 (8 December 1934), 849.

Sylvia Lynd, "Tales of Long Ago in New Novels." *News Chronicle*, No. 27630 (12 November 1934), p. 4.

Reviewing three novels, Lynd finds "no fault" with *Voyage in the Dark* and calls the "treatment ... brilliant." She thinks that the technique derives from that of Ernest Hem-

ingway. While the story of "the making of a prostitute"
is "less of a novelty now [than] in the 'nineties," the
novel is "a perfect thing of its kind, with the intensity
and force which belong to genius."

"New Books--A Selected List." *London Mercury*, 31 (December
1934), 189.

The reviewer describes the novel in three sentences of
praise.

"Recommended Novels." *Saturday Review* (London), 158 (1 December 1934), 468.

In a list of ten novels with a paragraph notice for each,
Voyage in the Dark is referred to as "a strangely moving
pitiful little tale" in which the narrative style "softens
the effect of sordidness and gloom."

A4b. First American Edition, 1935

* | VOYAGE | IN THE DARK | * | JEAN RHYS | NEW YORK * MCMXXXV
| WILLIAM MORROW & CO. | *

Format: Seventeen gatherings of eight leaves. No signatures.

Pagination: [i] half title; [ii] ALSO BY MISS RHYS | * |
AFTER LEAVING MR. MACKENZIE | THE LEFT BANK | QUARTET; [iii]
title page; [iv] VOYAGE IN THE DARK | COPYRIGHT-1935 | BY JEAN
RHYS | PRINTED IN THE UNITED STATES | BY THE STRATFORD PRESS,
INC., NEW YORK; [1] PART I; [2] blank; 3-141, text; [142]
blank; [143] PART II; [144] blank; 145-192, text; [193] PART
III; [194] blank; 195-256, text; [257] PART IV; [258] blank;
259-266, text; one blank leaf.

Contents: Identical with A4a.

Binding: Orange, linen-weave cloth boards lettered in black
on the spine: VOYAGE | IN THE | DARK | JEAN | RHYS | * | MOR-
ROW | * . On the front cover a circular design printed in
black and incorporating the words: VOYAGE IN THE DARK JEAN
RHYS. Top and bottom edges trimmed, and top edges stained.
White end-papers. 7 1/2 x 5 inches.

Publication: March 1935 at $2.00.

Copy examined: Perkins Library (Rare Book Room).

Reviews:

T.P.,Jr. *Saturday Review of Literature*, 11 (16 March 1935), 556.

The reviewer begins with balanced generalizations about Rhys's books, asserting that the novelist "is primarily a realistic writer, but a realist of the emotions, free from that tendency to exaggerate the importance of detail which used to be characteristic of the school." There is little variety in her characters or subject matter: "She specializes in young girls who have come to Paris or London ... and who are either about to go astray or already in that undefinable state." Her style is "well adapted to her subject matter." The critic shows his knowledge of Rhys's earlier novels as he briefly outlines the plot of *Voyage in the Dark* in which "Miss Rhys has done a very nearly perfect job."

Florence Haxton Britten, "Recent Leading Fiction." *New York Herald Tribune Books*, 11 (17 March 1935), 10.

In this enthusiastic, discursive essay focussed on the artistic perfection of the novel Britten compares the style to the method of the Imagist poets: "Put into words the thing itself.... Out of that will come new, original beauty of a high order.... So it is when the method is instinctively adhered to by a novelist of fresh, sensitive vision and rare artistry." The reviewer recounts the story of the novel in detail, concluding that it is "a stream-of-consciousness account of the futile effort of a bewildered child to orient herself in a confusing world" which ultimately forces one-- although the novel "is no social document"--to consider one's responsibility "for the weak."

Jane Spence Southron, "A Girl's Ordeal." *New York Times Book Review*, 17 March 1935, p. 7.

In this important review Southron sketches in the details of Rhys's earlier books, unequivocally stating that the novelist has concerned herself with prostitutes and their world while seeing them as individuals at the mercy of their personalities and the cruelty of the world. The reviewer analyzes the narrative techniques used in *Voyage in the Dark*, realizing that the "mental flash-backs" heighten "the drama by vivid contrast." She recounts the events of the novel in detail and stresses the novelist's satire which

is mainly "directed at hypocrisy." She writes with sympathy of Anna's situation and calls her "this smirched and
unhappy child." This totally enthusiastic review ends with
the evaluation, "Aside altogether from its undeniable artistic excellence the book displays unusually broad sympathy
and quite exceptional insight."

Hazel Hawthorne, "Some Spring Novels." *New Republic*, 82 (10
April 1935), 260.

Calling Rhys "one of the finest writers of this time,"
Hawthorne compares her to Schnitzler because she too "is
irradiated with pity for the woman who is victimized by
either too much or not enough feeling, or perhaps ... the
woman in whom the very excess of feeling causes an atrophy
of itself whenever action ... is required of her." The
reviewer provides a brief account of the novel.

A4c. Second English Edition, 1936

[In May 1936 Constable issued a "cheap edition" priced
at two shillings and sixpence. I have not been able to
locate a copy of the novel which could be positively
identified as this edition; the copy in the Connolly
Collection described in A4a: Copies Examined may possibly be this "cheap edition."]

A4d. Third English Edition, 1967

VOYAGE | IN THE | DARK | JEAN RHYS | * | ANDRE DEUTSCH

Format: [ ]$_4$, VID•A★$_{12}$, VID•B$_4$, VID•B★$_{12}$, VID•C$_4$, VID•C★$_{12}$,
VID•D$_4$, VID•D★$_{12}$, VID•E$_4$, [ ]$_{12}$, VID•F$_4$, VID•F★$_{12}$.

Pagination: [1] half title including a two-paragraph précis of
the novel; [2] BY THE SAME AUTHOR | WIDE SARGASSO SEA | GOOD
MORNING, MIDNIGHT | POSTURES | AFTER LEAVING MR. MACKENZIE |
THE LEFT BANK; [3] title page; [4] THIS EDITION PUBLISHED 1967
BY | ANDRE DEUTSCH LIMITED | 105 GREAT RUSSELL STREET | LONDON
WC 1 | FIRST PUBLISHED 1934 BY | CONSTABLE AND COMPANY LIMITED
| ALL RIGHTS RESERVED | PRINTED IN GREAT BRITAIN BY | EBENEZER

BAYLIS AND SON LTD | THE TRINITY PRESS | WORCESTER AND LONDON;
[5] PART ONE; [6] blank; [7]-100, text; [101] PART TWO; [102]
blank; 103-135, text; [136] blank; [137] PART THREE; [138]
blank; 139-179, text; [180] blank; [181] PART FOUR; [182]
blank; 183-188, text; two blank leaves.

Contents: Identical with A4a.

Binding: Light brown, paper-covered boards, lettered on the
spine in gilt: * | VOYAGE | IN THE | DARK | * | JEAN | RHYS |
* | * | ANDRE | DEUTSCH. All edges trimmed. White end-papers.
7 9/10 x 5 inches.

Publication: June 1967 at twenty-one shillings.

Copies examined: British Library deposit copy, pressmark X.
909/10312, received June 1967; University of London Library
copy; Jean Rhys Collection, University of Tulsa. The Tulsa
copy was given by Jean Rhys to her brother-in-law Alec Hamer
and is inscribed by her on the front free end-paper: WITH
LOVE | JEAN RHYS | JULY 2ND 1968. The color of the binding
of this copy is a dark maroon.

Notes: The volume was issued with a pictorial dust-jacket
designed by Barbara Brown.

Reviews:

Francis Hope, "Women Beware Everyone." *Observer*, No. 9178
(11 June 1967), p. 26.

   Introducing Rhys as the author of *Wide Sargasso Sea*, Hope
   discusses *Voyage in the Dark* in terms of its portrayal of Anna, whose "progress--chorus-girl to kept woman to prostitute
   --is like a Salvation Army tract rewritten from the inside,
   with no hint of salvation." He comments on the style that
   "it is like (well, fairly like) a story by Doris Lessing re-
   worked by Virginia Woolf." Turning to *Good Morning, Midnight* the reviewer considers it "more completely hopeless;"
   he notes the events of the novel (it is "a short story
   rather than a novel") and considers that the "dénouement
   ... is ... a very thorough pay-off for anyone bridling at
   the book's lapses into artificiality of manner or content."

Julian Jebb, "Painful Eyes." *Financial Times*, 14 June 1967.

   A review of *Voyage in the Dark* and *Good Morning, Midnight*
   in which Francis Wyndham is praised for his part in the
   "discovery" of Jean Rhys.

"Neurotic Women." *Times Literary Supplement*, No. 3412 (20
July 1967), p. 644.

The reviewer declares that "All Jean Rhys's novels deal essentially with the same unhappy situation in different
guises.... The case for neurotic woman has rarely been put
with such artistry or seemed so hopeless." After summariz-
ing very briefly the contents of *Voyage in the Dark* and *Good
Morning, Midnight*, the writer comments on the "distinct, but
not disagreeable, element of tear-jerking.... *Voyage in the
Dark* ... just misses being sentimental by a narrow margin of
irony and might well seem monotonous were it not for precise
construction and a slightly acid charm."

Neville Braybrooke, "Between Dog and Wolf." *Spectator*, 219
(21 July 1967), 77-78.

Writing on the occasion of Rhys's being given a Royal Society of Literature award, Braybrooke studies all of the novelist's literary works in detail. He begins with biographical details with the stress placed upon Rhys's West Indian
origins and her role in the expatriate Parisian world of the
'twenties. He sees that *Voyage in the Dark* and *Good Morning, Midnight*, "written in the first person, ... explore,
though in greater depth, the territory of the two earlier
books written in the third person." Having described the
contents of *The Left Bank*, he summarizes in detail the plots
of the four pre-World War II novels and draws comparisons
between the four heroines who all "belong to an in-between
world.... [T]hey are flotsam floating between the rich and
the poor, just as, in the West Indies, the Creole belongs
to neither white nor black." In these novels the "lovely,
foolish women" are at the mercy of "cruel, deceiving men."
This "injustice" is less one-sided in *Wide Sargasso Sea*,
which work Braybrooke studies with care, showing its historical relationships to *Jane Eyre*. The essayist concludes
by noting the twenty-seven years of no publications and
asserts that Rhys's "books and stories show the assured
touch of a master, and are among the most original and memorable of our time."

Martin Shuttleworth, "Mrs Micawber." *Punch*, 253 (16 August
1967), 253.

After noting that Rhys has "never caught on," the critic
sums up her work: "There is really only one Jean Rhys book,
one Jean Rhys heroine. She is a girl and/or woman Micawber;
the book is the story of what life does to a female utterly

impractical, incompetent, generous, passive." Shuttleworth
praises Rhys's accomplishment and summarizes the plots of
Voyage in the Dark, *Good Morning, Midnight*, and *Wide Sargasso Sea*.

A4e.   Second American Edition, 1968

VOYAGE | IN THE | DARK | JEAN RHYS | * | W.W. NORTON & COMPANY.
INC. | NEW YORK

Format: Six gatherings of sixteen leaves. No signatures.

Pagination: [i-ii] blank; [1] half title; [2] BY THE SAME
AUTHOR | WIDE SARGASSO SEA | GOOD MORNING, MIDNIGHT | POSTURES
| AFTER LEAVING MR MACKENZIE | THE LEFT BANK; [3] title page;
[4] ALL RIGHTS RESERVED | LIBRARY OF CONGRESS CATALOG CARD NO.
68-16564 | PRINTED IN THE UNITED STATES OF AMERICA | 1 2 3 4
5 6 7 8 9 0; [5] PART ONE; [6] blank; [7]-100, text; [101]
PART TWO; [102] blank; 103-135, text; [136] blank; [137] PART
THREE; [138] blank; 139-179, text; [180] blank; [181] PART
FOUR; [182] blank; 183-188, text; two blank leaves.

Contents: Identical with A4a.

Binding: Mustard yellow, paper-covered boards, the spine and
one-quarter of the boards bound in dark green, smooth cloth.
Spine lettered in gilt from head to tail: RHYS VOYAGE IN THE
DARK, and horizontally at the tail: NORTON. Top edges trimmed.
End-papers. 8 1/4 x 5 3/4 inches.

Publication: April 1968 at $4.95.

Copies examined: Library of Congress copy, call number PZ3.
R3494. Vo 5; and University of Tulsa Library copy, call num-
ber 820.81 | R479 | Vo.

Reviews:

Publishers Weekly, 193 (8 January 1968), 65.

This carefully written summary of the novel calls attention to the skillfully drawn characters--"even relatively
minor ones pulsate with desperate life." The novel "well
deserves to be brought back again."

Carmen P. Collier. *Best Sellers*, 28 (1 May 1968), 58-59.

Collier briefly reviews Rhys's literary career and recapit-
ulates the story of the novel which, though "pitiful," is
"neither gloomy nor sordid." Throughout the review Collier
suggests that Rhys was ahead of her time and that "her ability to create an atmosphere and her power to express an
emotion and to present life will be better understood today
and more widely acclaimed than thirty years ago."

Elizabeth W. Frazer. *Library Journal*, 93 (1 May 1968), 1919.

The critic calls the "reissue ... just as marvelously contemporary as when the book was first published" and summarizes the action, concluding with the judgement: "A work of
high quality."

New Yorker, 44 (24 August 1968), 119.

The reviewer briefly summarizes this "captivating short
novel," compares Anna Morgan to Colette's Mitsou, and declares that "this book is a classic of the small--which is
only to say extra-precious--kind."

A4f. First English Paperback, 1969

JEAN RHYS | VOYAGE IN THE DARK | PENGUIN BOOKS

Format: [   ]$_{10}$, V.I.D$^\bullet$2$_{10}$ - V.I.D$^\bullet$8$_{10}$.

Pagination: [1] PENGUIN BOOK 2960 | VOYAGE IN THE DARK | [nine-
teen line description of Jean Rhys's literary career] | * ;
[2] blank; [3] title page; [4] PENGUIN BOOKS LTD, HARMONDS-
WORTH, | MIDDLESEX, ENGLAND | PENGUIN BOOKS AUSTRALIA LTD,
RINGWOOD, | VICTORIA, AUSTRALIA | FIRST PUBLISHED BY CONSTABLE
1934 | THIS EDITION PUBLISHED BY ANDRÉ DEUTSCH 1967 | PUBLISHED
IN PENGUIN BOOKS 1969 | MADE AND PRINTED IN GREAT BRITAIN BY |
HAZELL WATSON & VINEY LTD, AYLESBURY, BUCKS | SET IN LINOTYPE
BASKERVILLE | THIS BOOK IS SOLD SUBJECT TO THE CONDITION THAT |
IT SHALL NOT, BY WAY OF TRADE OR OTHERWISE, BE LENT, | RE-SOLD,
HIRED OUT, OR OTHERWISE CIRCULATED WITHOUT | THE PUBLISHER'S
PRIOR CONSENT IN ANY FORM OF | BINDING OR COVER OTHER THAN
THAT IN WHICH IT IS | PUBLISHED AND WITHOUT A SIMILAR CONDI-
TION | INCLUDING THIS CONDITION BEING IMPOSED ON THE | SUB-
SEQUENT PURCHASER; [5] PART ONE; [6] blank; 7-[86] text; [87]

PART TWO; [88] blank; 89-[115] text; [116] blank; [117] PART
THREE; [118] blank; 119-[152] text; [153] PART FOUR; [154]
blank; 155-[159] text; [160] ALSO BY JEAN RHYS [advertisements
for the Penguin editions of *Wide Sargasso Sea* and *Good Morning,
Midnight,* with the note: NOT FOR SALE IN THE U.S.A.]

Contents: Four parts divided into chapters without titles and
numbered with Arabic numerals.

Binding: White paper covers printed in black, orange, and
aqua. On the front cover, a drawing of a girl in front of a
dressing-table and the words: BY THE AUTHOR OF WIDE SARGASSO
SEA | JEAN RHYS | VOYAGE IN THE DARK. On the spine from head
to tail: JEAN RHYS VOYAGE IN THE DARK; and horizontally at
the tail: 2960 | * . On the back cover, a three-paragraph de-
scription of the novel, followed by: COVER ILLUSTRATION BY
FAITH JACQUES | FOR COPYRIGHT REASONS THIS EDITION IS NOT FOR
SALE IN THE U.S.A. | UNITED KINGDOM 20P 4/- | AUSTRALIA
$0.70 | NEW ZEALAND $0.65 | SOUTH AFRICA R0.50 | CANADA $0.85.
All edges trimmed. 7 x 4 3/8 inches.

Publication: May 1969 at twenty pence or four shillings.

Copies examined: Personal copy; copy in the Cyril Connolly
Collection, University of Tulsa Library.

Notes: Later impressions were issued in 1975 and 1981.

Reviews:

"Paperbacks." *Times* (London), No. 57586 (14 June 1969), p. 23.

   After briefly noting the plot details, the reviewer remarks:
   "There is a Colette-like air to Jean Rhys's novel. Her
   style is succinct, tender, idiomatic; at its best, very
   good indeed."

"Paperbacks." *Observer*, No. 9608 (28 September 1975), p. 22.

   The reviewer writes one-sentence summaries of *Voyage in
   the Dark* and *Good Morning, Midnight,* commenting that
   "Although the books sank noiselessly soon after their
   original publication, they seem now two of the finest
   novels of the thirties."

A4g. First American Paperback, 1975

JEAN RHYS | * | VOYAGE | IN THE | DARK | POPULAR LIBRARY. NEW
YORK

Format: Perfect binding.

Pagination: [1] [seventeen-line quotation from and description
of the novel]; [2] blank; [3] title page; [4] ALL POPULAR LIB-
RARY BOOKS ARE CAREFULLY SELECTED BY THE | POPULAR LIBRARY
EDITORIAL BOARD AND REPRESENT TITLES BY THE | WORLD'S GREATEST
AUTHORS. | POPULAR LIBRARY EDITION | THIS BOOK IS FULLY PRO-
TECTED IN ALL COUNTRIES BELONGING TO THE | INTERNATIONAL COPY-
RIGHT UNION. | PUBLISHED BY ARRANGEMENT WITH W.W. NORTON AND
COMPANY, INC. | PRINTED IN THE UNITED STATES OF AMERICA | ALL
RIGHTS RESERVED, INCLUDING THE RIGHT TO REPRODUCE THIS BOOK, |
OR PARTS THEREOF, EXCEPT FOR THE INCLUSION OF BRIEF QUOTATIONS
IN A | REVIEW. ; [5] PART ONE; [6] blank; 7-85, text; [86]
blank; [87] PART TWO; [88] blank; 89-116, text; [117] PART
THREE; [118] blank; 119-154, text; [155] PART FOUR; [156]
blank; 157-160, text.

Contents: Identical with A4f.

Binding: Paper covers. The front cover is rose, printed in
black, blue, and white; the design includes a wreath encircling
the words: "THE BEST LIVING ENGLISH NOVELIST"--NEW YORK TIMES.
Above the wreath: * $1.25 445-00250-125; and below it: JEAN
RHYS | * | VOYAGE | IN THE | DARK | "EXCEPTIONAL"--NEW YORK
TIMES | "PERFECT" | --SATURDAY REVIEW OF LITERATURE. On the
spine, horizontally at the head: * | POPULAR | LIBRARY | FIC-
TION; and from head to tail: VOYAGE IN THE DARK JEAN RHYS
445-00250-125. The back cover is white, printed in rose and
black: LONDON, 1914-- | A WORLD OF SEDUCTIVE | OPULENCE AND |
ULTIMATE CORRUPTION | [two-paragraph description of the novel]
| "MARVELOUS!"--NEW YORK TIMES | FIRST TIME IN PAPERBACK |
POPULAR * LIBRARY. All edges trimmed and stained yellow.
6 7/8 x 4 1/8 inches.

Publication: February 1975 at $1.25.

Copy examined: Personal copy.

Notes: According to Alice K. Turner, *Publishers Weekly*, 206 (1
July 1974), 56, the first printing of this edition consisted of
100,000 copies. The design of the cover matches that of *Wide
Sargasso Sea*, A6d: 3rd impression.

Reviews:

Gail and Paul Doherty, "Spring Paperback Parade." *America*,
134 (20 March 1976), 230.

In this review of *Voyage in the Dark* and *Tigers Are Better
Looking* the writers give an inaccurate summary of the novel
and report that Rhys "has been writing stories since the
1920's but is just now being widely noticed." This unin-
formed review concludes that "many" of the stories "are told
in a most eerie way by the heroine, without feeling, almost
clinically."

A4h. Second American Paperback, 1982

VOYAGE | IN THE | DARK | JEAN RHYS | * | W.W. NORTON & COMPANY
| NEW YORK. LONDON

Format: Perfect binding.

Pagination: [1] half title; [2] BY JEAN RHYS IN | NORTON PAPER-
BACK | VOYAGE IN THE DARK | WIDE SARGASSO SEA; [3] title page;
[4] NO PART OF THIS PUBLICATION MAY BE | REPRODUCED OR TRANS-
MITTED IN ANY FORM OR BY ANY MEANS, | ELECTRONIC OR MECHANICAL,
INCLUDING PHOTOCOPY, RECORDING, OR | ANY INFORMATION STORAGE
AND RETRIEVAL SYSTEM, WITHOUT | PERMISSION IN WRITING FROM THE
PUBLISHER. | FIRST PUBLISHED AS A NORTON PAPERBACK 1982 | BY
ARRANGEMENT WITH WALLACE & SHEIL AGENCY, INC. | ALL RIGHTS RE-
SERVED | ISBN 0 393 00083 4 | W.W.NORTON & COMPANY, INC., 500
FIFTH AVENUE, | NEW YORK, N.Y. 10110 | PRINTED IN THE UNITED
STATES OF AMERICA | 1 2 3 4 5 6 7 8 9 0; [5] PART ONE | * ;
[6] blank; [7]-100, text; [101] PART TWO | * ; [102] blank;
103-135, text; [136] blank; [137] PART THREE | * ;[138] blank;
139-179, text; [180] blank; [181] PART FOUR | * ; [182] blank;
183-188, text; two blank leaves.

Contents: Identical with A4f.

Binding: Paper covers. The front cover is black, printed in
white and grey with the words: A NOVEL $3.95 | JEAN RHYS |
VOYAGE | IN THE | DARK; and includes silhouettes of the faces
of a man and a woman with red highlights. The black spine is
printed in red, white, and grey from head to tail: RHYS VOYAGE
IN THE DARK NORTON * . The back cover is white, printed in

black, with the heading: JEAN RHYS IN NORTON PAPERBACK; there
are one-paragraph descriptions of *Wide Sargasso Sea* and *Voyage
in the Dark*, as well as one paragraph about Jean Rhys; at the
bottom: COVER DESIGN BY TIM GAYDOS | * NORTON * | W.W. NOR-
RON & COMPANY NEW YORK . LONDON | ISBN 0 393 00083 4. All
edges trimmed. 7 x 4 1/8 inches.

Publication: January 1982 at $3.95.

Copy examined: Personal copy.

Reviews:

"New in Paperback." *Book World* [*Chicago Tribune* and *Washing-
ngton Post*], 12 (28 February 1982), 12.

In this announcement of Norton's publication of *Voyage in
the Dark* and *Wide Sargasso Sea* the anonymous reviewer succinctly details Rhys's literary career as "an object-lesson
for all those who dream of a literary life," concluding
(without having said anything about the titles under review) by asking, "who knows what she might have gone on to
do, given the acclaim she merited?"

Translation. 1. Dutch, 1935 (Not seen)

Melodie in Mineur, translated by Edouard de Nève, with Preface
by Victor E. van Vriesland. Amsterdam: Uitgeveriu de Steenuil.

Translation. 2. Dutch and Belgian, 1969 (Not seen)

Reis Door Het Duister, translated by Henriëtte van Eyk. Ant-
werp: A. W. Bruna; Utrecht: Bruna & Zoon. Pp. 168. Second
edition: Utrecht: Bruna & Zoon, 1975. Pp. 175.

Translation. 3. French, 1974

JEAN | RHYS | VOYAGE | DANS | LES | TÉNÈBRES | ROMAN | TRADUIT
DE L'ANGLAIS | PAR RENÉ DAILLIE | LES LETTRES NOUVELLES |
26, RUE DE CONDÉ, PARIS 6E | DENOËL

Format: [ ]$_{16}$, 2_{16} - 7_{16}.

Pagination: [1] blank; [2] [publisher's advertisement]; [3]
LES LETTRES NOUVELLES | PUBLICATION | DIRIGÉE PAR MAURICE
NADEAU; [4] DU MÊME AUTEUR | DANS LA COLLECTION "LES LETTRES
NOUVELLES" | BONJOUR, MINUIT | LA PRISONNIÈRE DES SARGASSES
| QUATUOR ; [5] title page; [6] TITRE EN ANGLAIS: VOYAGE IN
THE DARK | ©ANDRÉ DEUTSCH, LONDRES, 1967 | PREMIÈRE ÉDITION,
CONSTABLE AND CO, 1934 | © BY EDITIONS DENOËL, 1973; [7]
PREMIÈRE PARTIE; [8] blank; [9]-117, text; [118] blank; [119]
DEUXIÈME PARTIE; [120] blank; [121]-157, text; [158] blank;
[159] TROISIÈME PARTIE; [160] blank; [161]-207, text; [208]
blank; [209] QUATRIÈME PARTIE; [210] blank; [211]-216, text;
[217]-[220] [alphabetical list of authors and their titles
in this series (Rhys included with titles as given above for
p. [4])]; [221] ACHEVÉ D'IMPRIMER SUR LES PRESSES DE | L'IM-
PRIMERIE AUBIN 86 LIGUGÉ/VIENNE | LE 5 FÉVRIER 1974 [lines
1 and 2 are divided in the center by printer's device]; [222]
blank; [223] D.L., 1ER TRIM. 1974--EDIT., 3985.--IMPR., 7527.
| IMPRIMÉ EN FRANCE; [224] 3985.

Contents: Identical with A4f.

Binding: White, glossy paper covers. On the front in black:
JEAN | RHYS | [in red] VOYAGE | DANS LES | TÉNÈBRES |
[a red bar with white printing imposed] ROMAN | TRADUIT DE
L'ANGLAIS PAR | RENÉ DAILLIE | LES LETTRES NOUVELLES LN | [in
black] DENOËL. On the back cover, two-paragraph description
of the novel and its author; at bottom: IMP. PRIESTER. PARIS
2-74. All edges trimmed. 7 1/2 x 4 3/8 inches.

Publication: February 1974.

Copy examined: Perkins Library copy.

Notes: Second edition: Paris: Gallimard (Folio), 1978. Pp.
217. (Not seen)

Translation. 4. Hungarian, 1974 (Not seen)

A Sötétség Utasa (with *Jó reggelt, éjfél!* [*Good Morning, Mid-*
night]), translated by Hanna Udvarhelyi. Budapest: Europa.
Pp. 385.

A5a. First English Edition, 1939

JEAN RHYS | * | GOOD MORNING | MIDNIGHT | LONDON | * | CON-
STABLE & COMPANY LTD

Format: [ ]$_8$, B$_8$ - I$_8$, K$_8$ - P$_8$, R$_8$ - T$_8$.

Pagination: [i-ii] blank; [iii] half title; [iv] BY THE SAME
AUTHOR | * | STORIES AND SKETCHES | THE LEFT BANK | NOVELS |
POSTURES | AFTER LEAVING MR. MACKENZIE | VOYAGE IN THE DARK;
[v] title page; [vi] PUBLISHED BY | CONSTABLE AND COMPANY LTD
| LONDON | THE MACMILLAN COMPANY | OF CANADA, LIMITED | TORON-
TO | FIRST PUBLISHED 1939 | PRINTED IN GREAT BRITAIN BY | EB-
ENEZER BAYLIS & SON LTD. WORCESTER AND LONDON; [vii] [two-
quatrain quotation] Good morning, Midnight! | I'm coming
home, | Day got tired of me-- | How could I of him? | Sunshine
was a sweet place, | I liked to stay-- | But Morn didn't want
me--now-- | So good night, Day! | Emily Dickinson. ; [viii]
blank; [ix] Contents; [x] blank; [1] PART ONE; [2] blank; 3-
112, text; [113] PART TWO; [114] blank; 115-151, text; [152]
blank; [153] PART THREE; [154] blank; 155-207, text; [208]
blank; [209] PART FOUR; [210] blank; 211-[273] text; [274-
278] blank.

Contents: Four parts titled Part One, Part Two, Part Three,
and Part Four, each part further divided into sections of
varying lengths by double paragraphing.

Binding: Purple, linen-weave cloth boards, lettered on the
spine in light green: GOOD | MORNING | MIDNIGHT | * | JEAN |
RHYS | AUTHOR OF | "A VOYAGE | IN THE DARK" | * | CONSTABLE.
All edges trimmed. White end-papers. 7 3/10 x 4 8/10 inches.

Publication: April 1939 at seven shillings and sixpence.

Copies examined: British Library deposit copy, pressmark NN
30204, received 19 April 1939; also copies in the Jean Rhys
Collection and the Cyril Connolly Collection, University of
Tulsa Library. The copy in the Rhys Collection is identical
to that in the British Library; it bears the inscription: FOR
SELMA | FROM JEAN RHYS | GRATEFULLY | * . The hand-writing
is that of the novelist in the early nineteen-fifties. The

volume has been heavily marked throughout, presumably by Selma Vaz Dias for her dramatic recitation (see below, E. 1 and F. 3: 1949).
The copy in the Cyril Connolly Collection differs from the other two in its binding. There are no end-papers; rather the blank leaves [i-ii] and [277-278] have been pasted down to form the end-papers. This copy has been bound in light green, textured cloth on limp boards, and the lettering on the spine is in dark blue or purple.

Reviews:

John Mair, "New Novels." *New Statesman*, 17 (22 April 1939), 614.

Reviewing *Good Morning, Midnight* with two now-forgotten proletarian novels and R. C. Sherriff's *The Hopkins Manuscript*, Mair gives first place to Rhys's "study in accidie" in which the novelist "has drawn a portrait that is very near perfection, and is as profoundly depressing as it is possible for a work of art to be." The critic considers Sasha to have been "copied from life," but the gigolo "is merely facsimilied from fiction, ... the second-rate international novel." Yet Rhys through her literary skill makes even such a puppet tolerable, for "she chooses her words like a poet." Even though the subject matter is distasteful to Mair, he finds the novel "quite remarkably impressive."

"Lost Years." *Times Literary Supplement*, No. 1942 (22 April 1939), p. 231.

Although the review is accompanied by a boxed list of "Recommended" novels in which *Good Morning, Midnight* is "First Choice," the writer clearly has rather mixed feelings about the novel which appears to him "doggedly tough in a feminine way ... always clever and ... sometimes poignant." Analyzing Sasha's character he considers "it is a weakness of the tale that ... Rhys" does not specify what "has crushed Sasha." Sentimentality is always threatened, and the self-consciousness manifested by the "subjective manner" becomes monotonous. Indeed, while responding favorably to the novel as a whole, the reviewer is so repulsed by Sasha that he cannot forbear expressing his disgust at her life.

Frank Swinnerton, "New Novels. All Sorts." *Observer*, No. 7717 (23 April 1939), p. 6.

Remembering the earlier novels, Swinnerton writes of Rhys's
"several ruthlessly disagreeable studies of women whose
lives, casual, improvident, and inescapably draggled, have
fallen into misery." Because of her earlier treatment of
the subject *Good Morning, Midnight* does not have "the fizz
of novelty of *After Leaving Mr Mackenzie*." The brief account of *Good Morning, Midnight* reveals Swinnerton's care-
less reading, although his novelist's eye appreciates
Rhys's "impressionistic gift" of picturing "a room or a
street." While admitting that her "work is not for optim-
ists," he finds "its quality as black-and-white craftsman-
ship ... quite exceptional."

"Literary Supplement Recommendations. Monthly Summary for
April." *Times Literary Supplement*, No. 1944 (6 May 1939),
p. 270.

    Good Morning, Midnight is listed under "Fiction: First
    Choices."

[Publisher's advertisement]. *Times Literary Supplement*, No.
1944 (6 May 1939), p. 265.

    Good Morning, Midnight is one of four books advertised.
    Rhys is identified as "the author of *Voyage in the Dark*"
    and five lines of Swinnerton's *Observer* review are quoted.

Birmingham Post. Quoted in publisher's advertisement, *Sunday
Times*, No. 6057 (14 May 1939), p. 7.

    (Original not seen)

Ralph Straus, "New Fiction. Black and White." *Sunday Times*,
No. 6061 (11 June 1939), p. 8.

    Most of the review consists of Straus's not-altogether-
    accurate summary of the novel which concludes with the
    somewhat grudging admission, "if one finds Miss Rhys's
    technique at times irritating, one can understand why it
    has been used, and must admire the considerable effect
    which it produces."

Kate O'Brien, "Fiction." *Spectator*, 162 (16 June 1939), 1062.

    After using the first half of the full-page review to
    praise W. J. Turner's *The Duchess of Popocatapetl*, O'Brien
    gives three paragraphs to *Good Morning, Midnight* which she
    finds to be "so very modish as almost in its moment of ap-

pearance to be already out of date." She dislikes the
style and considers Rhys, "for a sophisticated writer, odd-
ly dependent on dots." After sketching in some of the details of the plot she notes Rhys's "great powers of bitterness and of humour.... The whole effect is femininely acute
and painful, and the end very pitiful, very bitter."

"Recommended New Novels." *Times Literary Supplement*, No. 1954
(15 July 1939: Summer Reading Supplement), p. iv.

In a listing of recently published titles *Good Morning, Midnight* is given a three-sentence comment. According to the
writer its "story ... is always clever and ... sometimes
poignant. There is not a lot of it, but what there is goes
a little in advance of, say, Mr. Hemingway, the father of
all such as wear a hard-boiled heart on their sleeve."

Dublin Magazine, 15 (January-March 1940), 58-59.

Reviewing *Good Morning, Midnight* and Kathleen Norris's *The
Runaway* the anonymous writer considers *Good Morning, Midnight* primarily a study in character and declares that Rhys
strikes "the proper balance between over-description and
brevity;" yet he much prefers the Norris novel because of
its healthier attitude to life.

A5b. Second English Edition, 1967

GOOD | MORNING, | MIDNIGHT | JEAN RHYS | * | ANDRE DEUTSCH

Format: [   ]$_{16}$, GMM • B$_{16}$ - GMM • F$_{16}$.

Pagination: [1] half title including a two-paragraph précis
of the novel; [2] BY THE SAME AUTHOR | WIDE SARGASSO SEA |
VOYAGE IN THE DARK | POSTURES | AFTER LEAVING MR MACKENZIE |
THE LEFT BANK; [3] title page; [4] THIS EDITION PUBLISHED
1967 BY | ANDRE DEUTSCH LIMITED | 105 GREAT RUSSELL STREET |
LONDON WC 1 | FIRST PUBLISHED 1939 BY | CONSTABLE AND COMPANY
LIMITED | ALL RIGHTS RESERVED | PRINTED IN GREAT BRITAIN BY |
EBENEZER BAYLIS AND SON LTD | THE TRINITY PRESS | WORCESTER
AND LONDON; [5] [two-line quotation] Good morning, Midnight!
| I'm coming home, | Day got tired of me-- | How could I of
him? | Sunshine was a sweet place, | I liked to stay-- | But
Morn didn't want me--now-- | So good night, Day! | Emily Dic-

kinson; [6] PUBLISHER'S NOTE [three paragraphs acknowledging
and thanking Selma Vaz Dias for her part in the "rediscovery"
of Jean Rhys; [7] PART ONE | * ; [8] blank; 9-81, text; [82]
blank; [83] PART TWO | * ; [84] blank; 85-109, text; [110]
blank; [111] PART THREE | * ; [112] blank; 113-145, text; [146]
blank; [147] PART FOUR | * ; [148] blank; 149-[190], text; one
blank leaf.

Contents: Four parts titled Part One, Part Two, Part Three,
and Part Four; each part subdivided into sections of varying
lengths by triple paragraphing and a centered printer's orna-
ment; and these subdivisions further divided by double paragraphing.

Binding: Dark blue, textured paper-covered boards, lettered
on spine in gilt: * GOOD | MORNING, | MIDNIGHT | * | JEAN |
RHYS | * | * | ANDRE | DEUTSCH. All edges trimmed. End-papers.
7 9/10 x 5 inches.

Publication: June 1967 at twenty-one shillings.

Copies examined: British Library deposit copy, received June
1967; University of London Library; Perkins Library; Jean Rhys
Collection, University of Tulsa Library. The copy in the Rhys
Collection has the following inscription on the front free
end-paper: WITH LOVE TO ALEC | JEAN RHYS | JULY 2ND 1968
(Alec is Alec Hamer, Jean Rhys's brother-in-law).

Notes: The volume was issued with a pictorial dust-jacket designed by Barbara Brown and incorporating quotations from reviews by Braybrooke (*Spectator*), Chambers (*Daily Express*), and
Massingham (*Sunday Express*).

Reviews:

Francis Hope, "Women Beware Everyone." *Observer*, No. 9178
(11 June 1967), p. 26.

    See above, A4d: Reviews.

Julian Jebb, "Painful Eyes." *Financial Times*, 14 June 1967.

    See above, A4d: Reviews.

"Neurotic Women." *Times Literary Supplement*, No. 3412 (20
July 1967), p. 644.

    See above, A4d: Reviews.

Neville Braybrooke, "Between Dog and Wolf." *Spectator*, 219
(21 July 1967), 77-78.

See above, A4d: Reviews.

Martin Shuttleworth, "Mrs. Micawber." *Punch*, 253 (16 August
1967), 253.

See above, A4d: Reviews.

Manchester Guardian, 97 (21 December 1967), 11.

(Not seen)

A5c. First English Paperback, 1969

JEAN   RHYS | GOOD   MORNING,   MIDNIGHT | PENGUIN   BOOKS

Format: [   ]$_{10}$,   G.M.M. $\cdot$ 2_{10} - G.M.M. $\cdot$ 8_{10}.

Pagination: [1] PENGUIN BOOK 2961 | GOOD MORNING, MIDNIGHT
[nineteen-line description of Jean Rhys's literary career];
[2] blank; [3] title page; [4] PENGUIN BOOKS LTD, HARMONDS-
WORTH, | MIDDLESEX, ENGLAND | PENGUIN BOOKS AUSTRALIA LTD,
RINGWOOD, | VICTORIA, AUSTRALIA | FIRST PUBLISHED BY CONSTABLE
1939 | THIS EDITION PUBLISHED BY ANDRÉ DEUTSCH 1967 | PUBLISHED
IN PENGUIN BOOKS 1969 | ALL RIGHTS RESERVED | MADE AND PRINTED
IN GREAT BRITAIN BY | HAZELL WATSON & VINEY LTD, AYLESBURY,
BUCKS | SET IN LINOTYPE BASKERVILLE | THIS BOOK IS SOLD SUB-
JECT TO THE CONDITION THAT | IT SHALL NOT, BY WAY OF TRADE OR
OTHERWISE, BE LENT, | RE-SOLD, HIRED OUT, OR OTHERWISE CIRCU-
LATED WITHOUT | THE PUBLISHER'S PRIOR CONSENT IN ANY FORM OF |
BINDING OR COVER OTHER THAN THAT IN WHICH IT IS | PUBLISHED
AND WITHOUT A SIMILAR CONDITION | INCLUDING THIS CONDITION
BEING IMPOSED ON THE | SUBJEQUENT PURCHASER; [5] [two-quatrain
quotation] Good morning, Midnight! | I'm coming home, | Day
got tired of me-- | How could I of him? | Sunshine was a sweet
place, | I liked to stay-- | But Morn didn't want me--now-- |
So good night, Day! | Emily Dickinson; [6] PUBLISHER'S NOTE
IN THE 1967 ANDRÉ DEUTSCH | EDITION [three paragraphs acknow-
ledging and thanking Selma Vaz Dias for her part in the "rediscovery" of Jean Rhys]; [7] PART ONE; [8] blank; 9-[68] text;
[69] PART TWO; [70] blank; 71-[91] text; [92] blank; [93] PART
THREE; [94] blank; 95-[121] text; [122] blank; [123] PART FOUR;

[124] blank; 125-[159] text; [160][publisher's advertisement
for *Wide Sargasso Sea* and *Voyage in the Dark*].

Contents: Identical with A5b.

Binding: White paper covers, printed in black, orange, and
russet. On the front cover a drawing of a woman seated at a
table against a Parisian street scene; at the top: BY THE AUTH-
OR OF WIDE SARGASSO SEA | JEAN RHYS | GOOD MORNING, | MIDNIGHT.
On the spine, from head to tail: JEAN RHYS GOOD MORNING, MID-
NIGHT; and horizontally at the tail: 2961 | * . On the back
cover, a three-paragraph description of the novel; at the bot-
tom: COVER ILLUSTRATION BY FAITH JACQUES | FOR COPYRIGHT REAS-
ONS THIS EDITION IS NOT FOR SALE IN THE U.S.A. | UNITED KING-
DOM 20P 4/- | AUSTRALIA $0.70 | NEW ZEALAND $0.65 | SOUTH
AFRICA R0.50 | CANADA $0.85. All edges trimmed. 7 1/8 x
4 3/8 inches.

Publication: May 1969 at twenty pence or four shillings.

Copy examined: Personal copy.

Notes: Later impressions were issued in 1975, 1980, and 1981.

Reviews:

"Paperbacks." *Observer*, No. 9608 (28 September 1975), p. 22.

   See above, A4f: Reviews.

          A5d. First American Edition, 1970

GOOD | MORNING, | MIDNIGHT | BY JEAN RHYS | * | HARPER & ROW,
PUBLISHERS | NEW YORK AND EVANSTON

Format: Six gatherings of sixteen leaves. No signatures.

Pagination: [1] half title; [2] BY THE SAME AUTHOR | WIDE
SARGASSO SEA | VOYAGE IN THE DARK | POSTURES | AFTER LEAVING
MR MACKENZIE | THE LEFT BANK; [3] title page; [4] GOOD MORN-
ING, MIDNIGHT. ALL RIGHTS RESERVED. PRINTED IN THE UNITED |
STATES OF AMERICA. NO PART OF THIS BOOK MAY BE USED OR RE-
PRODUCED IN ANY | MANNER WHATSOEVER WITHOUT WRITTEN PERMIS-
SION EXCEPT IN THE CASE OF BRIEF | QUOTATIONS EMBODIED IN
CRITICAL ARTICLES AND REVIEWS. FOR INFORMATION ADDRESS |

HARPER & ROW, PUBLISHERS, INC., 49 EAST 33RD STREET, NEW YORK,
N.Y. 10016 | FIRST U.S. EDITION | LIBRARY OF CONGRESS CATALOG
CARD NUMBER: 78-96002; [5] [two-quatrain quotation] Good morn-
ing, Midnight! | I'm coming home, | Day got tired of me-- |
How could I of him? | Sunshine was a sweet place, | I liked
to stay-- | But Morn didn't want me--now-- | So good night,
Day! | Emily Dickinson; [6] blank; [7] PART ONE | * ; [8]
blank; 9-81, text; [82] blank; [83] PART TWO | * ; [84] blank;
85-109, text; [110] blank; [111] PART THREE | * ; [112] blank;
113-145, text; [146] blank; [147] PART FOUR | * ; [148] blank;
149-[190] text; [191] blank; [192] blank except for code numbers at bottom: 70 71 72 73 10 9 8 7 6 5 4 3 2 1.

Contents: Identical with A5b.

Binding: Aqua, cloth-covered boards lettered in magenta. On
the front cover, bottom right-hand corner, publisher's device.
On the spine, from head to tail: GOOD MORNING, MIDNIGHT; horizontally at the head: RHYS; and horizontally at the tail:
HARPER | & ROW. Top edges trimmed and stained magenta. End-
papers. 8 x 5 1/2 inches.

Publication: April 1970 at $4.95.

Copies examined: Perkins Library; personal copy.

Notes: Issued with a dust-jacket designed by Jacqueline
Schuman. Re-issued in 1981 at $8.95.

Reviews:

Publishers Weekly, 197 (26 January 1970), 268.

  The reviewer stresses the thematic connection of the novel
  to "the fiction of the Lost Generation," noting that it is
  not, because of Rhys's exploration of Sarah Jansen's [*sic*]
  psychology, "just a period piece." Although the novel is
  "small in scope, for what it sets out to do, it is very
  nearly perfect."

Martin Levin. *New York Times Book Review*, 22 March 1970,
p. 39.

  Good Morning, Midnight reminds Levin of "Billie Holiday's
  blues ode ... 'Good Morning, Heartache.'" He considers
  the novel "a classic, as alive today as when it was written," and he gives a spare outline of its events, concen-
  trating on Rhys's creation of "so complete a personality

that its abasement and destruction linger with the reader
long after he has put down this unforgettable book."

Sara Blackburn, "Women's Lot." *Book World* [*Chicago Tribune*
and *Washington Post*], 4 (5 April 1970), 6.

Blackburn reads the novel as a study in the despair of a
woman who has lost her youth and who sees herself as destined to be exploited. After an impressionistic summary
of the novel Blackburn writes of Sasha: "Her eventual fate
is even worse than the shattering finish of her relationship with [the gigolo], and marks the moment of her final
surrender to the grotesque, defeated image she's consented
to see as herself." The reviewer points to the fact "that
this thirty-year-old novel could become a strong weapon in
the current and growing movement toward women's liberation"
and speculates that "perhaps thousands of women in this
country today will read this book and, horribly, identify
with the image of its intelligent, attractive, aging,
beaten and bereft heroine."

John Leonard, "What men don't know about women...." *New York
Times*, 119 (12 May 1970), 37.

In the "Books of the Times" column *Good Morning, Midnight*
is given the first half (Christopher Brookhouse's *Running
Out* is also reviewed); and Leonard writes perceptively about
Rhys's insights: the novel is "the expression of a sensibility that seems in its turn to have informed the sensibilities
of later writers like Doris Lessing and Joan Didion." He
understands that "the Paris [of the novel] ... is actually
the city of [Sasha's] self. She explores the architecture
of her own ego." The reviewer enthusiastically praises
the novel.

Geoffrey Wolff. *Newsweek*, 75 (1 June 1970), 91-92.

The critic succinctly describes Sasha's actions and attitudes, deciding that the main character "succeeds in de-
feating herself." He marvels that "it has taken so long
to rediscover Jean Rhys: her writing is clear, her focus
sharp, her characterizations swift, her representations of
states of mind persuasive." *Good Morning, Midnight* exem-
plifies the novelist's "grim and impressive art."

"A Selection of Recent Titles." *New York Times Book Review*,
7 June 1970, p. 2.

A brief summary of *Good Morning, Midnight* in a listing of
other new books. This paragraph is repeated in a similar
listing of significant titles: "1970: A Selected List from
Books of the Year." *New York Times Book Review*, 6 December 1970, pp. 100-101.

Barbara Raskin, "Classic Female." *New Republic*, 163 (4 July
1970), 27.

Writing from the standpoint of the feminist, Raskin treats
Good Morning, Midnight as "a very contemporary novel" in
which Rhys "portrays that particular brand of female helplessness and hopelessness that has only recently been im-
aginatively possessed and described...." Raskin describes
the events of the novel from Sasha's point of view, for
Sasha is "the classic modern female caught in the vicious
circle of her own suffering--unable or unwilling to cease
and desist, to reject her own pain, which is the only pos-
sibility of freedom for a woman." The exploration of "the
psychological wilderness women inhabit in literature" began only recently, and "Rhys was one of the first to begin
decoding the secret message of female existence, and her
novel is an important emotional and artistic legacy for us."

Christopher Ricks, "Female and Other Impersonators." *New York
Review of Books*, 15 (23 July 1970), 12-13.

In trying to understand the novel Ricks points to verbal
parallels between it and T.S. Eliot's poems, and compares
Rhys and Christina Stead, preferring the latter. Without
much insight he describes Sasha in general terms and concludes by expressing his difficulties with the novel: "it
all ends with a desperate 'Yes--yes--yes ... ' which is a
grimly anaphrodisiac counterpart to Molly Bloom's dying
fall. Even so, it is hard even to sense with any precision
just what it is about this fiercely unforgiving book which
so sends it under one's skin. Perhaps there are rather few
such evocations of pain which find no pleasure whatsoever
in it."

A5e. First American Paperback, 1974

GOOD | MORNING, | MIDNIGHT | BY JEAN RHYS | * | VINTAGE BOOKS
| A DIVISION OF RANDOM HOUSE | NEW YORK

Format: Perfect binding.

Pagination: [1] half title; [2] blank; [3] title page; [4]
VINTAGE BOOKS EDITION, MARCH 1974 | ALL RIGHTS RESERVED. PUB-
LISHED IN THE UNITED STATES BY | RANDOM HOUSE, INC., NEW YORK.
PUBLISHED BY ARRANGE- | MENT WITH HARPER & ROW, PUBLISHERS,
INC. | LIBRARY OF CONGRESS CATALOGING IN PUBLICATION DATA |
RHYS, JEAN. | GOOD MORNING, MIDNIGHT. | I. TITLE. | [PZ3.R3494
Go10] [PR6035.H96] 823'.9'.2 73-16280 | ISBN 0-394-71042-8
| MANUFACTURED IN THE UNITED STATES OF AMERICA ; [5] [two-quat-
rain quotation] Good morning, Midnight! | I'm coming home, |
Day got tired of me-- | How could I of him? | Sunshine was a
sweet place, | I liked to stay-- | But Morn didn't want me--
now-- | So good night, Day! | Emily Dickinson; [6] blank; [7]
PART ONE | * ; [8] blank; 9-81, text; [82] blank; [83] PART
TWO | * ; [84] blank;85-109, text; [110] blank; [111] PART
THREE | * ; [112] blank; 113-145, text; [146] blank; [147]
PART FOUR | * ; [148] blank; 149-[190] text; [191] [eight-line
description of Jean Rhys's literary career]; [192] blank.

Contents: Identical with A5b.

Binding: Glossy, plastic-treated paper covers. On the front
cover a photograph of a girl's face printed in tones of orange,
yellow, and brown, with lettering in white or black imposed:
GOOD MORNING, | MIDNIGHT | BY JEAN RHYS | 394-71042-8 *
$1.65 V-42. The light green spine and back cover are printed
in black and aqua: on the spine from head to tail: GOOD MORN-
ING, MIDNIGHT * JEAN RHYS; and horizontally at the tail:
* | V-42 | VINTAGE. On the back cover: "No one who reads
'Good Morning, Midnight' will ever forget it." --Anatole Broyard, *The New York Times*; and a fifteen-line description of the
novel. All edges trimmed. 7 1/8 x 4 3/8 inches.

Publication: March 1974 at $1.65.

Copy examined: Personal copy.

Notes: According to Alice K. Turner, *Publishers Weekly*, 206
(1 July 1974), 56, there had been, by July 1974, three printings of this edition, each of 10,000 copies.

Reviews:

Anatole Broyard, "A Difficult Year for Hats." *New York Times*,
123 (26 March 1974), 39.

   The entire "Books of the Times" column is given over to
   the reviewer's impressionistic and somewhat elliptical re-

port of the novel in which its theme of "a beautiful woman
growing old" is stressed.   Broyard declares that "nobody
has evoked the Paris of the nineteen-thirties better than
Jean Rhys" and, further, that the ending of the novel presents "one of the most devastating encounters between two
human beings in the literature of this century."   The reviewer has only praise for the novel.

A5f.   Second American Paperback, 1982

GOOD | MORNING, | MIDNIGHT | BY JEAN RHYS | * | PERENNIAL
LIBRARY | HARPER & ROW, PUBLISHERS | NEW YORK, CAMBRIDGE,
PHILADELPHIA, SAN FRANCISCO | LONDON, MEXICO CITY, SÃO PAULO,
SYDNEY

Format: Perfect binding.

Pagination: [1] half title; [2] BOOKS BY JEAN RHYS | QUARTET
| AFTER LEAVING MR MACKENZIE | VOYAGE IN THE DARK | GOOD MORN-
ING, MIDNIGHT | WIDE SARGASSO SEA | TIGERS ARE BETTER LOOKING
(STORIES) | SLEEP IT OFF, LADY | SMILE PLEASE (AUTOBIOGRAPHY);
[3] title page; [4]   THIS WORK WAS ORIGINALLY PUBLISHED IN
ENGLAND IN 1938. | GOOD MORNING, MIDNIGHT.   ALL RIGHTS RESERVED.
PRINTED IN THE UNITED STATES OF | AMERICA.   NO PART OF THIS
BOOK MAY BE USED OR REPRODUCED IN ANY MANNER | WHATSOEVER WITHOUT
WRITTEN PERMISSION EXCEPT IN THE CASE OF BRIEF QUOTATIONS |
EMBODIED IN CRITICAL ARTICLES AND REVIEWS.   FOR INFORMATION
ADDRESS HARPER & ROW, | PUBLISHERS, INC., 10 EAST 53RD STREET,
NEW YORK, N.Y. 10022. | FIRST PERENNIAL LIBRARY EDITION PUB-
LISHED 1982. | ISBN:0-06-080580-3 | 82 83 84 85 86 10 9 8 7 6
5 4 3 2 1; [5]   [two-quatrain quotation] Good morning, Mid-
night! | I'm coming home, | Day got tired of me-- | How could
I of him? | Sunshine was a sweet place, | I liked to stay-- |
But Morn didn't want me--now-- | So good night, Day! | Emily
Dickinson; [6] blank; [7] PART ONE | * ; [8] blank; 9-81, text;
[82] blank; [83] PART TWO | * ; [84] blank; 85-109, text; [110]
blank; [111] PART THREE | * ; [112] blank; 113-145, text; [146]
blank; [147] PART FOUR | * ; [148] blank; 149-[190] text; one
blank leaf.

Contents: Identical with A5b.

Binding: Glossy, plastic-treated, white paper covers.   On the
front cover a design including a woman's head and shoulders
against an orange-striped background with imposed white let-
ters: GOOD | MORNING, | MIDNIGHT | JEAN RHYS; and at the bot-

tom in black print: P580 * PERENNIAL LIBRARY $2.95. On
the spine in black letters, horizontally at the head: P580 |
* ; and from the head to the tail: GOOD MORNING, MIDNIGHT
JEAN RHYS. On the back cover a panel outlined in blue: FIC-
TION | GOOD MORNING, MIDNIGHT | JEAN RHYS | [one-paragraph
description of the novel] | [quotations of four reviews (by
Anatole Broyard, *New York Times*; Barbara Raskin, *New Repub-
lic*; Martin Levin, *New York Times Book Review*; and *Financial
Times*)] PERENNIAL LIBRARY * HARPER & ROW, PUBLISHERS |
[at bottom left] COVER DESIGN | © BY FRED MARCELLINO |
[at bottom right] >>$2.95 | ISBN 0-06-080580-3 | 0128482.
All edges trimmed. 7 x 4 1/8 inches.

Publication: 1982 at $2.95.

Copy examined: Personal copy.

Translation. 1. Dutch and Belgian, 1969 (Not seen)

Goodemorgen, Middernacht, translated by Max Schuchart. Ant-
werp: A.W. Bruna; Utrecht: Bruna & Zoon (Grote Beren. No.
58). Pp. 153. Second edition: Utrecht: Bruna & Zoon, 1975.
Pp. 174.

Translation. 2. French, 1969

JEAN | RHYS | BONJOUR | MINUIT | ROMAN | TRADUIT DE L'ANGLAIS
PAR | JACQUELINE BERNARD | LES LETTRES NOUVELLES | 26, RUE DE
CONDÉ, PARIS-6E

Format: [ ]$_{16}$, 2_{16} - 7_{16}, 8_8.

Pagination: [1-2] blank; [3] LES LETTRES NOUVELLES | PUBLIC-
ATION | DIRIGÉE PAR MAURICE NADEAU; [4] DU MÊME AUTEUR, À
PARAÎTRE | DANS LA MÊME COLLECTION: | VASTE MER DES SARGASSES,
ROMAN; [5] title page; [6] © 1969, BY EDITIONS DENOËL, POUR
L'ÉDITION FRANÇAISE. ; [7] [two-quatrain quotation] Bonjour,
Minuit! | Je rentre chez moi, | Le Jour s'est lassé de moi-- |
Comment pouvais-je me lasser de lui? | Le soleil était un doux
endroit, | J'aimais y demeurer--| Mais le Matin n'a plus voulu
de moi--désormais-- | Alors bonne nuit, Jour! | Emily Dickin-

son; [8] blank; [i]-x, text of Introduction; [9] PREMIÈRE
PARTIE; [10] blank; [11]-97, text; [98] blank; [99] DEUXIÈME
PARTIE; [100] blank; [101]-130, text; [131] TROISIÈME PARTIE;
[132] blank; [133]-171, text, [172] blank; [173] QUATRIÈME
PARTIE; [174] blank; [175]-223, text; [224] blank; [225-226]
[alphabetical list of authors and their books in this series];
[227] ACHEVÉ | D'IMPRIMER | [printer's device] | SUR LES |
PRESSES D'AUBIN | LIGUGÉ (VIENNE) | LE 30 OCT. | 1969 | D.L.,
4E TRIM. 1969.--EDITEUR, NO 3016.--IMPRIMEUR, NO 5306. |
IMPRIMÉ EN FRANCE; [228] blank; one blank leaf.

Contents: Four parts, each subdivided into sections of varying lengths by blank spaces.

Binding: Light green paper covers, printed in black. On the
front cover: JEAN | RHYS | BONJOUR | MINUIT ROMAN | DENOËL
LN. On the back cover, a two-paragraph description of the
novel and of Jean Rhys. At the bottom: IMPRIMÉ EN FRANCE 20,
30 F | 19-50-11-69. All edges trimmed. 7 3/4 x 4 1/2 inches.

Publication: October 1969.

Copy examined: Perkins Library copy.

Notes: The Introduction is that written by Francis Wyndham
and first published in *Art and Literature* (see below, F.3:
1964); the translation is by Yvonne Davet.

Translation. 3. German, 1969   (Not seen)

Guten Morgen, Mitternacht, translated by Grete Felten.   Hamburg: Hoffmann & Campe. Second edition: Munich: Deutscher
Taschenbuch Verlag, 1971. Pp. 138.

Translation. 4. Turkish, 1972   (Not seen)

Günaydin Geceyarisi, translated by Nuray Kermen. Istanbul:
Dilek Matbaasi. Pp. 305.

Translation. 5. Italian, 1973 (Not seen)

Buongiorno, Mezzanotte, translated by Miro Silvera. Milan: Bompiani. Pp. 203.

Translation. 6. Hungarian, 1974 (Not seen)

Jó reggelt, éjfél! (with *A Sötétség Utasa* [*Voyage in the Dark*]), translated by Hanna Udvarhelyi. Budapest: Europa. Pp. 385.

Translation. 7. Spanish, 1975 (Not seen)

Buenos Dias, Medianoche, translated by Andrés Bosch. Barcelona: Noguer (Nueva Galería Literaria). Pp. 206.

Translation. 8. Swedish, 1977 (Not seen)

Godmorgon, Midnatt!, translated by Annika Preis. Göteborg: Stegeland. Pp. 179.

A6   WIDE SARGASSO SEA   1966

A6a. First English Edition, 1966

* | WIDE | * | SARGASSO | * | SEA | * | JEAN RHYS | INTRODUC-
TION BY FRANCIS WYNDHAM | * | ANDRE DEUTSCH

Format: [ ]$\bigstar_4$, A$\bigstar_{12}$, B$_4$, B$\bigstar_{12}$, C$_4$, C$\bigstar_{12}$, D$_4$, D$\bigstar_{12}$, E$_4$, E$\bigstar_{12}$, F$_4$, F$\bigstar_{12}$.

Pagination: [1] half title with a three-paragraph description of the novel; [2] BY THE SAME AUTHOR | THE LEFT BANK | CAPE,

1927 | POSTURES | CHATTO & WINDUS, 1928 | AFTER LEAVING MR
MACKENZIE | CAPE, 1930 | VOYAGE IN THE DARK | CONSTABLE, 1934
| GOOD MORNING, MIDNIGHT | CONSTABLE, 1939 | (VOYAGE IN THE
DARK AND | GOOD MORNING, MIDNIGHT ARE | SOON TO BE REISSUED
| BY ANDRÉ DEUTSCH); [3] title page; [4] FIRST PUBLISHED 1966
BY | ANDRE DEUTSCH LIMITED | 105 GREAT RUSSELL STREET | LONDON
WC 1 | COPYRIGHT © 1966 BY JEAN RHYS | ALL RIGHTS RESERVED |
PRINTED IN GREAT BRITAIN BY | EBENEZER BAYLIS AND SON LTD |
THE TRINITY PRESS | WORCESTER AND LONDON; 5-13, Introduction
by Francis Wyndham; [14] blank; [15] PART ONE | * ; [16]
blank; [17]-61, text; [62] blank; [63] PART TWO | * ;[64]
blank; [65]-173, text; [174] blank; [175] PART THREE | * ;
[176] blank; [177]-[190] text; one blank leaf.

Contents: Eight-page Introduction by Francis Wyndham, reprinted from *Art and Literature*, No. 1 (March 1964), pp. 173-
177 (see below, F.3: 1964). Text of the novel: three parts
titled Part One, Part Two, and Part Three, each part further
divided into sections of varying length by double paragraphing.

Binding: Light-red, paper-covered boards, the spine lettered
in gilt: * | WIDE | SARGASSO | SEA | * | JEAN | RHYS | * | * |
ANDRE | DEUTSCH. All edges trimmed. End-papers. 7 3/4 x
5 inches.

Publication: 27 October 1966 at twenty-one shillings.

Copies examined: British Library deposit copy, received October 1966; and copy in the Jean Rhys Collection, University
of Tulsa Library. The copy in the Rhys Collection was sent
by the publisher to Rhys's brother-in-law, Alec Hamer. On the
front pasted down end-paper there is a printed slip beginning
"With the compliments of Diana Athill ... " and with the typed
words: "Jean asked me to send you this. Isn't it wonderful
that the book is getting such a good reception." Pasted on
the front free end-paper is a half-sheet inscribed: TO ALEC |
FROM YOURS WITH LOVE | JEAN RHYS | NOV. 3RD 1966.

Notes: The volume was issued with a pictorial dust-jacket
designed by Eric Thomas. A second impression appeared in
December 1966 and a third, in March 1968.

Reviews:

Norman Shrapnell, "The Gift and Some Skills." *Guardian*, 28
October 1966, p. 9.

     Reviewing *Wide Sargasso Sea* along with five other novels,

Shrapnell praises it and puns: "*Wide Sargasso Sea* is eerie, not to say Jane Eyrie."

Francis Hope, "The First Mrs Rochester." *New Statesman*, 72 (28 October 1966), 638-639.

Hope outlines the story of *Wide Sargasso Sea* and points to its connections with *Jane Eyre*: "There are resonances, but no borrowings." Relying on Wyndham's "Introduction" he sketches the literary career of the novelist, shows the connections between her personal story and that of the "Creole wife" of the novel, and points out that, "as in *The Sound and the Fury*, her scatterbrained narrative is a commentary on itself. It is also a work of some power, and some poetry."

Neville Braybrooke, "Shadow and Substance." *Spectator*, 217 (28 October 1966), 560-561.

Braybrooke points out that the "shadow" of Charlotte Brontë's *Jane Eyre* now "takes on substance" and he provides a full, straight-forward account of the plot of the novel. He concludes: "After a silence of twenty-seven years, except for a few short stories, this much-praised novelist who was the protégée of Ford Madox Ford, has made a magnificent comeback."

[Deutsch advertisement]. *Bookseller*, 29 October 1966, p. 2129.

The publisher quotes in this advertisement the opinions of six London editors or publishers concerning *Wide Sargasso Sea*: the six are John Guest (Longmans), Tom Maschler (Jonathan Cape), David Farrer (Secker and Warburg), Norah Smallwood (Chatto and Windus), Walter Neurath (Thames and Hudson), and John Murray (John Murray).

Peter Chambers, *Daily Express*. (Not seen)

This review is quoted in the publisher's advertisement, *Sunday Times*, No. 7484 (30 October 1966), p. 48, and No. 7488 (27 November 1966), p. 53.

Robert Baldick, "Decadence in the Downs." *Daily Telegraph*.

A review of *Wide Sargasso Sea* and four other novels. Quoted in the publisher's advertisements in the *Sunday Times* noted above.

Colin MacInnes, "Nightmare in Paradise." *Observer*, No. 9147
(30 October 1966), p. 28.

MacInnes gives a straight-forward, complete account of the
plot and subject of the novel, stressing Rhys's use of "natural description ... to evoke the moods of" her characters.
He points to the description of the honeymoon as "the most
powerful section" because the novelist can force the reader
"into the nightmare world with which she enfolds him." The
reviewer expresses no reservations as he praises the novel.

Elizabeth Smart, *Queen*. (Not seen)

This review is quoted in the publisher's advertisement in
the *Sunday Times* noted above.

Kay Dick, "Wife to Mr. Rochester." *Sunday Times*, No. 7484
(30 October 1966), p. 50.

Dick reports on Rhys's pre-World War II novels, maintaining that "they are as unique in their way as the stories of
Katherine Mansfield, though they lack her beautiful discipline." She gives a short account of *Wide Sargasso Sea* and
calls the work "successful ... enormous fun," even though
she wishes the novelist had returned to writing "with an
aspect of life she has observed and experienced rather than
by annotating Charlotte Brontë." This issue of the *Sunday
Times* also includes a two-column publisher's advertisement
for the novel in which the reviews in the *Daily Express*,
Spectator, *Daily Telegraph*, *London Magazine*, and *Queen*
are quoted.

Alan Ross. *London Magazine*, 6 (November 1966), 99, 101.

Ross recounts Rhys's literary history, describing *Voyage
in the Dark* and *Good Morning, Midnight* as "two of the most
remarkable novels of their time" which "have gloomy subjects,
gloomily treated. Romantic and sexual love are given a foul
aftertaste, squalor a fine detail." He calls attention to
the four Rhys stories published in the *London Magazine* and
welcomes the new novel which he describes in general terms,
noticing "a striking thematic affinity to Herbert de Lis-
ser's popular romance *The White Witch of Rose Hall*." He
calls the novel "astonishingly convincing" and sees that
its heroine is similar to Anna Morgan and Sasha Jensen, "a-
like victims of their own attractiveness, predatory temper-
aments and unyielding honesty...."

Hunter Davis, "Atticus: Rip van Rhys." *Sunday Times*, No. 7485 (6 November 1966), p. 13.

On the occasion of the publication of *Wide Sargasso Sea*, the columnist writes a human-interest story about the novelist based on publicity handouts, Wyndham's introduction to the novel, and a personal interview with Rhys. The title indicates the "angle:" the rediscovered artist.

Sally Williams, "Mr. Rochester's First Wife." *Evening Standard*, 15 November 1966, p. 14.

A brief notice.

"New Fiction." *Times*, No. 56,791 (17 November 1966), 16.

The anonymous reviewer examines four new novels, giving the first third of his essay to *Wide Sargasso Sea*. He calls it the "pre-history" of *Jane Eyre*, a "romanticism snatched from the grave of literary history." But the novel "doesn't quite work. It remains whatever the opposite of a sequel is, and doesn't snatch a life of its own."

"A Fairy-Tale Neurotic." *Times Literary Supplement*, No. 3377 (17 November 1966), p. 1039.

This long (almost one-half page) essay on the novel presents an in-depth study of the work with particular attention given to the psychology of the characters. The anonymous reviewer defines the relationship of *Wide Sargasso Sea* to *Jane Eyre*: the latter "is the happy tale of an English Cinderella, *Wide Sargasso Sea* the tragedy of a West Indian heiress. Although the origins of her main characters are in Charlotte Brontë, Miss Rhys's work exists entirely in its own right." He gives a detailed account of the novel and then analyzes the characters. Antoinette's alienation, like that of Virginia Woolf's Mrs. Dalloway, "is to a large extent aesthetic. A Creole narcissus, she sees the world in terms of its beauty, but the only beauty she understands derives from the experiences and fantasies of her own childhood; and above all from the exotic landscape. It is that which gives her a sense of herself and of her own beauty; and with it belongs safety and happiness." The reviewer shows her similarities to Rhys's other heroines: their purpose is "to love and be loved," and they are all dependent upon the men they love--who always abandon them. "Reduced to the bare narrative outline, her novels are about the injustice done by cruel men to lovely women." He quotes extensively from *Wide Sargasso Sea* to show that it expands the situation in earlier novels, particularly in its presentation of the man: "Miss Rhys makes us understand his bewilderment as clearly as hers. He [too] is the victim of ... society...." In this enthusiastic and altogether positive review the writer makes no mention of the "rediscovery" of Rhys and focusses his attention solely on the novel.

Robert Ottoway, *Daily Sketch*.   (Not seen)

Quoted in the publisher's advertisement, *Sunday Times*, 27 November 1966 (see below).

[Deutsch advertisement]. *Sunday Times*, No. 7488 (27 November 1966), p. 53.

The following reviews are quoted in this advertisement: Alan Ross (*London Magazine*), Elizabeth Smart (*Queen*), Peter Chambers (*Daily Express*), Robert Baldick (*Daily Telegraph*), Francis Hope (*New Statesman*), Norman Shrapnell (*Guardian*), Neville Braybrooke (*Spectator*), Colin MacInnes (*Observer*), Rivers Scott (*Sunday Telegraph*), Robert Ottoway (*Daily Sketch*), Sally Williams (*Evening Standard*), *Times Literary Supplement*.

John Knowler, "Return of Jean Rhys." *Books and Bookmen*, 12 (December 1966), 84, 96.

Knowler gives a detailed account of the events of *Wide Sargasso Sea*, noting that after the first sixty page--"perfect in pitch, in pace, in tone, in the exact deployment of fact and atmosphere"--the "back of the book breaks" with the introduction of the husband's narrative. This summary leads to Knowler's revelation that Rhys is making use of *Jane Eyre*, although her work is not a "Brontean pastiche." Knowler credits Francis Wyndham with the discovery of Rhys in 1959, outlines her biography, and surveys the earlier novels (*Postures* is the only one named and discussed: he guesses that the Heidlers are "based on the Fords"). He declares that in *Wide Sargasso Sea* Rhys "has written a novel of the past in a language of lyrical matter-of-factness that seems immediately present." This issue also includes a publisher's advertisement in which the reviews in the *London Magazine, Queen, New Statesman, Observer*, and *Sunday Telegraph* are quoted.

Marghanita Laski, "Books of the Year. Some Personal Choices." *Observer*, No. 9154 (18 December 1966), p. 23.

In this annual, end-of-the-year feature, Laski chooses
Wide Sargasso Sea as one of her three choices.

Hilary Corke, "New Fiction." *Listener*, 77 (19 January
1967), 103.

Reviewing *Wide Sargasso Sea* along with four other novels,
Corke dismisses it in one paragraph.

Martin Shuttleworth, "Mrs.Micawber." *Punch*, 253 (16 August
1967), 253.

See above, A4d: Reviews.

A6b. First American Edition, 1967

WIDE │ SARGASSO │ SEA │ JEAN RHYS │ INTRODUCTION BY FRANCIS
WYNDHAM │ * │ NEW YORK │ W.W. NORTON & COMPANY. INC.

Format: Six gatherings of sixteen leaves. No signatures.

Pagination: [1] half title; [2] BY THE SAME AUTHOR │ THE LEFT
BANK │ WITH A PREFACE BY FORD MADOX FORD │ QUARTET │ VOYAGE IN
THE DARK │ GOOD MORNING, MIDNIGHT; [3] title page; [4] COPY-
RIGHT © 1966 BY JEAN RHYS │ LIBRARY OF CONGRESS CATALOG CARD
NO. 67-15822 │ PRINTED IN THE UNITED STATES OF AMERICA │ 1 2
3 4 5 6 7 8 9; 5-13, Introduction, by Francis Wyndham; [14]
blank; [15] PART ONE │ * ; [16] blank; [17]-61, text; [62]
blank; [63] PART TWO │ * ; [64] blank; [65]-173, text; [174]
blank; [175] PART THREE │ * ; [176] blank; [177]-[190] text;
one blank leaf.

Contents: Identical with A6a.

Binding: Light grey, paper-covered boards with dull, blue-
green linen-weave cloth spine extending to the center of the
covers; the spine lettered in gilt from head to tail: RHYS
WIDE SARGASSO SEA; and horizontally at the tail: NORTON. Top
edges trimmed. End-papers of the same color as the spine.
8 3/8 x 5 1/2 inches.

Publication: April 1967 at $4.50.

Copies examined: Perkins Library (two copies); personal copy.

Notes: The volume was issued with a pictorial dust-jacket designed by Bill Logan; the outside back cover bears six quotations from the British reviews of the novel.

Reviews:

Publishers Weekly, 191 (13 February 1967), 75-76.

Introducing *Wide Sargasso Sea* as "a literary curiosity that has received top critical attention in England, the reviewer describes the story of the novel. He considers the first part to be the "most successful" and describes Rhys as "a writer of sensitivity and delicate precision."

Genevieve M. Casey. *Best Sellers*, 27 (15 May 1967), 75.

Relying heavily on Wyndham's introduction, Casey inaccurately recounts the details of Rhys's literary career; she stresses the similarities between the heroines of the different novels: "Essentially, these are all depictions of the same woman." The reviewer tells the story of *Wide Sargasso Sea*, noting that "Antoinette is in the pattern of Jean Rhys's heroines--feckless, unhappy, promiscuous, victimized by the men in her life, redeemed as she is destroyed by terrible objectivity." The novelist is never "sentimental or discursive. As only a woman can, she looks the human situation squarely in the face and finds it utterly horrible."

Elizabeth W. Frazer. *Library Journal*, 92 (15 May 1967), 1951.

Frazer succinctly summarizes the novel and stresses that it "will be received with interest by the growing numbers of Jean Rhys aficionados." The novel is "Highly recommended for public and academic libraries."

Walter Allen, "Bertha the Doomed." *New York Times Book Review*, 18 June 1967, p. 5.

Noting that *Wide Sargasso Sea* is Rhys's first novel since 1939, Allen remembers that Rhys was "much admired by other contemporary novelists" and contends that she was "very much a writer of her period, one who had come to maturity in the 1920's and whom one might expect to be taken up by Ford." After describing in detail the origin of the novel in *Jane Eyre* he calls it "a triumph of ... Caribbean Gothic atmosphere" and sketches in the character of "Bertha Mason"

as Rhys has recreated it. He realizes that "Bertha Mason
seems to sum up in herself, more closely than ever before,
the nature of the heroine who appears under various names
throughout Jean Rhys's fiction. She is a young woman, generally Creole in origin and artistic in leanings, who is
hopelessly and helplessly at sea in her relations with men,
a passive victim, doomed to destruction. It is remarkable
that after so many years Miss Rhys should have pinned her
down in a character, however sketchily presented, from another novelist." Yet the novel is not a success, for Mr.
Rochester is too "shadowy a figure" and the work is not independent of *Jane Eyre*.

Gerald Kersh, "The Second Time Around." *Saturday Review*, 50
(1 July 1967), 23.

In the first third of this full-page review Kersh retells
the story of the Rhys "rediscovery," leaning heavily on
Wyndham's introduction and writing to attract the larger
reading public. He provides a lengthy and rather lurid description of the events of the plot. In his conclusion he
stresses the unity of the novel: "To quote from it would
be like offering a sample snipping of a tapestry--it might
convey something of the texture, but it wouldn't enlighten
the reader as to the pattern;" and he declares that the
novel is "a work of high art and profound perception...."

Booklist, 63 (15 July 1967), 1182.

A brief description of the novel which is summed up as "an
imaginative but grim psychological tale of encroaching madness and the contributing factors."

"Nation Book Marks." *Nation*, 205 (2 October 1967), 317.

The anonymous reviewer welcomes the reappearance of Rhys,
summarizes the story of the novel while praising the novelist's creation, and declares that "Working a stylistic range
from moody introspection to formal elegance, Miss Rhys has
us traveling under Antoinette's skin. It is an eerie and
memorable trip."

A6c. First English Paperback, 1968

JEAN RHYS | WIDE SARGASSO SEA | INTRODUCTION BY FRANCIS WYND-
HAM | PENGUIN BOOKS

Format: Perfect binding.

Pagination: [1] PENGUIN BOOK 2878 | WIDE SARGASSO SEA | [twen-
ty-line description of Jean Rhys's literary career]; [2] blank;
[3] title page; [4] PENGUIN BOOKS LTD, HARMONDSWORTH, | MID-
DLESEX, ENGLAND | PENGUIN BOOKS AUSTRALIA LTD, RINGWOOD, | VIC-
TORIA, AUSTRALIA | FIRST PUBLISHED BY ANDRE DEUTSCH 1966 | PUB-
LISHED IN PENGUIN BOOKS 1968 | COPYRIGHT © JEAN RHYS, 1966 |
MADE AND PRINTED IN THE NETHERLANDS BY | N. V. DRUKKERIJ BOSCH
UTRECHT | SET IN MONOTYPE BASKERVILLE | THIS BOOK IS SOLD SUB-
JECT TO THE CONDITION THAT | IT SHALL NOT, BY WAY OF TRADE OR
OTHERWISE, BE LENT, | RE-SOLD, HIRED OUT, OR OTHERWISE CIR-
CULATED WITHOUT | THE PUBLISHER'S PRIOR CONSENT IN ANY FORM
OF | BINDING OR COVER OTHER THAN THAT IN WHICH IT IS | PUB-
LISHED AND WITHOUT A SIMILAR CONDITION | INCLUDING THIS CON-
DITION BEING IMPOSED ON THE | SUBSEQUENT PURCHASER; 5-[11]
Introduction by Francis Wyndham; [12] blank; [13] PART ONE;
[14] blank; 15-[51], text; [52] blank; [53] PART TWO; [54]
blank; 55-[142] text; [143] PART THREE; [144] blank; 145-[156]
text; [157][advertisement for Penguin books headed MORE ABOUT
PENGUINS]; [158-159] [advertisement for the Penguin editions
of *Jane Eyre* and *Wuthering Heights*]; [160] blank.

Contents; Identical with A6a.

Binding: White paper covers printed in black, orange, and
blue. On the front cover: WINNER OF 1967 W.H. SMITH & SON
ANNUAL LITERARY AWARD | * | JEAN RHYS | WIDE | SARGASSO |
SEA; and a drawing of a girl's head against a tropical landscape. On the spine, from head to tail: JEAN RHYS WIDE SAR-
GASSO SEA; and horizontally at the tail: 2878 | * . On the
back cover, a three-paragraph description of the novel, fol-
lowed by: 'AN IMAGINATIVE FEAT ALMOST UNCANNY IN ITS VIVID |
INTENSITY'--FRANCIS WYNDHAM | COVER ILLUSTRATION BY FAITH
JAQUES | FOR COPYRIGHT REASONS THIS EDITION IS NOT FOR SALE
IN THE U.S.A. | UNITED KINGDOM 5'- | AUSTRALIA $0.85 | NEW
ZEALAND $0.75 | SOUTH AFRICA R0.65 | CANADA $1.25. All edges
trimmed. 7 1/8 x 4 3/8 inches.

Publication: September 1968 at five shillings.

Copy examined: Personal copy.

Notes: Later impressions were issued in June 1970, 1975, and 1981.

A6d.   First American Paperback, 1973

WIDE │ SARGASSO │ SEA BY JEAN RHYS │ INTRODUCTION BY FRANCIS
WYNDHAM │ POPULAR LIBRARY . NEW YORK

Format: Perfect binding.

Pagination: [1] [thirteen-line quotation from the novel, two-
paragraph description of the novel, and quotation of two re-
views: "INTENSE AND HAUNTING!" QUEEN MAGAZINE │ "STUNNING,
VIVID AND HYPNOTIC!" │ DAILY EXPRESS (LONDON); [2] blank; [3]
title page; [4] ALL POPULAR LIBRARY BOOKS ARE CAREFULLY SE-
LECTED BY THE │ POPULAR LIBRARY EDITORIAL BOARD AND REPRESENT
TITLES BY │ THE WORLD'S GREATEST AUTHORS. │ POPULAR LIBRARY
EDITION │ COPYRIGHT © 1966 BY JEAN RHYS │ LIBRARY OF CONGRESS
CATALOG CARD NUMBER: 67-15822 │ PUBLISHED BY ARRANGEMENT WITH
W.W. NORTON & COMPANY, INC. │ PRINTED IN THE UNITED STATES OF
AMERICA │ ALL RIGHTS RESERVED; 5-[13] Introduction by Francis
Wyndham; [14] blank; [15] PART ONE; [16] blank; 17-62, text;
[63] PART TWO; [64] blank; 65-174, text; [175] PART THREE;
[176] blank; 177-190, text; at bottom right: 5-73; unnumbered
leaf with Popular Library advertisement for six "widely acclaimed reference paperbacks" and including a shipping label
to be cut out.

Contents: Identical with A6a.

Binding: Glossy, plastic-treated covers. The front cover is a
painting (primarily in tones of green) of a ruined building in
a mountainous jungle setting; imposed is a female figure draped
in white. Lettering in white or yellow: * 445-00459-095
95¢ │ A NOVEL OF │ UNFORGETTABLE ROMANCE │ AND TERROR. "A TRI-
UMPH... │ A CARIBBEAN GOTHIC!" ¦ --NEW YORK TIMES │ WIDE │ SAR-
GASSO │ SEA BY JEAN RHYS. Black spine with white lettering from
head to tail: * POPULAR │ LIBRARY WIDE SARGASSO SEA JEAN
RHYS 445-00459-095. The back cover is black with lettering
in white or yellow: THE │ HEIRESS │ [three-paragraph description of the novel] │ "LUSH, CAPTIVATING, BRILLIANT AND FRIGHT-
ENING ... HIGHLY │ RECOMMENDED!"--LIBRARY JOURNAL │ FIRST TIME
IN PAPERBACK │ POPULAR * LIBRARY. All edges trimmed and

stained green. 6 7/8 x 4 1/4 inches.

Publication: [?May] 1973 at $0.95.

Copies examined: Personal copies.

Notes: According to Alice K. Turner, *Publishers Weekly*, 206
(1 July 1974), 56, the sudden popularity of Rhys in 1974--
sparked by Alvarez's *New York Times Book Review* essay--occas-
ioned a "reprinting of 20,000 copies without risking delay for
a more dignified cover" (the article includes a photograph of
the cover of the first impression with the caption "pre-Alvar-
ez"). In February 1975 *Wide Sargasso Sea* and *Voyage in the
Dark* were issued in matching covers (see above, A4g, for the
description of *Voyage in the Dark*). The description of the
binding of the third impression of *Wide Sargasso Sea* is as
follows: Glossy, plastic-treated paper covers. Yellow front
cover, printed in black and red; the design includes a wreath
encircling the words: "THE BEST LIVING ENGLISH NOVELIST"--NEW
YORK TIMES. Above the wreath: * $1.25 445-00251-125; and
below it: JEAN RHYS | * | WIDE | SARGASSO | SEA | "A MASTER-
PIECE"--NEW YORK TIMES | "CAPTIVATING AND BRILLIANT" | --LIB-
RARY JOURNAL. The white spine is printed in black, horizontal-
ly at the head: * | POPULAR | LIBRARY; and from head to tail:
WIDE SARGASSO SEA JEAN RHYS 445-00251-125. The back cover
is white, printed in red and black: "AN EXQUISITE WEST INDIAN
ISLAND ... | AN HEIRESS ON THE BORDERLINE | BETWEEN INNOCENCE
AND DECADENCE ... | A NOVEL AS UNDENIABLE AS A DREAM" | --NEW
YORK TIMES | [two-paragraph description of the novel] | POPU-
LAR * LIBRARY | LITHO. IN U.S.A. All edges trimmed and stained
green. 6 3/4 x 4 1/8 inches. In addition to the new cover;
there are the following changes in the third impression: [1]
POISONED PARADISE | [three-paragraph description of the novel]
| WIDE SARGASSO SEA; [3] JEAN RHYS | * | WIDE | SARGASSO |
SEA | POPULAR LIBRARY . NEW YORK; 13, page number added to the
last page of Wyndham's Introduction; 190, no number at bottom
of page; the unnumbered leaf has been reset; it still adver-
tises the six reference books, but the price has advanced from
$4.25 to $6.25.

A6e. Second American Paperback, 1982

WIDE | SARGASSO | SEA | JEAN RHYS | INTRODUCTION BY FRANCIS
WYNDHAM | * | W. W. NORTON & COMPANY | NEW YORK . LONDON

Format: Perfect binding.

Pagination: [1] half title; [2] BY JEAN RHYS IN │ NORTON PAP-
ERBACK │ VOYAGE IN THE DARK │ WIDE SARGASSO SEA; [3] title
page; [4] FIRST PUBLISHED AS A NORTON PAPERBACK 1982 │ BY AR-
RANGEMENT WITH WALLACE & SHEIL AGENCY, INC. │ COPYRIGHT © 1966
BY JEAN RHYS │ ISBN 0 393 00056 7 │ W. W. NORTON & COMPANY,
INC., 500 FIFTH AVENUE │ NEW YORK, N.Y. 10110 │ PRINTED IN THE
UNITED STATES OF AMERICA │ 1 2 3 4 5 6 7 8 9; 5-13, Introduction by Francis Wyndham; [14] blank; [15] PART ONE │ * ; [16]
blank; [17]-61, text; [62] blank; [63] PART TWO │ * ; [64]
blank; [65]-173, text; [174] blank; [175] PART THREE │ * ;
[176] blank; [177]-[190] text; one blank leaf.

Contents: Identical with A6a.

Binding: Glossy paper covers. The front cover printed in
shades of red, brown, and green with an abstract design of
faces and foliage; imposed lettering: $3.95 │ A NOVEL │ JEAN
RHYS │ * │ WIDE SARGASSO │ SEA. The abstract design continues
on the spine which is lettered from head to tail: RHYS   WIDE
SARGASSO SEA   NORTON; and horizontally at the tail: * .
White back cover, printed in green: JEAN RHYS IN NORTON PAPER-
BACK │ [[three paragraphs describing *Wide Sargasso Sea, Voyage
in the Dark,* and Jean Rhys's literary career] │ COVER DESIGN
BY TIM GAYDOS │ * NORTON * │ W.W. NORTON & COMPANY NEW YORK
. LONDON │ ISBN 0 393 00056 7. All edges trimmed. 7 x 4 1/8
inches.

Publication: January 1982 at $3.95.

Copy examined: Personal copy.

Reviews:

"New in Paperback." *Book World,* 12 (28 February 1982), 12.

See above, A4h: Reviews.

Translation. 1. Danish, 1967 (Not seen)

Langt Over Havet, translated by Lotte Eskelund.   Copenhagen:
Fremad.

Translation. 2. Finnish, 1968 (Not seen)

Siintää Sargassomer, translated by Eva Siikarla. Porvoo, Helsinki: Werner Söderström.

Translation. 3. Norwegian, 1969 (Not seen)

Kreolerinnen på Thornfield Hall, translated by Liv Malling. Oslo: H. Aschehoug.

Translation. 4. French, 1971

La Prisonnière des Sargasses, translated by Yvonne Davet. Paris: Denoël (Les Lettres Nouvelles). Pp. 224. Second edition: Paris: Gallimard (Folio), 1977. Pp. 209.

Translation. 5. Hungarian, 1971 (Not seen)

Széles Sargasso-Tenger, translated by Dezsö Tandori. Budapest: Európa Kiadó.

Translation. 6. Italian, 1971 (Not seen)

Il Grande Mare dei Sargassi, translated by Adriana Motti. Milan: Adelphi. Second edition: Milan: Adelphi (Piccola Biblioteca), 1980. Pp. 207.

Review:

Adriano Bon, "Jean Rhys: Dominatori e Devianti." *Uomini e Libri*, 16, No. 80 (September-October 1980), 28.

Writing to introduce the new edition of *Wide Sargasso Sea* to the Italian public, Bon notes that the translation first appeared in 1971 and that *Good Morning, Midnight* has also been translated. He expresses a high regard for Rhys, whose life he briefly describes; his appreciation for *Wide Sargasso Sea* is based on its exotic qualities; he shows no knowledge of its link to *Jane Eyre*. Half of the review is given over to quotation of the novel. (In Italian)

Translation. 7. Yugoslavian, 1971 (Not seen)

Široko Sargaško Morje, translated by Olga Šiftar. Murska Sobota: Pomurska založba.

Translation. 8. Japanese, [?1972] (Not seen)

Hiroi Mo No Umi, translated by Shinoda Ayako. Tokyo: Shobō Shinsa. Pp. 256.

Translation. 9. Czech, 1973 (Not seen)

Šire Sargasové More, translated by Kornélia Richterová. Bratislava: Smena. Pp. 147.

Translation. 10. Dutch and Belgian, 1974 (Not seen)

Sargasso Zee, translated by W.A. Dorsman-Vos. Utrecht: Bruna & Zoon. Pp. 157.

Translation. 11. Spanish, 1976 (Not seen)

Ancho Mar de los Sargazos, translated by Andrés Bosch. Barcelona: Noguer (Galería literaria contemporánea). Pp. 186.

Translation. 12. German, 1980 (Not seen)

Sargasso-Meer, translated by Anna Leube. Munich: Rogner & Bernhard. Pp. 223.

A7   TIGERS ARE BETTER-LOOKING,   1968

                WITH A SELECTION FROM THE LEFT BANK

                A7a.   First English Edition, 1968

TIGERS ARE | BETTER-LOOKING | WITH A SELECTION FROM | THE
LEFT BANK | * | STORIES BY | JEAN RHYS | * | ANDRE DEUTSCH

Format: [$]_{16}$, 2_{16} - 7_{16}, 8_8.

Pagination: [1-2] blank; [3] half title; [4] BY THE SAME AUTH-
OR | WIDE SARGASSO SEA | GOOD MORNING, MIDNIGHT | VOYAGE IN
THE DARK | AFTER LEAVING MR MACKENZIE | POSTURES; [5] title
page; [6] FIRST PUBLISHED 1968 BY | ANDRE DEUTSCH LIMITED |
105 GREAT RUSSELL STREET | LONDON WC 1 | ALL RIGHTS RESERVED |
PRINTED IN GREAT BRITAIN BY | EBENEZER BAYLIS AND SON LTD |
THE TRINITY PRESS | WORCESTER AND LONDON | 'TILL SEPTEMBER
PETRONELLA', 'THE DAY THEY BURNED THE BOOKS', | 'TIGERS ARE
BETTER-LOOKING' AND 'LET THEM CALL IT JAZZ' WERE FIRST | PUB-
LISHED IN THE LONDON MAGAZINE (COPYRIGHT © JEAN RHYS, 1960, |
1960, 1962 AND 1962); 'THE SOUND OF THE RIVER' AND 'THE LOTUS'
| WERE FIRST PUBLISHED IN ART AND LITERATURE NUMBERS 9 AND 11
(COPY- | RIGHT © JEAN RHYS, 1966 AND 1967); 'OUTSIDE THE MACH-
INE' WAS | FIRST PUBLISHED IN WINTER'S TALES, MACMILLAN (COPY-
RIGHT © JEAN | RHYS, 1960); 'A SOLID HOUSE' WAS FIRST PUBLISHED
IN VOICES, MICHAEL | JOSEPH (COPYRIGHT © JEAN RHYS, 1963). |
THE STORIES FROM THE LEFT BANK WERE FIRST PUBLISHED BY JONATHAN
| CAPE IN 1927. | SBN 233 95987 4; [7] Contents; [8] blank; [9]
half title; [10] blank; [11]-144, text; [145] half title: THE
LEFT BANK; [146] blank; [147]-150, PREFACE TO A SELECTION OF
STORIES FROM THE LEFT BANK, by Ford Madox Ford; [151]-236,
text; two blank leaves.   [There are no numbers on the first
page of each story; the unnumbered pages are 11, 40, 47, 68,
83, 107, 120, 138, 147, 151, 156, 160, 167, 173, 177, 181, 185,
and 202.]

Contents: *Tigers are Better-Looking*:   Till September Petronella.
The Day They Burned the Books. Let Them Call it Jazz.   Tigers
Are Better-Looking.   Outside the Machine.   The Lotus.   A Solid
House.   The Sound of the River.   *The Left Bank*: Preface to a
Selection of Stories from *The Left Bank* by Ford Madox Ford.
Illusion.   From a French Prison. Mannequin.   Tea with an Art-
ist.   Mixing Cocktails.   Again the Antilles.   Hunger.   La
Grosse Fifi.   Vienne.

Binding: Rose, paper-covered boards, the spine lettered in
gilt: * | TIGERS | ARE | BETTER- | LOOKING | * | JEAN | RHYS
| * | * | ANDRE | DEUTSCH. All edges trimmed. End-papers.
7 3/4 x 5 inches.

Publication: March 1968 at twenty-five shillings.

Copies examined: University of London Library; University of
Tulsa Library, Perkins Library; and University of Kentucky
Library.

Notes: The "Preface to a Selection of Stories from *The Left
Bank*" begins with a two-paragraph note pointing out that this
selection was made by the publisher and approved by Jean Rhys.
Ford's original "Preface" is here reduced to the last five
pages (pp. 23-27 in *The Left Bank*) with the penultimate paragraph omitted.

Reviews:

Montague Haltrecht, "More from Jean Rhys." *Sunday Times*, No.
7556 (24 March 1968), p. 52.

   Considering *Tigers Are Better-Looking* with two other novels,
   Haltrecht gives almost half of his review to the Rhys stories, welcoming them in terms that evoke comparisons with
   Colette and Scott Fitzgerald and that suggest a kinship between the reader's response to them and the "masochistic
   pleasure that provides the romantic swell in the operas of
   Puccini." He describes the contents of the volume and
   praises the writer's accomplishment in general terms.

A. S. Byatt, "Trapped." *New Statesman*, 75 (29 March 1968),
421-422.

   Reviewed along with five other novels, *Tigers Are Better-
   Looking* is given one paragraph of generalizations, most of
   them contrasting the 1927 stories to the post-1939 ones.
   The reviewer points to the similar nature of the characters
   and writes: "I am moved by her prose, but a whole series of
   stories in which it is always Them against a Me seen with a
   very indulgent irony begins to seem limited."

Julian Jebb, "Sensitive Survivors." *Times*, No. 57,214 (30
March 1968), p. 21.

   Welcoming the re-publication of her earlier novels, Jebb
   calls Rhys "a twentieth-century master" and sees that the

chronologically separated stories in *Tigers Are Better-
Looking* are the work of "very much the same woman." He
describes the "vulnerable" heroines of the stories who,
though "acutely" sensitive, have "a capacity to survive."
Rhys does not have "wide" sympathies and "the majority of
the central suffering figures are girls...." They may be
dismissed by some readers as "paranoid case-histories,"
but they are the product of a writer who has been "uncom-
promisingly truthful to [her] vision of life."

Francis Hope, "Did You Once See Paris Plain?" *Observer*, No.
9220 (31 March 1968), p. 29.

Hope provides an account of the stories in the collection,
writing of "The Lotus," for example, that "the cutting between the three [characters] is so quick that the reader
never settles into comfortable identification or equally
comfortable scorn." Evaluating the work as a whole he
points out that "this is not art which consoles, or explains, or even constructs anything beyond itself."

Rayner Heppenstall, "Bitter-sweet." *Spectator*, 220 (5 April
1968), 446-447.

Heppenstall ponders some of the reasons why his generation
(the young writers of the 'thirties) did not recognize Rhys;
he considers that her early novels have been over-valued and
prefers *Wide Sargasso Sea* and "Let Them Call It Jazz" because "neither is at all directly autobiographical. Both
required a detachment and an imaginative effort not always
evident elsewhere." The early sketches are "less than brilliant," and from "Vienne" through the later stories there
is the same "composite heroine." Heppenstall discusses the
title story in some detail, largely because it allows him
to call up the names of other writers and figures of the
'thirties.

Mary Sullivan, "All Underdogs." *Listener*, 79 (25 April 1968),
549.

Reviewing *Tigers Are Better-Looking* with three other novels, Sullivan devotes almost half of her essay to it, writing primarily about Rhys's attitude to life: "life is bat-
tering ... each of us is stuck in our particular situation
.... Rhys [is] ... interested in individual responses ...
as signs of hope and strength." She stresses Rhys's detachment, comedy, and "hard, sympathetic gaze." The review is
an enthusiastic response to the collection of stories.

"Losing Battles." *Times Literary Supplement*, No. 3453 (2 May 1968), p. 466.

> The anonymous reviewer describes the contents of the volume, finding that the work "has the slightly acid charm and the wryly poetic style that characterize [Rhys's] writing." Over the years the "tone has become more sophisticated, more completely disenchanted, but her interests have not changed," and the "heroines ... reappear in a variety of guises." The reviewer describes these women and concludes by stating that "Miss Rhys isn't interested in anything fashionable or accepted: this is one reason why her work has dated so little."

R. Baker. *Books and Bookmen*, 13 (June 1968), 34.

> (Not seen)

Paul Bailey. *London Magazine*, 8 (June 1968), 110-111.

> Bailey quotes "'A Solid House,' the best story ...a beautiful, ironic study," to show how Rhys can write "about the condition known as death-in-life with an authority born obviously of experience." The characters in the stories are all very similar, and Bailey prefers the novels to the stories. Comparing the early and late stories, he finds that the "later writing is the result of considerable self-denial, a deliberate paring down by a novelist of wide-ranging gifts, rather than the product of a limited, if talented sensibility."

A7b.   First English Paperback, 1973   (Not seen)

(2nd Impression, 1977; 3rd Impression, 1981;
4th Impression, 1982: described below)

JEAN RHYS | TIGERS ARE BETTER-LOOKING | WITH A SELECTION FROM | THE LEFT BANK | * | PENGUIN BOOKS

Format: [ ]$_{12}$, T.B.L.•2$_{12}$, T.B.L.•3$_{10}$, T.B.L.•4$_{10}$, T.B.L.•5$_{12}$, T.B.L.•6$_{12}$, T.B.L.•7$_{10}$, T.B.L.•8$_{10}$, T.B.L.•9$_{12}$, T.B.L.•10$_{12}$.

Pagination: [1] PENGUIN BOOKS | TIGERS ARE BETTER-LOOKING [one-paragraph description of Jean Rhys's life and literary career];

[2] blank; [3] title page; [4] PENGUIN BOOKS LTD, HARMONDS-
WORTH, MIDDLESEX, ENGLAND | PENGUIN BOOKS, 625 MADISON AVENUE,
NEW YORK, NEW YORK 10022, U.S.A. | PENGUIN BOOKS AUSTRALIA
LTD, RINGWOOD, VICTORIA, AUSTRALIA | PENGUIN BOOKS CANADA LTD,
2801 JOHN STREET, MARKHAM, ONTARIO, CANADA L3R 1B4 | PENGUIN
BOOKS (N.Z.) LTD, 182-190 WAIRAU ROAD, AUCKLAND 10, NEW ZEA-
LAND | FIRST PUBLISHED BY ANDRÉ DEUTSCH 1968 | PUBLISHED IN
PENGUIN BOOKS 1972 | REPRINTED 1977, 1981, 1982 | TYPESET,
PRINTED AND BOUND IN GREAT BRITAIN BY | HAZELL WATSON & VINEY
LTD, AYLESBURY, BUCKS | SET IN INTERTYPE BASKERVILLE | 'TILL
SEPTEMBER PETRONELLA', 'THE DAY THEY BURNED THE BOOKS', 'TIGERS
ARE BETTER-LOOKING' | AND 'LET THEM CALL IT JAZZ' WERE FIRST
PUBLISHED IN THE LONDON MAGAZINE (COPYRIGHT © JEAN | RHYS,
1960, 1960, 1962, AND 1962); 'THE SOUND OF THE RIVER' AND 'THE
LOTUS' WERE FIRST | PUBLISHED IN ART AND LITERATURE NUMBERS
9 and 11 (COPYRIGHT © JEAN RHYS, 1966 AND 1967); | 'OUTSIDE THE
MACHINE' WAS FIRST PUBLISHED IN WINTER'S TALES, MACMILLAN
(COPYRIGHT © JEAN | RHYS, 1960); 'A SOLID HOUSE' WAS FIRST
PUBLISHED IN VOICES, MICHAEL JOSEPH (COPYRIGHT © | JEAN
RHYS, 1963). | THE STORIES FROM THE LEFT BANK WERE FIRST PUB-
LISHED BY JONATHAN CAPE IN 1927. | ALL RIGHTS RESERVED | EX-
CEPT IN THE UNITED STATES OF AMERICA, THIS BOOK IS SOLD SUB-
JECT | TO THE CONDITION THAT IT SHALL NOT, BY WAY OF TRADE OR
OTHERWISE, BE LENT, | RE-SOLD, HIRED OUT, OR OTHERWISE CIRCUL-
ATED WITHOUT THE | PUBLISHER'S PRIOR CONSENT IN ANY FORM OF
BINDING OR COVER OTHER THAN | THAT IN WHICH IT IS PUBLISHED
AND WITHOUT A SIMILAR CONDITION | INCLUDING THIS CONDITION
BEING IMPOSED ON THE SUBSEQUENT PURCHASER; [5] Contents; [6]
blank; [7] half title; [8] blank; [9]-134, text; [135] half
title; [136] blank; [137]-220, text; [221] advertisement for
Penguin Books; [222] blank; [223] advertisement for Penguin
editions of *Wide Sargasso Sea, After Leaving Mr Mackenzie,*
and *Voyage in the Dark,* headed by the (significantly altered)
quotation: 'ONE OF THE FINEST BRITISH WRITERS OF THIS CENTURY'
--A.ALVAREZ; [224] advertisement for Penguin editions of *Good
Morning, Midnight, Sleep It Off Lady,* and *Quartet,* headed by
the quotation: 'SHE IS LOVED NOT JUST FOR A TALENT THAT SEEMS
AS SPONTANEOUS AND INDIVIDUAL IN ITS PERSONALITY AS PHYSICAL
BEAUTY BUT FOR A SPECIAL KIND OF COURAGE'--GUARDIAN.

Contents: Identical with A7a.

Binding: Glossy brown paper covers. On the front a photograph of a young girl with lettering in white imposed: JEAN
RHYS * | * | TIGERS ARE | BETTER-LOOKING | BITTER-SWEET STOR-
IES BY THE AUTHOR | OF WIDE SARGASSO SEA. Spine lettered in
white and red from head to tail: JEAN RHYS TIGERS ARE BETTER-
LOOKING ISBN 0 14 | 00.3512 5 * . The back cover is printed

in white: 'ONE OF THE FINEST BRITISH WRITERS OF | THIS CEN-
TURY'--A.ALVAREZ   * | [eleven-line description of the collec-
tion] | COVER PHOTOGRAPH BY SUE WILKS | [at bottom left:] U.K.
£1.50 | AUST. $4.50 | (RECOMMENDED) | CAN. $3.50 | [at bottom
right:] FICTION | ISBN 0 14 | 00.3512 5. All edges trimmed.
7 x 4 3/8 inches.

Publication: First impression of the edition: April 1973 at
thirty-five pence; fourth impression: 1982 at one pound and
fifty pence.

Copy examined: Personal copy.

Notes: On the Contents page the story "Vienne" is listed as
"Vienna."

A7c. First American Edition, 1974

TIGERS ARE | BETTER-LOOKING | WITH A SELECTION FROM | THE LEFT
BANK | * | STORIES BY | JEAN RHYS | HARPER & ROW, PUBLISHERS |
NEW YORK, EVANSTON, SAN FRANCISCO, LONDON

Format: Six gatherings of sixteen leaves, one gathering of
eight leaves, and one gathering of sixteen leaves. No signatures.

Pagination: [1-2], blank; [3] half title; [4] BY THE SAME
AUTHOR | WIDE SARGASSO SEA | GOOD MORNING, MIDNIGHT | VOYAGE
IN THE DARK | AFTER LEAVING MR MACKENZIE; [5] title page; [6]
THIS BOOK WAS FIRST PUBLISHED IN 1968 BY ANDRE DEUTSCH LIMIT-
ED. | 'TILL SEPTEMBER PETRONELLA,' 'THE DAY THEY BURNED THE
BOOKS,' 'TIGERS | ARE BETTER-LOOKING' AND 'LET THEM CALL IT
JAZZ' WERE FIRST PUBLISHED IN | THE LONDON MAGAZINE (COPYRIGHT
© JEAN RHYS, 1960, 1960, 1962 AND | 1962); 'THE SOUND OF THE
RIVER' AND 'THE LOTUS' WERE FIRST PUBLISHED | IN ART AND LIT-
ERATURE NUMBERS 9 AND 11 (COPYRIGHT © JEAN RHYS, 1966 | AND
1967); 'OUTSIDE THE MACHINE' WAS FIRST PUBLISHED IN WINTER'S
TALES, | MACMILLAN (COPYRIGHT © JEAN RHYS, 1960); 'A SOLID
HOUSE' WAS FIRST | PUBLISHED IN VOICES, MICHAEL JOSEPH (COPY-
RIGHT © JEAN RHYS, 1963). | THE STORIES FROM THE LEFT BANK
WERE FIRST PUBLISHED BY JONATHAN CAPE | (LONDON) AND HARPER &
BROTHERS (NEW YORK) IN 1927. | TIGERS ARE BETTER-LOOKING. ALL
RIGHTS RESERVED. PRINTED IN THE UNITED | STATES OF AMERICA.
NO PART OF THIS BOOK MAY BE USED OR REPRODUCED IN ANY | MAN-
NER WHATSOEVER WITHOUT WRITTEN PERMISSION EXCEPT IN THE CASE

OF BRIEF | QUOTATIONS EMBODIED IN CRITICAL ARTICLES AND RE-
VIEWS. FOR INFORMATION | ADDRESS HARPER & ROW, PUBLISHERS,
INC., 10 EAST 53RD STREET, NEW YORK, | N.Y. 10022. | FIRST U.
S. EDITION | ISBN: 0-06-013561-1 | LIBRARY OF CONGRESS CATALOG
CARD NUMBER: 72-9175;[7] Contents; [8] blank; [9] half title;
[10] blank; [11]-144, text; [145] half title: THE LEFT BANK;
[146] blank; [147]-150, PREFACE TO A SELECTION OF STORIES FROM
THE LEFT BANK, by Ford Madox Ford; [151]-236, text; [237-239]
blank; [240] [at bottom right] 74 75 10 9 8 7 6 5 4 3 2 1.
[There are no numbers on the first page of each story; the unnumbered pages are 11, 40, 47, 68, 83, 107, 120, 138, 147, 151,
156, 160, 167, 173, 177, 181, 185, and 202.]

Contents: Identical with A7a.

Binding: Maroon, paper-covered boards with maroon, linen-weave
cloth spine extending over one-quarter of the front and back
covers. On the lower right quarter of the front cover, the
publisher's device stamped in silver. The spine is lettered
in silver from head to tail: TIGERS ARE BETTER-LOOKING JEAN
RHYS; and horizontally at the tail: HARPER | & ROW. Top and
bottom edges trimmed. End-papers of the same maroon paper as
on the covers. 7 7/8 x 5 1/2 inches.

Publication: October 1974 at $6.95.

Copy examined: Perkins Library copy.

Reviews:

Kirkus Reviews, 42 (15 August 1974), 299.

    (Not seen)

Publishers Weekly, 206 (26 August 1974), 299.

    Having described the contents of *Tigers Are Better-Looking*,
the reviewer points to the stylistic differences between
the early and late stories and decides that one remembers
primarily the girls in the stories. "They are really aspects of the same anxious, feckless, hard-drinking, penni-
less girl, walking the tightrope between respectability
and semi-sluttishness...."

New York Times Book Review, 20 October 1974, pp. 5-6.

    The reviewer generalizes about the earlier works and *Tigers
Are Better-Looking* to show that Rhys "has one character and

one subject: the tribulations of her heroine in a cruel
world of selfish men and respectable women." This heroine
is described through details taken from the earlier novels
and the stories in this collection ("in one story she is
put into the body of a man and in another put into the body
of a black woman from the West Indies"). The reviewer maintains that the heroine "is no feminist," but rather holds a
solipsistic view of life. His negative attitude is fully
revealed in the last paragraph of the review: "I do not like
this heroine or the fiction in which she appears.... The
prose is sharp, rapid, without affection; and there are
moments of clammy fascination, moments when the author gets
you to share her obsessions.... The heroine's self-pity
and self-absorption wash back over the image we form of the
author ... after having read the fiction, you realize how
often you have met its heroine and just why you wish you
hadn't."

Diane Johnson, "Overdrawn at the Left Bank of the World."
Book World [*Chicago Tribune* and *Washington Post*], 3 November 1974, pp. 1-2.

In this thoughtful, discursive essay Johnson writes to introduce Rhys to new readers. She points to Alvarez's judgement, "'the best living English novelist,'" as a seemingly
"smug cultish" verdict which is actually "a bold perceptive
remark" and speculates on the reasons for the tardy recognition of Rhys, one being that she is a woman who "writes
mostly about women." She is "not exactly an English writer but something more cosmopolitan and alienated" who like
Ford and Conrad "belongs to a distinguished group of expatriate, somewhat French novelists-in-English." Johnson surveys Rhys's biography and literary career and then turns to
Tigers Are Better-Looking which she introduces by remarking
that Orwell's title "Down and out in Paris and London" would
be appropriate for the collection since Rhys "is the chron-
icler of the seedy, cold and cruel." Developing the idea
that the volume is like "a gallery of Impressionist paint-
ings," Johnson quotes or describes significant passages.
These stories provide an "admirable introduction to the
even more finely sustained novels" in which "Rhys takes up
a story where another novelist might have left off." She
"has the courage to look behind the scenes, and an extraordinary power to paint what she sees there."

Bruce Allen. *Library Journal*, 99 (15 November 1974), 2983.

Allen describes the stories of the collection in general
terms, always with praise: "The best exemplify [Rhys's]

work's distinctive paradox: beyond the rigidly held tone
and restricted viewpoint, convincingly dense imagery and
narrative momentum make even quiet vignettes probe
startling depths of character."

Booklist, 71 (1 December 1974), 367.

A brief description of the contents of the collection.

Robert Leiter. *New Republic*, 171 (7 December 1974), 22-24.

Noting that in the four early novels "the same story is repeated, each time with greater depth and technical assurance" and that the four heroines are "a composite, the same
woman at various stages of physical and psychological development," Leiter retells the stories of these novels with
perceptive comments on Rhys's artistic development. "These
four books are like separate panels in a narrowly confined,
coldly etched landscape painting." The new stories are "important additions" to the "ongoing saga." Leiter first discusses the earlier pieces in some detail and then studies
"Till September Petronella" and "'Outside the Machine,'"
the best story in the collection." This volume is "acidly
humorous and more varied in technique than one would imag-
ine." Since her subjects and techniques are now "routine
fare in present-day fiction, ... a historical perspective
is a prerequisite in evaluating this exceptional artist."

Howard Moss, "Going to Pieces." *New Yorker*, 50 (16 December
1974), 161-164.

See below, F.3: 1974.

Ralph Tyler, "Luckless Heroines, Swinish Men." *Atlantic*,
235 (January 1975), 81-84.

This review is actually a discursive essay on Rhys's life
and literary career in which Tyler makes use of the various
interviews and biographical essays published after 1966,
generalizing in sometimes sweeping statements. He suggests
that Rhys's slow acceptance may have been due to the fact
that "she hid her careful art behind an offhand manner; or
it could have been that the world wasn't ready to learn about
woman as underdog unless that dog had a pet's winning ways.
Miss Rhys's underdogs bite, most particularly the hands that
feed them." Taking exception to the critical acclaim for
Wide Sargasso Sea, Tyler writes that "it seems feverish and
strained" and that the novelist "is better out of crinolines
and into those chic little dresses her luckless heroines of

the twenties and thirties covet so hungrily." Although
her work has been taken up by contemporary feminists, "her
heroines are passive, distrustful of other women, only too
eager to be kept by a man...." He describes these women,
declaring that Rhys "is admittedly all her heroines ... "
and that "her books are her own story slightly askew." He
writes of the novels in terms of their biographical relationships to Rhys's life, a critical ploy which brings him
to the realization that "Perhaps it wasn't the war alone
that broke off this series of semi-autobiographical novels.
Good Morning, Midnight ... marks some final inner shattering." Only at the end of the essay Tyler turns to *Tigers
Are Better-Looking* in which he finds "at times ... a broad-
er humanity" in the sense that Rhys employs a more varied
cast of characters; and he suggests that "there is not all
that much difference between Jean Rhys women and some
modern men."

Walter Sullivan, "Erewhon and Eros. The Short Story Again."
Sewanee Review, 83 (July 1975), 539-540.

Reviewing eight collections of short stories, Sullivan ad-
mits that he knows little about Rhys; he describes the stories in *Tigers Are Better-Looking* with few comments, with the
exception of "Outside the Machine," for which he gives half
a page of detailed criticism. In the volume "no other single piece [is] quite so fine," although "there are other
fine moments."

A7d. First American Paperback, 1976

JEAN RHYS | * | TIGERS ARE BETTER-LOOKING | WITH A SELECTION
FROM | THE LEFT BANK | POPULAR LIBRARY . NEW YORK

Format: Perfect binding.

Pagination: [1] THE IMPRINT OF TRUTH, | THE STAMP OF GENIUS
| [one-paragraph description of the collection, followed by
brief quotations from reviews of A7c which appeared in *Publishers Weekly, Seattle Post-Intelligencer, Library Journal,*
and *Raleigh News & Observer*]; [2] OTHER TITLES BY JEAN RHYS |
AVAILABLE FROM POPULAR LIBRARY | WIDE SARGASSO SEA | VOYAGE IN
THE DARK; [3] title page; [4] ALL POPULAR LIBRARY BOOKS ARE
CAREFULLY SELECTED BY THE | POPULAR LIBRARY EDITORIAL BOARD
AND REPRESENT TITLES BY THE | WORLD'S GREATEST AUTHORS. |

POPULAR LIBRARY EDITION | FEBRUARY, 1976 | LIBRARY OF CONGRESS
CATALOG CARD NUMBER: 72-9175 | PUBLISHED BY ARRANGEMENT WITH
HARPER & ROW, PUBLISHERS, INC. | "TILL SEPTEMBER PETRONELLA,"
"THE DAY THEY BURNED THE BOOKS," | "TIGERS ARE BETTER-LOOKING"
AND "LET THEM CALL IT JAZZ" WERE FIRST | PUBLISHED IN THE LON-
DON MAGAZINE (COPYRIGHT © JEAN RHYS, 1960, | 1960, 1962 AND
1962); "THE SOUND OF THE RIVER" AND "THE LOTUS" | WERE FIRST
PUBLISHED IN ART AND LITERATURE NUMBERS 9 AND 11 (COPY- |
RIGHT © JEAN RHYS, 1966 AND 1967); "OUTSIDE THE MACHINE" WAS
FIRST | PUBLISHED IN WINTER'S TALES, MACMILLAN (COPYRIGHT ©
JEAN RHYS, | 1960); "A SOLID HOUSE" WAS FIRST PUBLISHED IN
VOICES, MICHAEL | JOSEPH (COPYRIGHT © JEAN RHYS, 1963). | THE
STORIES FROM THE LEFT BANK WERE FIRST PUBLISHED BY JONATHAN |
CAPE (LONDON) AND HARPER & BROTHERS (NEW YORK) IN 1927. | PRINT-
ED IN THE UNITED STATES OF AMERICA | ALL RIGHTS RESERVED. NO
PART OF THIS BOOK MAY BE USED OR REPRODUCED | IN ANY MANNER
WHATSOEVER WITHOUT WRITTEN PERMISSION EXCEPT IN THE | CASE OF
BRIEF QUOTATIONS EMBODIED IN CRITICAL ARTICLES AND REVIEWS. |
FOR INFORMATION ADDRESS HARPER & ROW, PUBLISHERS, INC., 10
EAST | 53RD STREET, NEW YORK, N.Y. 10022. ; [5] Contents; [6]
blank; [7] half title; [8] blank; 9-39, text; [40] blank; 41-
71, text; [72] blank; 73-113, text; [114] blank; 115-127, text;
[128] blank; 129-147, text; [148] blank; 149-155, text; [156]
blank; [157] half title: THE LEFT BANK; [158] blank; 159-162,
PREFACE TO A SELECTION OF STORIES FROM THE LEFT BANK, by Ford
Madox Ford; 163-253, text; [254-256] [advertisements for Popular
Library books].

Contents: Identical with A7a.

Binding: Glossy, orange-red paper covers printed in white and
yellow. On the front an abstract design incorporating a
woman holding a mask; at the top: * $1.50 445-03107-150 |
AUTHOR OF GOOD MORNING, MIDNIGHT | AND WIDE SARGASSO SEA |
JEAN RHYS | * | TIGERS ARE BETTER-LOOKING | THE INNERMOST HEART
OF A WOMAN LAID BARE. | A DAZZLING FICTION TRIUMPH BY "A | RE-
MARKABLE, TERRIFYING AND | IMPORTANT WRITER WHO | DELIVERS THE
TRUTH!" | --BOSTON GLOBE. On the spine, horizontally at the
head: * | POPULAR | LIBRARY | FICTION; and from the head to
the tail: TIGERS ARE BETTER-LOOKING . JEAN RHYS 445-03107-150.
The back cover is printed in yellow and white: "THE BEST | LIV-
ING NOVELIST!" | --NEW YORK TIMES | [one-paragraph description
of Rhys, followed by quotations from reviews of A7c which appeared in the *Boston Globe, Los Angeles Times,* and the *New
York Times*] | FIRST TIME IN PAPERBACK | POPULAR * LIBRARY |
LITHO. IN U.S.A. All edges trimmed and stained yellow.
6 3/4 x 4 1/8 inches.

Publication: February 1976 at $1.50.

Copy examined: Personal copy.

                    Translation. 1. French, 1969

LES TIGRES │ SONT PLUS BEAUX │ A VOIR │ PAR JEAN RHYS │ AVANT-
PROPOS ET TRADUCTION │ DE PIERRE LEYRIS │ * │ MERCURE DE FRANCE

Pagination: [1-2] blank; [3] DOMAINE ANGLAIS │ DIRIGÉ PAR
PIERRE LEYRIS; [4] blank; [5] title page; [6] IL A ÉTÉ TIRÉ
│ SUR VÉLIN D'ARCHES │ DIX EXEMPLAIRES NUMÉROTÉS DE 1 À 10 │
ET QUELQUES EXEMPLAIRES HORS COMMERCE │ MARQUÉS H.C. │ TIGERS
ARE BETTER LOOKING. │ FIRST PUBLISHED BY ANDRÉ DEUTSCH LTD.│
© JEAN RHYS, 1968. │ © TRADUCTION FRANÇAISE: MERCURE DE FRANCE,
1969, │ 26, RUE DE CONDÉ, PARIS-VI E. ; [7] AVANT-PROPOS │ DU
TRADUCTEUR; [8] blank; [9]-12, text of Introduction; [13]-235,
text [Each story has its own title page on a recto, the verso
being blank; the text begins on the next recto.]; [236] blank;
[237] Contents; [238] blank; [239][list of ten titles in the
Domaine Anglais Series]; [240] ACHEVÉ D'IMPRIMER │ LE 16 OC-
TOBRE 1969 │ PAR L'IMPRIMERIE FLOCH │ A MAYENNE (FRANCE │
(9067) .

Contents: Avant-propos du traducteur. *La Rive Gauche* (1927):
Illusion. D'Une Prison Française. La Grosse Fifi. *Les Tigres
Sont plus Beaux a Voir* (1963): A Septembre, Petronella. Qu'ils
Appellent ça du Jazz. Les Tigres Sont plus Beaux à Voir. En
dehors de la Machine. Le Lotus.

Binding: Green paper covers lettered in black. On the front
cover: LES TIGRES │ SONT │ PLUS BEAUX │ A VOIR │ PAR JEAN
RHYS │ DOMAINE ANGLAIS │ DIRIGÉ PAR PIERRE LEYRIS │ MERCURE
DE FRANCE. Spine labelled from tail to head: * JEAN RHYS.
On the back cover, a six-line quotation from "Qu'ils Appellent
ça du Jazz."

Copy examined: Jean Rhys Collection, University of Tulsa
Library.

Notes: The introduction consists mainly of quotations from
Francis Wyndham's introduction to *Wide Sargasso Sea* (A6a).

          Translation.   2.   German, 1971   (Not seen)

Die Dicke Fifi: Geschichten aus London und Paris,   translated
by Grete Felten.   Hamburg: Hoffmann & Campe.

A8   MY DAY   1975

                    A8a.   First Edition

MY DAY | * 3 PIECES BY * | JEAN RHYS | [line drawing of
daffodils within a rectangular frame, printed in green] |
FRANK HALLMAN | 1975

Format: Four gatherings of four leaves.   No signatures.   No
page numbers.

Pagination: [1-2] blank; [3] title page; [4] FIRST PUBLISHED
IN 1975 BY: | FRANK HALLMAN | BOX 246, COOPER STATION | NEW
YORK, NEW YORK 10003 | COPYRIGHT © 1975 BY JEAN RHYS.   ALL
RIGHTS | RESERVED.   L.C. CARD NO. 75-26292   GRATEFUL AC- |
KNOWLEDGEMENT IS MADE TO VOGUE, WHICH FIRST | PUBLISHED "MY
DAY," AND TO THE TIMES (LON- | DON), WHICH FIRST PUBLISHED
"CLOSE SEASON FOR | THE OLD?" IN SOMEWHAT DIFFERENT FORM.;
[5] Contents; [6] blank; [7-30] text; [31] MY DAY | IS PUB-
LISHED IN SEVEN HUNDRED FIFTY | HARDCOVER COPIES, TWENTY-SIX
SPECIALLY | BOUND COPIES SIGNED BY THE AUTHOR, | AND IN A
PAPERBOUND EDITION. ; [32] DESIGN: R. SCHAUBECK | PRINTED BY
THE STINEHOUR PRESS, LUNENBURG, VERMONT

Contents: Three essays entitled My Day; Invitation to the
Dance; and Close Season for the Old?

Binding: There are three bindings; the ordinary edition has
unbleached, loosely-woven cloth boards, lettered in brown. On
the front cover: MY DAY | JEAN RHYS; and on the spine from
head to tail: MY DAY. RHYS. All edges trimmed. White end-
papers. 7 1/4 x 5 inches. The signed edition is identical to
the ordinary edition with these exceptions: there is no printing on the spine; there is the signature JEAN RHYS on p. [1];
and there is a hand-written letter on p. [31]. The paperbound
edition is identical to the ordinary edition with the exception

that the dust-jacket for the ordinary edition is printed on heavy paper and is the cover.

Publication: December 1975 at $3.00 (paperbound edition) and $7.50 (ordinary edition).

Copies examined: Ordinary edition: personal copy and copy in the Jean Rhys Collection, University of Tulsa Library.   Signed edition: Copy No. F in the Tulsa Rhys Collection.   Paperbound edition: copy in the Tulsa Rhys Collection.

Notes: The dust-jacket for the ordinary edition (which is the cover for the paperbound edition) is an off-white paper with a black-and-white photograph of Jean Rhys on the front with the lettering: MY DAY │ JEAN RHYS; and on the spine from head to tail: MY DAY. RHYS; and on the back cover: PHOTOGRAPH BY JERRY BAUER.

The Tulsa Rhys Collection also includes the page proofs for this book.

Details of the first publication of these essays are given below: see C17 and C18.

Reviews:

Mary G. McBride.   *Library Journal*, 100 (1 December 1975), 2243.

McBride suggests that Rhys's "brisk and common-sense manner" should make this discussion of aging "appeal to readers of all ages."   The work "provides a sensitive and passionate context for understanding the process of aging."

Translation.   1.   French, 1981   (Not seen)

See above, A1.   Translation.   1.   French, 1981

A9   SLEEP IT OFF LADY   1976

A9a.   First English Edition, 1976

SLEEP IT OFF LADY │ STORIES BY │ JEAN RHYS │ * │ ANDRE DEUTSCH

Format: One gathering of eight leaves; four gatherings of
sixteen leaves; and two gatherings of eight leaves. No signatures.

Pagination: [1] half title; [2] BY THE SAME AUTHOR | VOYAGE IN
THE DARK | QUARTET | AFTER LEAVING MR MACKENZIE | GOOD MORNING,
MIDNIGHT | WIDE SARGASSO SEA | TIGERS ARE BETTER-LOOKING; [3]
title page; [4] FIRST PUBLISHED 1976 BY | ANDRÉ DEUTSCH LIM-
ITED | 105 GREAT RUSSELL STREET LONDON WC1 | COPYRIGHT © 1976
BY JEAN RHYS | ALL RIGHTS RESERVED | PRINTED IN GREAT BRITAIN
BY | COX & WYMAN LIMITED | LONDON, FAKENHAM AND READING | ISBN
0 233 96818 0; [5] ACKNOWLEDGMENTS | 'PIONEERS, OH, PIONEERS'
WAS FIRST PUBLISHED IN THE TIMES | UNDER THE TITLE 'DEAR DAR-
LING MR RAMAGE'. | 'SLEEP IT OFF LADY' WAS FIRST PUBLISHED IN
THE NEW REVIEW. | 'THE INSECT WORLD' WAS FIRST PUBLISHED IN
THE SUNDAY|TIMES MAGAZINE.; [6] blank; [7] Contents; [8]
blank; [9] story title; [10] blank; [11]-22 text; [23] story
title; [24] blank; [25]-30, text; [31] story title; [32]
blank; [33]-36, text; [37] story title; [38] blank; [39]-41,
text; [42] blank; [43] story title; [44] blank; [45]-62, text;
[63] story title; [64] blank; [65]-77, text; [78] blank; [79]
story title; [80] blank; [81]-85, text; [86] blank; [87] story
title; [88] blank; [89]-92, text; [93] story title; [94] blank;
[95]-99, text; [100] blank; [101] story title; [102] blank;
[103]-109, text; [110] blank; [111] story title; [112] blank;
[113]-122, text; [123] story title; [124] blank; [125]-136,
text; [137] story title; [138] blank; [139]-144, text; [145]
story title; [146] blank; [147]-156, text; [157] story title
[158] blank; [159]-172, text; [173] story title; [174] blank;
[175]-176, text.

Contents: Pioneers, Oh, Pioneers. Goodbye Marcus, Goodbye
Rose. The Bishop's Feast. Heat. Fishy Waters. Overture
and Beginners Please. Before the Deluge. On Not Shooting
Sitting Birds. Kikimora. Night Out 1925. The Chevalier of
the Place Blanche. The Insect World. Rapunzel, Rapunzel.
Who Knows What's Up in the Attic? Sleep It Off Lady. I
Used to Live Here Once.

Binding: Light-green, paper-covered boards, lettered on the
spine in gilt: * | SLEEP | IT OFF | LADY | * | JEAN | RHYS |
* | * | ANDRE | DEUTSCH. All edges trimmed. White end-
papers. 7 3/4 x 5 inches.

Publication: November 1976 at two pounds and ninety-five pence.

Copies examined: Personal copy; University of Tulsa Library copy.

Notes: The title page for the story "The Chevalier of the
Place Blanche" includes the note: "This story is a much-adapt-
ed translation of one written by Edouard de Nève" (p. [111]).
    The volume was issued with a pictorial dust-jacket designed
by Rosemary Honeybourne; on the back cover is a sixteen-line
quotation from A. Alvarez's essay in the *New York Times Book
Review* (see below, F.3: 1974).

Reviews:

Susannah Clapp, "Bleak Treats." *New Statesman*, 92 (22 October
1976), 568-569.

    Clapp gives the first third of her review of four works of
    fiction to *Sleep It Off Lady*, providing general comments
    about most of the stories in the collection. She sees them
    as investigations of "varieties of dislocation: ruin--moral
    and physical--in the West Indies; displacement and disen-
    chantment in London and Paris during and between the wars;
    the shrivelling worlds inhabited by the old and lonely,"
    and gives illustrations of these qualities. Clapp feels
    that "At times Jean Rhys seems on the point of self-parody
    .... But the wistfulness is always spiked with astringency
    --by a detachment of observation.... She is always capable
    of springing bleak treats."

Paul Bailey, "True Romance." *Times Literary Supplement*, No.
3893 (22 October 1976), p. 1321.

    In this long, appreciative essay Bailey analyzes the in-
    dividual stories in great detail, organizing his discussion
    around the chronological framework of the collection. The
    stories "read like a series of fragments from a single
    life" and are written in a prose that is "sprightly ... and
    ... piercingly exact." The reviewer summarizes and quotes
    the stories with praise for all of them except for the
    title story in which the "child is too much of a stock char-
    acter. She is too pointedly the deus ex machina." But this
    "lapse into convention is the only fault ... in the book."
    Rhys "is a romantic writer" and her subject matter is much
    the same as that of "Miss Cartland and Robins," but her
    characters, unlike theirs, "get involved with, and then are
    discarded by, Mr. Wrong." Rhys "deals with ... the real
    world ... where the true worth of the aspiring individual
    frequently goes unappreciated." She has written of such
    matters "for fifty years now, with increasing refinement."

Tony Gould, "In a Dark Wood." *New Society*, 38 (28 October 1976), 209.

> Gould provides a serious study of the collection in which he attempts to define Rhys's vision of the world: "the universe lours, the sky is the 'colour of no hope,' people are simultaneously smug and dangerous to know, nothing is quite what it seems--yet what can you do but accept?" *Sleep It Off Lady* is distinguished by "the peculiar blend of innocence and experience which is Jean Rhys's hall mark." The writer's "secret" is "her ability to view her other self-- at any stage of life--quite dispassionately." Gould examines "Goodbye Marcus, Goodbye Rose" in detail and calls the title story "the most memorable."

Nick Totton, "Speak, Memory." *Spectator*, 237 (30 October 1976), 22.

> Totton begins his review of three works of fiction with a lengthy, totally praising consideration of *Sleep It Off Lady*. It is "a kind of autobiography" in which "Rhys treads the boundary between fiction ... and history ... " because these "sharp, sudden images ... have been enriched through long immersion in that mysterious living element, the memory." The arrangement of the stories moves "according to the protagonist's age," from childhood to "beyond death." Extolling Rhys's style, he suggests that "an ambivalent perception of invisibility has played a central role in her life" and has "contributed to a subtle and unique literary personality." The collection may be viewed as an expression of "what one person has learnt from a long and varied life."

Lorna Sage, "Phantom Returns." *Observer*, No. 9665 (31 October 1976), p. 28.

> Sage gives half of this review of five works of fiction to *Sleep It Off Lady*, preferring it to the others (one of these being Rosamond Lehmann's *A Sea-Grape Tree*); she points out that in this volume "Rhys's life and fiction converge on each other" not merely because of the subject matter but because the stories "are concerned with vanishings, disappearances, phantom returns," qualities which have been evident in the writer's life. The reviewer describes the contents of the volume in general but always approving terms. She finds that "Miss Rhys has not mellowed" in the attitudes expressed in these late stories. "Her special people

are usually wretched, but if they think of surrendering or
adjusting, one thought deters them: their solitary, disor-
derly lives are of their own making."

Mary-Kay Wilmers, "Some Must Cry." *New Review*, 3 (November
1976), 51-52.

One of the most detailed and comprehensive reviews of *Sleep
It Off Lady*, this study gives paraphrases and analyses of
most of the contents, but particularly of the title story,
"The Insect World," "Mr Ramage," and "Fishy Waters." Wilmers notes the "autobiographical sequence" and suggests
the stories are "projections on the author's life." Although Rhys's attention is usually exclusively on the female characters, in several of these stories and in *Wide
Sargasso Sea* the male is the central figure; like the women
of the other tales, this man is also at the mercy of the
society in which he lives. Wilmers points out that "super-
stition accounts for a great deal of what happens in Jean
Rhys's fiction," yet for all of the belief in talismans and
good luck, such things never succeed in warding off the inevitable and inescapable evil: all innocence must end
"crabby and fatigued in a windy cottage at the back of beyond: that, roughly speaking, is the plot."

Pearl K. Bell, "Letter from London." *New Leader*, 59 (6 December 1976), 3-5.

In the context of a report on English literary life, Bell
observes that the most noteworthy writers are women: Mur-
doch, Spark, Drabble, Bainbridge, O'Brien, and Rhys--"the
oldest yet most fiercely original" who has just published
"a superb new book of stories...."

A. Alvarez, "Books of the Year." *Observer*, No. 9671 (12 December 1976), p. 26.

In this annual feature different critics write brief paragraphs in which they name the significant books of the year;
Alvarez chooses *Sleep It Off Lady* and E.L. Doctorow's *Rag-
time*.

John Mellors, "World Shrinkers." *Listener*, 96 (23 December
1976), 854.

Reviewing seven new books, Mellors begins by describing and
praising the stories in *Sleep It Off Lady* in general terms.
He stresses the unsentimental attitude of the writer as he

praises her "cool, clear prose" and her ability to make
the reader "feel everything was ...exactly as she tells it."

Joan Harcourt. *Queen's Quarterly*, 84 (1977), 512-513.

Providing inaccurate biographical details, the reviewer
praises the stories for both the writing ("It is as a stylist that Rhys excels") and the characters (the "women are
attractive and intelligent. They may be self-destructive,
but they are not self-deceiving. They always see the humor
of their various plights--no matter that the joke is on
them. They, and their creator, offer no judgments.") Harcourt concludes: "It is what she chooses *not* to say that
gives her work its final enigmatic appeal."

Peggy Crane, "Writers in an Alien Land." *Books and Bookmen*,
22 (February 1977), 60-61.

Most of this review is given over to a detailed treatment
of "Overture and Beginners, Please," "Dear Darling Mr Ramage," and the title story. Crane writes at length on "the
nightmarish quality of alienation ... [in] all the author's
work," realizing however that "at the heart of all her characters there is a core of innocence that prevents them from
degenerating into sodden sluts or mean-minded maniacs ...
there is always the flicker of hope that tomorrow will be
better." The reviewer recalls details of *Wide Sargasso Sea*
in order to write about the racial relationships explored
by Rhys in these stories. While her "earliest works" are
"modern in style and content," Rhys has a wider range than
Margaret Drabble, is as "sexually direct" as Edna O'Brien
"but less sentimental," and is "more self-centred than
Nadine Gordimer." The first novels recall early Hemingway,
but "no man could have written them. They are entirely
feminine and few writers have depicted so honestly, without self-pity, a woman struggling alone to be herself."
(Crane briefly considers Peggy Appiah's *Ring of Gold* in
order to show the superiority of Rhys's morality.)

G. Norton. *West Indies Chronicle*, 17 April 1977, 19 May 1977.

(Not seen)

Michael Thorpe, "Current Literature 1977. III. Commonwealth
Literature. Caribbean." *English Studies*, 60 (1979), 63-64.

Reviewing *Sleep It Off Lady* within a long survey of commonwealth literature, Thorpe finds it "fragmentary and insub-

stantial beside *Tigers Are Better-Looking*." He points out
that the protagonists appear to have only one life which
is "parallel in time and circumstance to the author's." The
"most fully developed" stories are those "that capture the
loneliness and pathos of old age."

A9b. First American Edition, 1976

SLEEP IT OFF, LADY | STORIES BY | JEAN RHYS | HARPER & ROW,
PUBLISHERS | NEW YORK, HAGERSTOWN, SAN FRANCISCO, LONDON

Format: Three gatherings of sixteen leaves; one gathering of
eight leaves; and two gatherings of sixteen leaves. No signatures.

Pagination: [1] half title; [2] blank; [3] BY THE SAME AUTHOR
| VOYAGE IN THE DARK | QUARTET | AFTER LEAVING MR MACKENZIE |
GOOD MORNING, MIDNIGHT | WIDE SARGASSO SEA | TIGERS ARE BETTER-
LOOKING; [4] blank; [5] title page; [6] 'PIONEERS, OH, PIONEERS'
WAS FIRST PUBLISHED IN THE TIMES (LONDON) UNDER THE TITLE 'DEAR
| DARLING MR RAMAGE.' | 'SLEEP IT OFF, LADY' WAS FIRST PUB-
LISHED IN THE NEW REVIEW. | 'THE INSECT WORLD' WAS FIRST PUB-
LISHED IN ENGLAND IN THE SUNDAY TIMES MAGAZINE AND FIRST | PUB-
LISHED IN THE UNITED STATES IN MADEMOISELLE. | 'GOODBYE MARCUS,
GOODBYE ROSE,' 'HEAT,' 'KIKIMORA,' AND 'ON NOT SHOOTING SITTING
| BIRDS' WERE FIRST PUBLISHED IN THE NEW YORKER. | SLEEP IT
OFF, LADY. COPYRIGHT © 1976 BY JEAN RHYS. ALL RIGHTS RE-
SERVED. PRINTED IN THE | UNITED STATES OF AMERICA. NO PART
OF THIS BOOK MAY BE USED OR REPRODUCED IN ANY MANNER | WHATSO-
EVER WITHOUT WRITTEN PERMISSION EXCEPT IN THE CASE OF BRIEF
QUOTATIONS EMBODIED | IN CRITICAL ARTICLES AND REVIEWS. FOR
INFORMATION ADDRESS HARPER & ROW, PUBLISHERS, INC., | 10 EAST
53RD STREET, NEW YORK, N.Y. 10022. | FIRST U.S. EDITION | ISBN:
0-06-013572-7 | LIBRARY OF CONGRESS CATALOG CARD NUMBER: 74-
15889 | 76 77 78 79 10 9 8 7 6 5 4 3 2 1; [7] Contents; [8]
blank; [9] [subsequent pagination is identical with that of
the first English edition: see above, A9a.]

Contents: Identical with A9a.

Binding: Cream-colored, linen cloth spine extending over one-
quarter of medium tan, paper-covered boards. Spine lettered
in bronze from head to tail: SLEEP IT OFF, LADY JEAN RHYS
HARPER & ROW. In the bottom right corner of the front cover,
the publisher's device stamped in bronze. Top and bottom

edges trimmed. White end-papers. 8 x 5 1/2 inches.

Publication: November 1976 at $7.95.

Copy examined: Personal copy.

Notes: The volume was issued with a tan dust-jacket printed in black, white, and dull blue and with a photograph of Jean Rhys by Fay Godwin on the back cover.

Reviews:

"Window on the Fall." *Book World* [*Chicago Tribune* and *Washington Post*], 29 August 1976, p. M2.

> In a two-page list of forthcoming books, some of the stories in *Sleep It Off, Lady* are described in general terms, while the entire collection is referred to as a gathering of "traditionally structured stories ... pared down to bare bones--a style that perfectly conveys [the] grim message."

Publishers Weekly, 210 (27 September 1976), 74.

> A description of the collection with special attention given to "Pioneers, Oh, Pioneers," "Rapunzel, Rapunzel," and the title story: "understatement illuminates elusive private moments with sensitivity and perception."

Booklist, 73 (1 November 1976), 392-393.

> A very brief description of the collection pointing out that "the central characters are females depicted in various stages of growth or defiance of a constricting environment."

Eve Auchincloss, "Lighting up the Inner Dark." *Washington Post Book World*, 10 (7 November 1976), G1-G2.

> In this long, front-page review, Auchincloss asserts that although Rhys writes about "victims of depression," her "ability to get inside the skins" of her characters and her "elegantly spare sense of form" combine to make "reading her ... an illumination." The reviewer tells the story of Rhys's life and literary career, noting that the novels dwell "on stages of her own life." Similarly *Sleep It Off, Lady* traces "the course of the author's life from the tropical childhood to a cold death and a moment of afterlife." The reviewer provides lengthy summaries of the stories, ac-

companied by critical evaluations. The close reading of
the text concludes with two paragraphs of significant generalizations about Rhys's accomplishments. "A loathing of
the hypocritical distinction between good and bad women is
an essential of everything Jean Rhys has written." Her
"true subject matter [is] the complicated relationship between men and women who are compelled to attract them,
sponge off them, yet [who] cannot" maintain the relationship. Rhys is "glacially honest in her self-appraisal,"
and while she pities the female victims, she "never roman-
ticizes them." Auchincloss notes that "If Jean Rhys were
really like the lonely, depressed women she writes about
she would have gone under long ago...." The writer's "ur-
gent creative intelligence" and artistic abilities enable
her "to transmute observation and experience into utterly
original, timeless works of art."

Michael Wood, "Endangered Species." *New York Review of Books*,
23 (11 November 1976), 30-32.

In this review of Muriel Spark's *The Takeover*, Francine
Gray's *Lovers and Tyrants* and *Sleep It Off, Lady*, Rhys's
work is treated second in a long, considered evaluation.
Wood quotes extensively from *Wide Sargasso Sea* to show that
for Rhys's characters "all communication is constantly en-
tangled in a mass of misinterpretation." He considers the
stories in fairly general terms, seeing that, together,
they make "neither a novel nor an autobiography ... " but
a "record of a maturing, darkening mind." While all of the
stories are not uniformly successful (there are "dips ...
into Rhys's particular form of sentimentality, a too simple
view of lonely sensibility adrift in a heartless world ...
and a sense of life as just too predictably elusive"), in
the main they express "'life as it is.'"

Katha Pollit, "Books in Brief." *Saturday Review*, 4 (13 November 1976), 40-41.

Writing of the vicissitudes of the novelist's literary
career, Pollit suggests that Rhys's new-found popularity
is due to "an odd combination of feminism and nostalgia."
She describes the stories in general terms and comments
that their "brevity ... arises not from slightness but from
an extreme artistic economy.... [A] few stories are perhaps *too* compressed."

Hara L. Seltzer. *Library Journal*, 101 (15 November 1976),
2395.

After briefly describing four of the sixteen stories,
Seltzer writes: "Some of the stories seem unfinished and
actually like plotless vignettes, but most have the usual
Jean Rhys charm and strength as they capture that moment
in which a life changes unalterably and irrevocably."

Robie Macauley, "Things unsaid and said too often." *New York
Times Book Review*, 21 November 1976, pp. 7, 50.

Briefly sketching in the story of Rhys's rediscovery and
the subsequent reprinting of her novels, Macauley points
out that she is "a gifted short-story writer" whose work
is described by Sean O'Faolain's statement: "the art of the
modern short story lies half in not-telling." Thus, in
Sleep It Off, Lady, the "good reader" will "supply the sil-
ent half, quickly and accurately, for himself." The reviewer discusses in detail "Pioneers, Oh, Pioneers," "Goodbye
Marcus, Goodbye Rose," "Fishy Waters," and "I Used to Live
Here Once"--the latter being "one of the best ghost stories
I know." Although the stories are set in far-off places in
a past time, they are "very modern stories written with a
quick, young sensibility."

Margo Jefferson, "Anatomy of Melancholy." *Newsweek*, 88 (6 December 1976), 90, 93.

Anne Tyler, "Boundaries and Bonds. Concerning Strangers in
Strange Lands." *National Observer*, 15 (11 December 1976), 18.

Reviewing *Sleep It Off, Lady* and Ruth Prawer Jhabvala's
How I Became a Holy Mother together because both writers
concern themselves with characters living in foreign lands,
Tyler shows that they have opposite attitudes to life.
Rhys's women are "eternally, wilfully foreign, and perverse-
ly proud of it," while Jhabvala's attain "deep and abiding
bonds with other people." The reviewer sketches in Rhys's
personal and literary background, declaring that she herself, while admiring the novelist's "stripped, pure prose,
[and] sense for a story's movement," questions whether "her
success today is not just as arbitrarily a matter of fashion as her failure was 30 years ago. Almost her sole concern, after all, is the abject misery of certain women, particularly at the hands of men. And that's not an unpopular
subject these days." The reviewer is baffled by Rhys's characters: her only clue to their behaviour lies in the story
"Goodbye Marcus, Goodbye Rose," in which the speaker "gives
herself up; she forfeits her vision of a respectable future
and awaits a life shaped wholly by that combination of

guilt, isolation, and rage."

"Felicitous Fictions." *Book World* [*Chicago Tribune* and *Washington Post*], 12 December 1976, p. H5.

This issue consists entirely of short notices of books which would appeal to the Christmas trade: *Sleep It Off, Lady* is listed alongside works by Anthony Powell and Kurt Vonnegut. The stories in the collection are described in general terms and referred to as "late leaves from the notebooks of an artist quite unique and unforgettable."

George Core, "Current Books in Review. Wanton life, Importunate Art." *Sewanee Review*, 85 (Winter 1977), ii-x.

Core considers that "Miss Rhys has ransacked her notebooks and has given her publisher the chaff from previous gleanings." He speculates if *Sleep It Off, Lady* consists of "fragments of several unfinished novels." "Insect World" is "one of the best of" these stories which "often show the hand of a master in their various incidental touches."

Peter Wolfe. *Studies in Short Fiction*, 14 (1977), 299-300.

Noting the connections of *Sleep It Off, Lady* to Rhys's earlier volumes, Wolfe praises the "honesty and accuracy of observation" which creates "poetical effects out of prosaic materials." He surveys the contents of the volume, pointing to the chronological sequence of the stories and writing at length about "I Used to Live Here Once."

"Briefly Noted." *New Yorker*, 52 (10 January 1977), 98.

The anonymous reviewer describes the contents of the collection as "nourishing stories about the ways in which people injure and comfort each other" and gives general information about some of them. He is most impressed by "the range of imagination ... one wonders how the author could have got under the skin of so many different sorts of people." There are no negative terms in this review.

Choice, 14 (March 1977), 65.

The anonymous reviewer describes the stories in general terms, noting that they "have the artlessness that bespeaks a master's hand," and declares that the volume is "A fine collection that should be in every library."

Paul Piazza, "The World of Jean Rhys." *Chronicle of Higher Education*, 14 (7 March 1977), 19.

In this full-page review Piazza introduces Rhys to new readers by surveying her literary career and her biography. He gains his information about her life from recently published interviews and from the novels, for her "life can readily be reconstructed by reading her fiction." In it she details the "downward spiral of the same woman, who appears under different names and at various stages.... The Rhys woman is a female Prufrock, unable to 'get on.'" The critic generalizes about the message in these novels, praises the style, and marvels that the effect of the stories upon the reader is "exhilarating." New readers might well begin with *Sleep It Off, Lady* which is "roughly sequential" and in which the title story and "I Used to Live Here Once" are "masterpieces of concision and irony."

Gerard C. Reedy, "Fiction." *America*, 136 (7 May 1977), 422.

Reviewing eleven new books, Reedy observes that in *Sleep It Off, Lady* the "best and most developed of these sixteen short stories concern the irruptions of something ugly and fearful into carefully measured lives." He describes two of the stories.

Dean Flower, "Fiction Chronicle." *Hudson Review*, 30 (Summer 1977), 299-312.

Sleep It Off, Lady is mentioned in a footnote to this survey of contemporary fiction.

"Notes on Current Books." *Virginia Quarterly Review*, 53 (Summer 1977), 103 [prefatory pages].

An enthusiastic if brief welcome to the volume by an anonymous reviewer who knows nothing about Jean Rhys.

John Heidenry. *Commonweal*, 104 (30 September 1977), 632, 634.

A discursive review of *Sleep It Off, Lady* and Philip Larkin's *A Girl in Winter* focussed on the nature of "English letters in the twilight of her second golden age" in which Rhys is denied the accolade of "greatest living novelist" but is praised, along with Larkin, for "hard-won, brilliantly subdued style." These novels "will alter the sensibility of anyone who reads them...."

Elgin W. Mellown. *World Literature Written in English*, 16
(November 1977), 473-474.

   This collection of stories is another segment in the continuing autobiography Rhys creates through her fiction.
The stories use the techniques of poetry, especially since
they set forth a "unified, consistent vision of life." The
critic points out that these autobiographical or factual
elements are transformed into literary form and metaphor by
Rhys's "ever-fertile imagination" as illustrated in the
title story. Mellown's emphasis on the poetry of the volume leads him to praise its "clarity and artistry that
never falter."

              A9c. First American Paperback, 1978

JEAN RHYS │ * │ SLEEP IT │ OFF, LADY │ POPULAR LIBRARY . NEW
YORK

Format: **Per**fect binding.

Pagination: [1] [Quotations from reviews of *Sleep It Off,
Lady* in the *Saturday Review, Newsday,* and *Best Sellers*]; [2]
ALSO BY JEAN RHYS AND │ AVAILABLE IN POPULAR LIBRARY EDITIONS:
│ TIGERS ARE BETTER-LOOKING │ VOYAGE IN THE DARK │ WIDE SAR-
GASSO SEA │ [at the bottom, in a ruled panel, a twelve-line
advertisement for Popular Library books]; [3] title page; [4]
PUBLISHED BY POPULAR LIBRARY, A UNIT OF CBS PUBLICATIONS, │
THE CONSUMER PUBLISHING DIVISION OF CBS INC., │ BY ARRANGE-
MENT WITH HARPER & ROW PUBLISHERS, INC. │ APRIL, 1978 │ COPY-
RIGHT © 1976 BY JEAN RHYS │ LIBRARY OF CONGRESS CATALOG CARD
NUMBER; 74-15889 │ ISBN: 0-445-04208-7 │ "PIONEERS, OH, PION-
EERS" WAS FIRST PUBLISHED IN THE TIMES (LONDON) │ UNDER THE
TITLE "DEAR DARLING MR. RAMAGE". │ "SLEEP IT OFF, LADY" WAS
FIRST PUBLISHED IN THE NEW REVIEW. │ "THE INSECT WORLD" WAS
FIRST PUBLISHED IN ENGLAND IN │ THE SUNDAY TIMES MAGAZINE AND
FIRST PUBLISHED IN THE UNITED STATES │ IN MADEMOISELLE. │
"GOODBYE MARCUS, GOODBYE ROSE", "HEAT", "KIKIMORA", AND │ "ON
NOT SHOOTING SITTING BIRDS" WERE FIRST PUBLISHED IN │ THE NEW
YORKER. │ PRINTED IN THE UNITED STATES OF AMERICA │ ALL RIGHTS
RESERVED. NO PART OF THIS BOOK MAY BE USED OR │ REPRODUCED IN
ANY MANNER WHATSOEVER WITHOUT WRITTEN PERMISSION │ EXCEPT IN
THE CASE OF BRIEF QUOTATIONS EMBODIED IN CRITICAL ARTICLES │
AND REVIEWS. FOR INFORMATION ADDRESS HARPER & ROW, PUBLISHERS,
INC., │ 10 EAST 53RD STREET, NEW YORK, N. Y. 10022.; [5] Con-

tents; [6] blank; 7-41, text; [42] blank; 43-91, text, [92]
blank; 93-97, text; [98] blank; 99-127, text; [128] blank;
129-145, text; [146] blank; 147-167, text; [168] blank; 169-
187, text; [188] blank; 189-191, text; [192] [advertisement
for "All Time Bestsellers From Popular Library" with an order
blank; at the bottom: "This offer expires 6/78."].

Contents: Identical with A9a.

Binding: Glossy paper covers. On the front cover, a photograph of a woman seated in a cane-backed arm-chair with imposed lettering in white, red, and black: *   0-445-04208-7
$1.95 | "THE BEST LIVING ENGLISH NOVELIST" | --NEW YORK TIMES
| JEAN RHYS | AUTHOR OF WIDE SARGASSO SEA | SLEEP IT | OFF,
LADY. White spine, lettered in red and black; at the head,
horizontally: * | POPULAR | LIBRARY | FICTION; and from head
to tail: SLEEP IT OFF, LADY JEAN RHYS 0-445-04208-7 $1.95.
The back cover is white, printed in black and red with a four-
line description of the novel and quotations from the *Boston
Globe, Charlotte Observer, Chicago Tribune,* and *Washington
Post*; at the bottom: POPULAR * LIBRARY | PRINTED IN U.S.A.
All edges trimmed and stained yellow. 6 7/8 x 4 1/8 inches.

Publication: April 1978 at $1.95.

Copy examined: Personal copy.

Reviews:

"Fiction Reprints." *Publishers Weekly,* 213 (13 February
1978), 126.

> Announcement of the April publication of *Sleep It Off,
> Lady* with quotations from the *Publishers Weekly* review of
> the first American edition (see above, A9b: Reviews).

"Paperbacks: New and Noteworthy." *New York Times Book Review,*
83 (2 April 1978), 41.

> A brief announcement of the paperback edition in which Rhys
> is referred to as "a gifted short-story writer."

A9d. First English Paperback, 1979 (Not seen)

(2nd Impression, 1980;
3rd Impression, 1981: described below)

SLEEP IT OFF LADY | STORIES BY JEAN RHYS | PENGUIN BOOKS

Format: Perfect binding. No signatures.

Pagination: [1] PENGUIN BOOKS | SLEEP IT OFF LADY | [one-par-
agraph description of Jean Rhys's life and literary career];
[2] blank; [3] title page; [4] PENGUIN BOOKS LTD, HARMONDS-
WORTH, MIDDLESEX, ENGLAND | PENGUIN BOOKS, 625 MADISON AVENUE,
NEW YORK, NEW YORK 10022, U.S.A. | PENGUIN BOOKS AUSTRALIA LTD,
RINGWOOD, VICTORIA, AUSTRALIA | PENGUIN BOOKS CANADA LTD, 2801
JOHN STREET, MARKHAM, ONTARIO, CANADA L3R 1B4 | PENGUIN BOOKS
(N.Z.) LTD, 182-190 WAIRAU ROAD, AUCKLAND 10, NEW ZEALAND |
FIRST PUBLISHED BY ANDRÉ DEUTSCH 1976 | PUBLISHED IN PENGUIN
BOOKS 1979 | REPRINTED 1980, 1981 | COPYRIGHT © THE ESTATE OF
JEAN RHYS, 1976 | ALL RIGHTS RESERVED | MADE AND PRINTED IN
GREAT BRITAIN BY | RICHARD CLAY (THE CHAUCER PRESS) LTD, BUN-
GAY, SUFFOLK | SET IN MONOTYPE BASKERVILLE | EXCEPT IN THE
UNITED STATES OF AMERICA, THIS BOOK IS SOLD SUBJECT | TO THE
CONDITION THAT IT SHALL NOT, BY WAY OF TRADE OR OTHERWISE, BE
LENT, | RE-SOLD, HIRED OUT, OR OTHERWISE CIRCULATED WITHOUT |
THE PUBLISHER'S PRIOR CONSENT IN ANY FORM OF BINDING OR COVER
OTHER THAN | THAT IN WHICH IT IS PUBLISHED AND WITHOUT A SIM-
ILAR CONDITION | INCLUDING THIS CONDITION BEING IMPOSED ON
THE SUBSEQUENT PURCHASER; [5] ACKNOWLEDGMENTS | 'PIONEERS, OH,
PIONEERS' WAS FIRST PUB- | LISHED IN THE TIMES UNDER THE TITLE
'DEAR | DARLING MR RAMAGE'. | 'SLEEP IT OFF LADY' WAS FIRST
PUBLISHED | IN THE NEW REVIEW. | 'THE INSECT WORLD' WAS FIRST
PUBLISHED | IN THE SUNDAY TIMES MAGAZINE.; [6] blank; [7] Con-
tents; [8] blank; [9] story title; [10] blank; 11-[21] text;
[22] blank; [23] story title; [24] blank; 25-[30] text; [31]
story title; [32] blank; 33-[36] text; [37] story title; [38]
blank; 39-[41] text; [42] blank; [43] story title; [44] blank;
45-[62] text; [63] story title; [64] blank; 65-[77] text; [78]
blank; [79] story title; [80] blank; 81-[85] text; [86] blank;
[87] story title; [88] blank; 89-[92] text; [93] story title;
[94] blank; 95-[99] text; [100] blank; [101] story title; [102]
blank; 103-[109] text; [110] blank; [111] story title; [112]
blank; 113-[122] text; [123] story title; [124] blank; 125-
[136] text; [137] story title; [138] blank; 139-[144] text;
[145] story title; [146] blank; 147-[156] text; [157] story
title; [158] blank; 159-[172] text; [173] story title; [174]
blank; 175-[176] text.

Contents: Identical with A9a.

Binding: Glossy brown paper covers. On the front a photograph of a woman and her mirrored reflection; in white let-
ters: JEAN RHYS * | 'ONE OF THE FINEST BRITISH WRITERS OF
THIS CENTURY' | --A. ALVAREZ | SLEEP IT OFF LADY. Orange
spine lettered in black and white from head to tail: JEAN RHYS
SLEEP IT OFF LADY   ISBN 0 14 | 00.4733.6 * . On the back
cover a four-line quotation from the *Guardian* and a one-paragraph description of the stories; COVER PHOTOGRAPH BY SUE
WILKS | [at bottom left] U.K. £1.50 | AUST. $4.50 | (RECOM-
MENDED) | CAN. $2.95 | [at bottom right] FICTION | ISBN
0 14 | 00.4733 6. All edges trimmed. 7 1/8 x 4 3/8 inches.

Publication: November 1979 at one pound and twenty-five pence;
2nd Impression: 1980 at one pound and twenty-five pence; 3rd
Impression: 1981 at one pound and fifty pence.

Copy examined: Personal copy.

Translation. 1. Dutch and Belgian, 1977 (Not seen)

Mens, Slaap Je Roes Uit: Verhalen, translated by W.A.Dorsman-
Vos. Utrecht: A.W. Bruna & Zoon. Pp. 158.

Translation. 2. French, 1978 (Not seen)

Il Ne Faut Pas Tirer les Oiseaux au Repos, translated by Maud
Perrin. Paris: Denoël (Arc-en-ciel). Pp. 196.

   Contents: Ah! valeureux pionniers. Adieu Marcus, adieu
   Rose. La fête de l'évêque. Canicule. Eaux troubles. Déb-
   utants, en place pour l'ouverture. Avant le déluge. Il ne
   faut pas tirer les oiseaux au repos. Kikimora. Sortie d'un
   soir en 1925. Le chevalier de la place Blanche. Le monde
   des insectes. Rapunzel, Rapunzel. Qui sait ce qui se passe
   dans le grenier? Cuvez donc en paix, ma chère. J'ai vécu
   ici jadis.

Translation. 3. Swedish, 1978 (Not seen)

Sov Av Sig Ruset, Damen! translated by Annika Preis. Göteborg: Stegeland. Pp. 159.

A10a. First English Edition, 1979

JEAN RHYS | * | SMILE PLEASE | AN UNFINISHED AUTOBIOGRAPHY |
* | ANDRE DEUTSCH

Format: [ ]$_{16}$, B$_{16}$ - E$_{16}$, F$_8$. Between C$_{15}$ and C$_{16}$ (that is,
between p. 94 and p. [95]) there is a gathering of four leaves
of black and white photographs; the gathering is sewn between
the second and third leaves. C$_{16}$ is a single leaf, tipped
onto D$_1$.

Pagination: [1] half title; [2] OTHER BOOKS BY JEAN RHYS |
QUARTET | AFTER LEAVING MR MACKENZIE | VOYAGE IN THE DARK |
GOOD MORNING, MIDNIGHT | WIDE SARGASSO SEA | TIGERS ARE BETTER
LOOKING | SLEEP IT OFF LADY; [3] title page; [4] FIRST PUB-
LISHED 1979 BY | ANDRÉ DEUTSCH LIMITED | 105 GREAT RUSSELL
STREET LONDON WC1 | COPYRIGHT © 1979 BY THE ESTATE OF THE LATE
JEAN RHYS | FOREWORD COPYRIGHT © 1979 BY DIANA ATHILL | ALL
RIGHTS RESERVED | PRINTED IN GREAT BRITAIN BY | EBENEZER BAY-
LIS AND SON LIMITED | THE TRINITY PRESS, WORCESTER, AND LON-
DON | ISBN 0 233 97213 7; 5-15, [text of Jean Rhys and her
Autobiography, A Foreword by Diana Athill]; [16] blank; [17]
half title: SMILE PLEASE; [18] blank; 19-94, text; four un-
numbered leaves of photographs; [95] half title: IT BEGAN |
TO GROW COLD | THE MATERIAL WHICH FOLLOWS | WAS NOT CONSIDERED
BY JEAN RHYS TO BE FINISHED WORK. | SOME OF IT IS LITTLE MORE
THAN NOTES.; [96] blank; 97-156, text; 157, half title: FROM
A DIARY: AT THE ROPEMAKERS' ARMS | [nine-line description];
[158] blank; 159-173, text; [174] blank; one blank leaf.

Contents: Jean Rhys and her Autobiography, a Foreword by Di-
ana Athill (includes a chronology of the life of Jean Rhys and
"A Note on the Publishing History of Jean Rhys's Books").
Smile Please: Smile Please. Books. Meta. Geneva. The Doll.
My Mother. Black/White. Carnival. St Lucia. Poetry. Facts
of Life. My Father. Sundays. The Religious Fit.   The
Zouaves. Leaving Dominica. *It Began to Grow Cold*: First
Steps. Chorus Girls. The Interval. Christmas Day. World's
End and a Beginning. Leaving England. Paris. Paris Again.
From a Diary: at the Ropemakers' Arms.

Binding: Red, linen-weave paper-covered boards, the spine
lettered in gilt: * | SMILE | PLEASE | * | JEAN | RHYS | * |

* ANDRE DEUTSCH. All edges trimmed. White end-papers.
8 1/2 x 5 1/2 inches.

Publication: 15 November 1979 at four pounds and ninety-five
pence.

Copy examined: Personal copy.

Notes: The volume was issued with a dust-jacket designed by
Splash Studies: glossy primrose paper printed in shades of
rose, blue, and grey with a black-and-white photograph of
Jean Rhys by Elizabeth Vreeland on the front cover and a list
of seven titles by Rhys published by Deutsch on the back
cover.
The significant differences between the English and American editions of *Smile Please* are noted below, A10b: Contents.

Reviews:

Hilary Spurling, "Werewolves and Zombies." *Observer*, No.
9821 (18 November 1979), p. 40.

Writing for the Sunday newspaper reader, Spurling recounts
several of the more sensational details from Rhys's life
in the West Indies; she notes the material in *Smile Please*
already familiar to readers of the novels; and she summarizes the contents of the volume. Turning to Thomas Staley's *Jean Rhys*, she appeals to the xenophobia of British
readers as she dismisses the study: in it Staley explains
"the meaning" and re-tells the plots "in the kind of un-
gainly, PR man's prose which never uses a simple expression
or a single sentence where a bogus neologism or a woffly
paragraph will do." Such "official Eng. lit. jargon ...
can make little of a writer as technically and intellect-
ually fastidious as Jean Rhys."

Marina Warner, "Jean Rhys: A Voyage into the Dark." *Sunday
Times*, No. 8108 (18 November 1979), p. 41.

The reviewer points out that *Smile Please* "is not a formal
autobiography but an admission into the real world of the
heroine familiar from Jean Rhys's masterpieces, 'Voyage in
the Dark,' 'Good Morning, Midnight,' and 'Wide Sargasso
Sea,'" and proceeds to tell the story of the novelist's
life, taking her information from the autobiography. She
concludes by noting that while *Smile Please* will frustrate
readers who want facts about the writer, it shows that "a
personality is not only a set of facts, a curriculum vitae,

but an atmosphere, a disposition."

Ronald Blythe, "A Girl from Dominica." *Listener*, 102 (6 December 1979), 789.

In this full-page study the reviewer provides a carefully considered summary of the facts in *Smile Please*, writing that "this slight, initially rich and finally sketchy book is partly an autobiography; partly an attempt to put some of the record straight ... ; and partly an apologia for her inability to write her 'life' in the conventional sense." He acknowledges the role which David Plante and Diana Athill played in the composition of the work and points out that "the result is tantalising rather than satisfactory." *Smile Please* leaves many questions unanswered: there is little explanation of how Rhys drifted into "the chorus of a dim touring company," of her affair with her first lover, or of her second and third husbands. Yet while factual details are absent, *Smile Please* explains "one important aspect of her personality, the absence in her of female narcissism. She seemed to possess little or no comprehension of what drew men to her." The review provides a full account of the autobiography and a balanced view of Rhys as both a writer and a human being.

Gabriele Annan, "Turned Away by the Tropics." *Times Literary Supplement*, No. 4005 (21 December 1979), p. 154.

In this long, seriously thought-out review Annan provides a detailed synopsis of Rhys's life story by bringing together facts from both *Smile Please* and Thomas Staley's *Jean Rhys*, as well as from unpublished sources; recounts the pertinent facts of Rhys's literary career; and outlines the critical reception of the novelist. The reviewer welcomes Staley's volume because it "sets a good example for the Rhys industry. His interpretations of the works are sensible and fairly free from jargon...." Annan stresses that "the psychological truth about [Rhys's] life is in her novels, as well as an unusually large proportion of facts, even if she changed these about a little," and shows some of the links between the fiction and the "vignettes" of *Smile Please*. The childhood material is closely related to *Wide Sargasso Sea* and to "the flashbacks to Anna Morgan's childhood" in *Voyage in the Dark*. The second section of *Smile Please* repeats material found in *Voyage in the Dark*. Yet *Smile Please* "is more explicit than the novel," and Annan quotes passages which reveal Rhys's unflinching view of herself. The reviewer is puzzled by the last section of

Smile Please ("From a Diary ... ") and describes these
parts as "a strange sting" in the "tail" of the autobiography "that cannot possibly be called exquisite or object-
ive."

Jeffrey Meyers, "Sense of Evil." *Spectator*, 243 (22 December
1979), 31-32.

Meyers, a biographer of Katherine Mansfield, bases his review on a series of comparisons between Rhys and Mansfield:
both came to England from colonial islands; both were beautiful in appearance; they had parallel experiences with men;
their literary careers were not unlike (Rhys even translated a novel by Mansfield's lover Francis Carco). In their
writing they share an "artistic integrity, sensitive style
and technical skill" and their work "is characterised by
subtle detail, precise phrasing, delicate observation and
concentrated emotion." Meyers describes *Smile Please* as a
"sketchy autobiography" held together by the theme of "the
child's discovery of evil, which changes from a threatening
force in Dominica (where she is protected by her family) to
a destructive force in England (where she is alone and vulnerable)." He concludes by noting the humiliation that
both Mansfield and Rhys experienced in their relationships
to men to whom they turned for "sympathy and protection."

Helen McNeil, "Broken Heart." *New Statesman*, 99 (15 February
1980), 253-254.

McNeil tells the story of Rhys's life, emphasizing the biographical origins of her "passion for loss" which arose
from her childhood experiences in the West Indies and her
young adult experiences of dispossession in England and
France. The Rhys heroine is "lost and victimized." *Smile
Please* does not "illuminate the differences between Rhys's
felt life and her fiction" but is rather a reworking of
"ingredients and perceptions which she had already written
several times." There are many verbal parallels and "thematic repetitions" between this autobiography and the novels,
and *Smile Please* provides very little "privileged information." The novels also reveal "a striking discrepancy between their emotional impact and their language, which,
while emotive, is simple and understated." The novelist
writes "unashamedly about female subjectivity" in cool,
modernistically controlled language." The novels are "feminine rather than feminist" and "like their heroines, present themselves as victims to the reader. McNeil suggests
that Rhys's "deference" has helped to make her "the think-

ing man's favourite woman writer." After studying *Smile
Please* at length and in detail, McNeil dismisses Thomas
Staley's *Jean Rhys* in one paragraph, noting drily that if
his book "is anything to go by, [Rhys's] work doesn't in-
terpret readily" and quoting one of Staley's sentences to
illustrate the dull nature of the volume.

A10b. First American Edition, 1980

[The title-page is enclosed by a double-ruled frame; in
the upper two-thirds is a black-and-white photograph of
Jean Rhys, and in the lower one-third:]

JEAN RHYS │ * │ SMILE PLEASE │ * │ AN UNFINISHED AUTOBIOGRAPHY

Format: Five gatherings of sixteen leaves. No signatures.
Four leaves of black-and-white photographs are tipped in between the third and fourth gatherings.

Pagination: [i] half title; [ii] blank; [iii] OTHER BOOKS BY
JEAN RHYS │ QUARTET │ AFTER LEAVING MR MACKENZIE │ VOYAGE IN
THE DARK │ GOOD MORNING, MIDNIGHT │ WIDE SARGASSO SEA │ TIGERS
ARE BETTER LOOKING │ SLEEP IT OFF, LADY; [iv] FOREWORD BY DI-
ANA ATHILL │ HARPER & ROW, PUBLISHERS │ * │ NEW YORK │ [pub-
lisher's device incorporating the date 1817 and to the left:]
CAMBRIDGE │ HAGERSTOWN │ PHILADELPHIA │ SAN FRANCISCO ͆ [and
to the right of the device:] LONDON │ MEXICO CITY │ SÃO PAULO
│ SYDNEY; [v] title page; [vi] "MY DAY" ORIGINALLY APPEARED IN
ENGLAND AND THE U.S. IN VOGUE. │ BRITISH VOGUE © 1975 BY THE
CONDE NAST PUBLICATION LTD. │ U.S. COPYRIGHT © 1975 BY THE CON-
DE NAST PUBLICATIONS INC. │ SMILE PLEASE: AN UNFINISHED AUTO-
BIOGRAPHY. COPYRIGHT © │ 1979 BY THE ESTATE OF JEAN RHYS.
FOREWORD COPYRIGHT © 1979 │ BY DIANA ATHILL. ALL RIGHTS RE-
SERVED. PRINTED IN THE UNITED │ STATES OF AMERICA. NO PART
OF THIS BOOK MAY BE USED OR │ REPRODUCED IN ANY MANNER WHAT-
SOEVER WITHOUT WRITTEN PER- │ MISSION EXCEPT IN THE CASE OF
BRIEF QUOTATIONS EMBODIED IN │ CRITICAL ARTICLES AND REVIEWS.
FOR INFORMATION ADDRESS HARPER │ & ROW, PUBLISHERS, INC., 10
EAST 53RD STREET, NEW YORK, N.Y. │ 10022. │ FIRST U.S. EDITION
│ DESIGNER: GLORIA ADELSON │ * │ LIBRARY OF CONGRESS CATALOG-
ING IN PUBLICATION DATA │ RHYS, JEAN. │ SMILE PLEASE. │ BIBLIO-
GRAPHY: P. │ 1. RHYS, JEAN--BIOGRAPHY. 2. NOVELISTS, ENGLISH--
│ 20TH CENTURY--BIOGRAPHY. I. TITLE │ PR6035.H96Z474 1980
823'.912 [B] 79-3666 │ ISBN 0-06-013602-2 │ * │ 80 81 82 83
84 85 10 9 8 7 6 5 4 3 2 1; vii-viii, Contents; [1] half title:

[within a double-ruled frame] FOREWORD; [2] blank; 3-9, text of Jean Rhys and Her Autobiography, by Diana Athill; [10] blank; [11] half title: [within a double-ruled frame] SMILE PLEASE | * ; [12] blank; 13-76, text; [77] half title: [within a double-ruled frame] IT BEGAN TO | GROW COLD | * | THE MATERIAL WHICH FOLLOWS WAS NOT | CONSIDERED BY JEAN RHYS TO BE FINISHED | WORK. SOME OF IT IS LITTLE MORE THAN NOTES. ; [78] blank; 79-88, text; four unnumbered leaves of photographs; 89-148, text; 149-150, Chronology; 151, Bibliography; [152] blank.

Contents: Identical with A10a, with the following exceptions: In the Foreword there are several revisions in the text which change the sense, and the "Chronology" and "Bibliography" are removed from the Foreword and placed at the end of the volume. The second part, "It Began to Grow Cold," includes after "Paris Again" a vignette entitled "The Dividing Line" (pp. 126-128) which is not in the English edition. The section "From a Diary" which, in the English edition, is separate from "It Began to Grow Cold" is in the American edition part of "It Began to Grow Cold." Following "From a Diary" there are two entries which are not in the English edition, "The Cottage" (pp. 142-143) and "My Day" (pp. 144-148). In addition, the photographs on the four unnumbered leaves are re-arranged and include the photograph of Jean Rhys which appears on the dust-jacket of A10a.

Binding: Spine covered in brown cloth extending over one-quarter of the covers; beige, paper-covered boards with end-papers of the same paper. Spine lettered from head to tail in gilt within a double-ruled frame: JEAN RHYS SMILE PLEASE HARPER & ROW. Blind-stamped rule on the front cover. All edges trimmed. 9 1/4 x 5 3/4 inches.

Publication: May 1980 at $10.95.

Copy examined: Perkins Library copy.

Reviews:

"Nonfiction." *Publishers Weekly*, 217 (4 April 1980), 68.

A brief description of the contents of this "unconventional, incomplete autobiography ... a series of vignettes.... This absorbing memoir is as mesmerizing as Rhys's other works."

Frances Esmonde de Usabel. *Library Journal,* 105 (15 April 1980), 983.

The reviewer briefly describes the contents of the autobiography, noting that "Athill ... provides an excellent foreword." The volume is "A necessary purchase for libraries
with sizable fiction and/or strong feminist collections."

Diana Trilling, "The Odd Career of Jean Rhys." *New York Times
Book Review,* 85 (25 May 1980), 1, 17.

Writing from a somewhat Olympian point of view, Trilling
uses the publication of *Smile Please* as an occasion to examine in detail the life and artistic achievement of Rhys
for the leading article of this issue. She provides a summary account of Rhys's life and works, pointing out that
since the novels all concern "the same woman at different
stages of experience," readers wish to know more about
Rhys's private life. But *Smile Please* does not provide the
information since it ends so early in Rhys's life. It is
a "nonfiction novel" which tells the story familiar from
the novels. Although there is some suggestion of "exploitation" in the publication, *Smile Please* has "the negative
usefulness of confirming the lack of invention in Miss
Rhys's world," even in *Wide Sargasso Sea.* Trilling describes the characteristics of the "Rhys woman" and Rhys's
understanding of "fate." In this area Rhys can be contrasted to Hemingway: he and other contemporaries of the
'twenties and 'thirties wrote for a world of possibilities,
while Rhys "was a premature spokeswoman for the psychological 'sixties and 'seventies ... [and] prefigured a period
that would be better prepared to receive her." Trilling
concludes with a fairly lengthy report of David Plante's
memoir in the *Paris Review* since it fills in the biographical gaps. She praises this memoir because Plante's "honesty as a writer" forces him not to dissemble and therefore
to reveal truly the "rage and hatred" of Rhys's life, from
which she "as a novelist distilled only the pathos, the
poison got rid of." His account enables one to see clearly the artistry in Rhys's work.

Samuel Hynes. *New Republic,* 182 (31 May 1980), 28-31.

In this important essay Hynes surveys the events of Rhys's
life and points out that her career was largely determined
by the fact that "she fit none of the standard categories
of writing women" and that her "extraordinary obscurity"
was caused by her colonial birth and her life in the demi-

mondaine, both of which "separated her entirely from the
centers of literary power, where reputations and careers
are made." Too, she was "completely without literary am-
bition" and "wrote out of private necessity, to exorcise
her demons." Although readers usually read her fiction as
autobiography, they err in doing so, for rather than "describing an entire life," the novels treat, "again and a-
gain, one human situation--the condition of absolute loneliness." Rhys the artist had only this one subject--"Her
myth of existence was made of the bad times"--and thus the
novels have a striking similarity. But while the "bad times
seem to have come pretty directly from Jean Rhys's own early life," Rhys has given them the shape and form that dis-
tinguishes art from the formlessness of life. She also discovered the "appropriate style" for the novel which is
"will-less and momentum-less," the form which is her "most
original achievement." Modern feminists have taken her up
because her female characters usually suffer at the hands
of men, but the novels actually show that she was concerned
with "the cruelty and the exploitation and the savagery of
human beings at large." *Smile Please* is "a marvelous book
in its own right" and differs from the novels in that it
provides "a more balanced account" of Rhys's life, "making
use of the good times that the novels have no room for."
Hynes praises the Dominica sketches in particular and singles out "The Trial" [part of "From a Diary"] as an important justification by the artist of her writing. While Rhys
is admittedly a "minor writer" who "played on one sad
string," she is also "one of our classics."

Phyllis Rose, "Jean Rhys in Fact and Fiction." *Yale Review*,
69 (Summer, 1980), 596-602.

Rhys's autobiography is in some ways superfluous since, unlike most modern writers, the novelist had used her life as
the subject of her stories. Her heroines, whatever they
may be named, "are always Jean Rhys," and the novels "express indelibly one aspect of the female condition--the lim-
itation, the dependence, the despair." If the four early
novels are viewed in terms of their internal chronology,
they tell the Rhys story (Rose places the events of *After
Leaving Mr Mackenzie* between *Quartet* and *Voyage in the
Dark*), yet the details within each are those demanded by
the "shape" of the novel at hand and are not the actual
facts of Rhys's life. *Smile Please* is supposed to be "a
repository of fact" which will correct the misinterpreta-
tions which the fiction allows, but Rhys was too old and in
too poor a physical condition to select significant facts.

Thus *Wide Sargasso Sea* is actually "more truly her autobiography," and the "best-written and most gripping parts"
of *Smile Please* are those covering "aspects of her life she
had already written about in her novels." The "querulous
speaking voice" of the novelist which David Plante "record-
ed so unnervingly" in his "appalling" memoir [in the *Paris
Review*] is too often heard in *Smile Please*, and it will
"win her no new readers." Indeed the autobiography points
up the faults of the fiction and the inadequacies of Rhys's
vision of social issues, particularly racial ones. The primary achievement of Rhys lies in her ability simply to record "so vividly the point of view of the victims" in their
struggle with the oppressors and "her sympathy with the experience of exile and alienation." Rhys's works either appeal to readers, or they do not; and in any case they cannot be read too often, even though they may "form an unforgettable part of one's experience." This "bad autobiography" does not matter since Rhys "wrote her life into existence in her fiction."

"Short Reviews." *Atlantic*, 245 (June 1980), 92.
     The anonymous reviewer describes the contents of the auto-
     biography, praising the work as "the best kind of personal
     account" in which "the only disappointment ... is that
     there is not more of it."

Joyce Carol Oates, "Books." *Mademoiselle*, 86 (June 1980), 50.

     Oates gives a brief account of Rhys's life and notes that
     "Rhys wrote so convincingly of victimized women because she
     had been one for much of her life.... [She] attributed her
     fear and distrust of the world not to cruel treatment by
     men ... but to the influence of her West Indies nurse...."
     The reviewer calls attention to the fragmented nature of
     Smile Please and writes: "One comes away as impressed by
     Jean Rhys's stubbornness and courage as by her gift for
     fiction."

Eve Auchincloss, "Jean Rhys. Voyage Through the Dark." *Book
World* [*Washington Post*], 10 (8 June 1980), 4.

     Auchincloss gives a detailed biographical sketch of Rhys
     based on material drawn from *Smile Please* and from Thomas
     Staley's *Jean Rhys*. She stresses the psychological forces
     in the novelist's childhood which helped to shape the ad-
     ult's attitudes, as well as the differences between the
     projected image of Rhys in the fiction and the actuality
     of the writer. "Her writing became her real life, the sup-

ple, quiet mechanism she perfected to order and expiate the
rooted sadness her early life had ordained." By the time
of her death "she was no longer an abject failure in anyone's eyes." The reviewer finds "it is strange that only
now has a critical examination of her work been written"
and pronounces that Thomas F. Stanley's [sic] Jean Rhys is
"excellent."

Agnes M. Kullman. *Best Sellers*, 40 (July 1980), 140.

A report on the contents of *Smile Please* in which Kullman
states that "each vignette is a story in itself" and that
"the book ... reads more like a novel than an autobiography."

Time, 116 (7 July 1980), 69.

The reviewer briefly summarizes the events of Rhys's life
and points to the "extraordinary freshness" of these unfinished memoirs which did not receive Rhys's usual "pol-
ish[ing] revisions." Even though the writer's memory often
fails her, "her prose style never [falls] below the high-
est standard."

John Updike, "Books: Dark Smile, Devilish Saints." *New Yorker*, 56 (11 August 1980), 82, 85-89.

Reviewing *Smile Please* and William Burroughs' *Port of
Saints*, Updike gives the first half of his lengthy essay
to a respectful consideration of Rhys's life and its influence upon her fiction. *Smile Please* is enhanced for him
because it is in a fragmentary state and therefore more in
keeping with our age of "relativity, indeterminacy, and ag-
nosticism." He contrasts Rhys's "resolute economy of style"
with "the recent gust of female confessionalism," and sees
that the accounts of Rhys's early life and of Antoinette's
girlhood (in *Wide Sargasso Sea*) both center on "the unreach-
able mother." The "socio-economic secrets" of the Caribbean, the background of *Wide Sargasso Sea*, are explained in
Smile Please, as are the novelist's personal attitudes and
personality: "The strikingly combined intensity and apathy
of Miss Rhys's world view have their seeds in the black/
white, fear-riddled atmosphere of Dominica." Using extensive quotations from both *Smile Please* and Athill's "Foreword" Updike follows Rhys's literary career, stressing her
commitment to the profession of writing. After discussing
Burroughs, Updike notes that Burroughs and Rhys "made good
acquaintance with those demons of self-destruction whose
entertainment is one of our modern luxuries," this demon

being for Rhys alcohol. Yet both writers survived this
self-destruction as did such modernists as Joyce and Proust;
but Rhys and Burroughs "have little of the idealist's ob-
ligatory optimism, or his passion for inner organization.
... A certain pragmatic dryness, which we feel in their
styles, a certain deadness even, permeates their burnt-out
worlds. This deadness, perhaps, proved their mundane sal-
vations, and makes them, as artists, post-modern." This
review is illuminated by insights which only another creative artist could provide.

V. S. Pritchett, "Displaced Person." *New York Review of
Books*, 27 (14 August 1980), 8, 10.

Pondering the difficulties faced by Rhys when she decided
to write her autobiography in order to establish the truth
about her life in London and Paris, Pritchett calls attention to the fact that she "had already written [her life]
out in her very autobiographical novels and stories. She
was being asked to winnow away her remarkable art and reveal, if she could remember them, the 'real' facts in a continuous narrative." Hence in *Smile Please* the reader is
"lost halfway between 'real life' and the novels. The
chief merit lies in her asides, in her fits of kindness or
temper, and forgiveness; they bring out the stoicism, courage, and honesty of her baffled fatalism." Pritchett retells the story of her life, pausing occasionally to make
his personal judgements. Rhys, he decides, "was not a feminist. She was simply feminine and took the rough with the
smooth, without foresight. She mistrusted women. She
worked through men, in the old way, carelessly, by instinct." He also notes that unlike Katherine Mansfield,
Rhys "did not move adroitly into a recognizable 'set....'
In Paris she was on the fringe.... Hers was the Paris of
failure" and he points out that the London and Paris vignettes "are best ... simply because her realism has no nostalgia in it. Her acceptance by later readers was based
on the fact that the "displacement" which she exemplified
"had become a norm."

Robert Phillips, "Pearls on a String." *Commonweal*, 107 (29
August 1980), 474-475.

Rhys's novels "are too narrow in range for greatness" and
the writer herself, "at different stages of development (or
disintegration)," is the female protagonist in each. But
Rhys was a "fine" writer with "an instinctive feeling for
form ... and ... total ... insight into the feminine sensibility." Phillips describes *Smile Please*, emphasizing that

Rhys thought that autobiography "must be literally true in every detail." Hence she presents a series of chronologic-al vignettes of "vital occasions which had involved her." But this "last book by this gifted prose stylist" presents "an incomplete portrait of the subject behind some of the most subjective fiction of our time."

"Noted by the Editors." *Antioch Review*, 39 (Spring, 1981), 264.

A short description of the autobiography with Rhys being called "a precise ... stylist" whose "fame continues" to grow.

Gail Pool, "Jean Rhys: Life's Unfinished Form." *Chicago Review*, 32 (Spring, 1981), 68-74.

The relationship of this autobiography to the writer's fic-tion contrasts the formlessness of life to the form of fic-tion. Since Rhys "was neither reflective nor analytical," she was unable to create a form when she treated her life directly, even though she could shape episodes in her life "to meet the aesthetic requirements of the work at hand." Her fiction is indeed characterized by form. The chronol-ogy which should unify the autobiography does not work be-cause it is "not really consistent with the way Rhys viewed her life." The autobiography is unfinished, but no amount of revision would have helped because Rhys was using mater-ial which was merely picturesque and about which she had nothing to say. The "listless" treatment of the West In-dian material has the negative value of showing "That Rhys was neither a political nor, directly a social writ-er." She was primarily a writer concerned with "Life on the edge, struggle, compromise, defeat." The autobiography makes the task of distinguishing the writer and her heroines even more difficult, as well as understanding her attitude to women and their position in life. It does show, how-ever, that Rhys may truly have believed that no decisions were possible, just as no analysis and no reflection of life were possible. While fiction can be made from such attitudes, autobiography cannot, for the reader turns to it for facts. Probably Rhys could never have written auto-biography for it "requires reflection, the formulation of an overview.... She did not work this way in her fiction, and it seems to have been a mode of thinking she found alien." Ultimately the autobiography is the biography of the persona Rhys had decided was Rhys, and thus "for an author who wrote almost exclusively about herself, Jean

Rhys revealed remarkably little about Jean Rhys." Pool
gives here an important study of Rhys and of autobiography
in general.

Mary Ann Klein, "Autobiography." *World Literature Today*, 55
(Spring, 1981), 324-325).

Since Rhys's "personal life infused her fiction," critics
have looked forward to her memoirs; but they will be disappointed by *Smile Please* which, even in its finished sections, is "fairly pedestrian" and lacks the "energy and intensity" that are characteristic of the fiction.   Thomas
Staley's "pioneering study" [*Jean Rhys*] acknowledges this
relationship of life and art by its use of biographical
material.   The organization of the study around the chronology of the novels leads to a certain repetitiveness, while
his treatment of "the images of the female" in the novels
is somewhat tentative.   "The chief significance of Staley's
work is its treatment of Rhys's entire canon and its legit-
imizing of Rhys as a writer who must be reckoned with by
critics."

         A10c.   First English Paperback, 1981   (Not seen)

              (2nd Impression, 1982: described below)

JEAN RHYS │ * │ SMILE PLEASE │ AN UNFINISHED AUTOBIOGRAPHY │
* │ PENGUIN BOOKS

Format: Perfect binding.

Pagination: [1]   PENGUIN BOOKS │ SMILE PLEASE │ [thirty-one
line description of Jean Rhys's life and literary career];
[2] blank; [3] title page; [4] PENGUIN BOOKS LTD, HARMONDS-
WORTH, MIDDLESEX, ENGLAND │ PENGUIN BOOKS, 625 MADISON AVENUE,
NEW YORK, NEW YORK 10022, U.S.A. │ PENGUIN BOOKS AUSTRALIA
LTD, RINGWOOD, VICTORIA, AUSTRALIA │ PENGUIN BOOKS CANADA LTD,
2801 JOHN STREET, MARKHAM, ONTARIO, CANADA L3R 1B4 │ PENGUIN
BOOKS (N.Z.) LTD, 182-190 WAIRAU ROAD, AUCKLAND 10, NEW ZEA-
LAND │ * │ FIRST PUBLISHED BY ANDRÉ DEUTSCH LTD 1979 │ PUB-
LISHED IN PENGUIN BOOKS 1981 │ REPRINTED 1982 │ * │ COPYRIGHT
© THE ESTATE OF THE LATE JEAN RHYS, 1979 │ FOREWORD COPYRIGHT
© DIANA ATHILL, 1979 │ ALL RIGHTS RESERVED │ * │ MADE AND
PRINTED IN GREAT BRITAIN BY │ RICHARD CLAY (THE CHAUCER PRESS),
LTD, BUNGAY, SUFFOLK │ SET IN MONOTYPE BELL │ EXCEPT IN THE

UNITED STATES OF AMERICA, | THIS BOOK IS SOLD SUBJECT TO THE
CONDITION | THAT IT SHALL NOT, BY WAY OF TRADE OR OTHERWISE,
| BE LENT, RE-SOLD, HIRED OUT, OR OTHERWISE CIRCULATED | WITH-
OUT THE PUBLISHER'S PRIOR CONSENT IN ANY FORM OF | BINDING OR
COVER OTHER THAN THAT IN WHICH IT IS | PUBLISHED AND WITHOUT
A SIMILAR CONDITION | INCLUDING THIS CONDITION BEING IMPOSED
| ON THE SUBSEQUENT PURCHASER; 5 [subsequent pagination is
identical with that of the first English edition with the exception that there are no photographs in this edition and that
the final blank leaf of A10a is here as follows:] [175] [ad-
vertisement for Penguin and Pelican books]; [176] [advertise-
ment for books by Jean Rhys, headed by a three-line quotation
from the *Guardian*; *Quartet* and *Sleep It Off Lady* are each
given eight-line descriptions, and *After Leaving Mr Mackenzie*,
Good Morning, Midnight, *Tigers are Better-Looking*, *Voyage in
the Dark*, and *Wide Sargasso Sea* are listed.]

Contents: Identical with A10a.

Binding: Glossy paper covers. The front cover is a sepia-
tinted photograph of Jean Rhys as a young woman; imposed in
the upper third of the cover is a rectangular frame of white,
pink, and black enclosing a cream-colored background for let-
tering in blue, green, red, and black: JEAN RHYS | SMILE
PLEASE | AN UNFINISHED AUTOBIOGRAPHY. At the bottom left of
the cover is the orange, white, and black Penguin symbol.
The orange spine is lettered in black and white from head to
tail: JEAN RHYS SMILE PLEASE   ISBN 0 14 | 00.5653 X   *.
The back cover is brown with a full-page frame repeating the
colors and design of the front-cover frame. Within the frame:
a two-line quotation from the *Financial Times*, a three-paragraph description of Jean Rhys's career, a three-line quotation from the *Daily Mail*, and a four-line quotation from the
Guardian; at the bottom left: U.K. £1.50 | AUST. $4.95 |
(RECOMMENDED) | CAN. $3.50; and at the bottom right: AUTO-
BIOGRAPHY | ISBN 0 14 | 00.5653 X. All edges trimmed.
7 1/8 x 4 3/8 inches.

Publication: December 1981 at one pound and fifty pence; 2nd
Impression: 1982 at one pound and fifty pence.

Copy examined: Personal copy.

Notes: This paperback edition is a line-by-line reproduction
of the text of the first edition in which the print and page
sizes are reduced by a little over eight per cent and the
signatures are omitted.

Reviews:

"Paperback Choice." *Observer*, No. 9929 (13 December 1981),
p. 31.

A one-sentence description of *Smile Please* ending "should
not be missed by anyone who likes ... Jean Rhys's novels."

On p. 29 of this issue of the *Observer* there is a double-
column, page-long advertisement for Penguin Books; *Smile
Please* heads the list and is accompanied by a quotation
from the *Guardian*:   "A treasure-house of keys that unlock
the sources of the pain and questionings of her novels."

Translation. 1. French, 1980 (Not seen)

Souriez, s'il vous plaît, autobiographie inachevée, translated by Jacques Tournier.   Paris: Denoël (Arc-en-ciel).
Pp. 224.

Reviews:

Pierre Kyria, "Jean Rhys, In Memoriam."   *Le Monde [des Livres]*,
No. 11036 (25 July 1980), pp. 11, 14.

   (Not seen)

Addenda

Section B
Contributions to Books

B. Contributions to Books

B1. *Winter's Tales, No. 6.* Edited by A. D. Maclean. London: Macmillan and Co., Ltd.; New York: St. Martin's Press, 1960. Pp. [viii], [322].

   A collection of short stories which includes Rhys's "Outside the Machine," pp. 189-219. The story is reprinted in A7.

B2. *Voices.* Edited by Robert Ruben. London: Michael Joseph, 1963. Pp. [264].

   A collection of twenty-one short stories which includes Rhys's "A Solid House," pp. 177-194. The story is reprinted in A7.

B3. *Penguin Modern Stories I.* Edited by Judith Burnley. Harmondsworth: Penguin Books Ltd., 1969. Pp. [128].

   A collection of stories by William Sansom, David Plante, and Bernard Malamud; and by Jean Rhys, "I Spy a Stranger," pp. 53-67, and "Temps Perdi," pp. 69-88. These stories were first printed in *Art and Literature*: see below, C8 and C11.

   Reviews:

   Frank Tuohy, "Fiction: Good News." *Times*, No. 57628 (2 August 1969), p. 20c.

"A brilliant introduction to one of our two best women writers." [Tuohy does not name the other writer.]

Oscar Turnhill, "Short Stories." *Sunday Times*, No. 7627 (3 August 1969), p. 45.

"Neither [of David Plante's stories] has quite the classic assurance of Jean Rhys's "I Spy a Stranger," in which the callous hounding of an elderly woman refugee seeps to light through the pleasantries of idle conversation...."

Stephen Wall, "New Short Stories." *Observer*, No. 9292 (17 August 1969), p. 20.

A negative review of the collection: "Jean Rhys contributes a couple of rather faded pieces."

B4.   [Letter by Jean Rhys] quoted by Helen Nebeker, *Jean Rhys. Woman in Passage*. Montreal: Eden Press Women's Publications, 1981, pp. vi-vii.

A letter "written in the last months" of Rhys's life (p. vi) commenting on Nebeker's study. See also below, F. 2: 1981.

B5.   [Letter by Jean Rhys] quoted in *The Presence of Ford Madox Ford, A Memorial Volume of Essays, Poems and Memoirs*, edited by Sondra J. Stang. Philadelphia: University of Pennsylvania Press, 1981.

(Not seen)

Addenda

Section C
Contributions to Periodicals

C. Contributions to Periodicals

C1.   "Vienne." *Transatlantic Review*, 2 (December 1924), 639-645.

Jean Rhys's first publication consists of three sketches entitled "The Dancer," "'Fischyl,'" and "The Spending Phase." A footnote to the title "Vienne" states: "From novel called *Triple Sec*." The sketches are reprinted, with some changes, as sections of "Vienne" in *The Left Bank* (A1). "The Dancer" is the untitled first section (pp. 193-194); "'Fischyl'" becomes "'Fischl' Winter 1920-Spring 1921" (pp. 215-217); and "The Spending Phase" is entitled "The Last Act of Vienna--The Spending Phase." The consistent changes between the periodical and the book publication are that the narrator "Ella" becomes "Frances" and her husband "John" is renamed "Pierre." The expletive *dam* in the *Transatlantic Review* is spelled *damn* in *The Left Bank* and is less frequently used.

C2.   "The Christmas Presents of Mynheer Van Rooz." *Time and Tide*, 12 (28 November 1931), 1360-1361.

Story: not reprinted. (Location of story found by Muriel J. Mellown)

C3.   "Till September Petronella." *London Magazine*, 7 (January 1960), 19-39.

Story: reprinted in A7.

C4.   "The Day They Burned the Books." *London Magazine*, 7 (July 1960), 42-46.

   Story: reprinted in A7.

C5.   "Let Them Call it Jazz." *London Magazine*, NS 1 (February 1962), 69-83.

   Story: reprinted in A7.   See also C13.

C6.   "Tigers are Better-Looking." *London Magazine*, NS 2 (October 1962), 24-34.

   Story: reprinted in A7.

C7.   "Wide Sargasso Sea." *Art and Literature*, No. 1 (March 1964), pp. 177-204.

   Extracts from the childhood sections of the novel of the same name and reprinted in it (A6).

C8.   "I Spy a Stranger." *Art and Literature*, No. 8 (Spring 1966), pp. 41-53.

   Story: reprinted in B3.

C9.   "The Sound of the River." *Art and Literature*, No. 9 (Summer 1966), pp. 192-197.

   Story: reprinted in A7.

C10.   "The Lotus." *Art and Literature*, No. 11 (Winter 1967), pp. 165-174.

   Story: reprinted in A7.

C11.   "Temps Perdi." *Art and Literature*, No. 12 (Spring 1967), pp. 121-138.

   Story: reprinted in B3.

C12.   "My Dear Darling Mr. Ramage." *The Times Saturday Review* [review section of the London *Times*], No. 57598 (28 June

1969), p. 19

> Story: published with a black-and-white illustration by
> Linnet Gotch. Reprinted in A9 under the title "Pioneers,
> Oh, Pioneers."

C13. "Qu'ils appellent ça du Jazz." *La Nouvelle Revue Française,* No. 202 (October 1969), pp. 484-507.

> Translation by Pierre Leyris of C5 and reprinted in A7.
> Translation. 1. The story is introduced (pp. 481-483) by
> three paragraphs taken from Francis Wyndham's "Introduction"
> to *Wide Sargasso Sea* and translated by Leyris; there are al-
> so references to the publication of A7. Translation. 1.

C14. "The Insect World." *The Sunday Times Magazine* [London].
19 August 1973, pp. 34, 37, 39.

> Story: published with a full-page black-and-white illus-
> stration by Franklin Wilson. Reprinted in A9; see also C25.

C15. "Sleep It Off, Lady." *New Review,* 1 (June 1974), 45-49.

> Story: reprinted in A9.

C16. "La Grosse Fifi." *Mademoiselle,* 79 (October 1974),
172-173.

> Story: introduced by a one-paragraph "Editor's Note" and
> identified as being "from the collection *Tigers Are Better-
> Looking* ... which Harper & Row will publish this month."
> First published in A1; reprinted in A7.

C17. "My Day." *Vogue,* 165 (February 1975), 186-187.

> Personal essay: reprinted in A8.

C18. "Whatever Became of Old Mrs. Pearce?" *Times* [London],
No. 59401 (21 May 1975), p. 16.

> Personal essay: introduced with the statement, "Novelist
> Jean Rhys contributes this week's guest column in our In-
> ternational Women's Year Series." Reprinted in A8, with

revisions, as "Close Season for the Old?"

C19. [Letter] quoted by Alice K. Turner, "Paperbacks in the
News. Jean Rhys Rediscovered: How it Happened." *Publishers
Weekly,* 206 (1 July 1974), 58.

   A letter written in response to an enquiry from *Publishers
   Weekly.* See below, F.3: 1974.

C20. "On Not Shooting Sitting Birds." *New Yorker,* 52 (26
April 1976), 35.

   Story: reprinted in A9.

C21. "Heat." *New Yorker,* 52 (17 May 1976), 36-37.

   Story: reprinted in A9.

C22. "Night Out, 1925." *Planet* [Llangeitho, Tregalon, Wales],
No. 33 (August 1976), pp. 32-34.

   Story: reprinted in A9. (Not seen: citation provided by
   Peter Hoy)

C23. "Kikimora." *New Yorker,* 52 (2 August 1976), 23-24.

   Story: reprinted in A9.

C24. "Goodbye Marcus, Goodbye Rose." *New Yorker,* 52 (30
August 1976), 26-27.

   Story: reprinted in A9.

C25. "The Insect World." *Mademoiselle,* 82 (October 1976),
175, 225-229.

   Story: introduced as being "from a new collection,
   Sleep It Off, Lady, which Harper & Row will publish next
   month." First published in C14; reprinted in A9.

C26. "Four Poems: Night on the River, All Through the Night, A Field Where Sheep were Feeding, and To Toni." *Observer*, No. 9680 (20 February 1977), p. 30.

Four poems of ten, eight, seven, and eight lines, respectively: not reprinted.

C27. "The Joey Blagstock Smile. September 7, 1974." *New Statesman*, 94 (23-30 December 1977), 890.

Sketch: not reprinted.

C28. "Q & A: Making Bricks Without Straw." *Harper's*, 257 (July 1978), 70-71.

Personal essay on the experience of giving interviews: not reprinted.

C29. "Whistling Bird." *New Yorker*, 54 (11 September 1978), 38-39.

Story: not reprinted. See also C30.

C30. "The Whistling Bird." *Harper's & Queen*, June 1979, pp. 160, 220.

Story: not reprinted. See also C29. (Not seen)

C31. [Letter by Jean Rhys to Alec Waugh, 30 December (?1952)] in Elaine Campbell, "Jean Rhys, Alec Waugh, and The Imperial Road." *Journal of Commonwealth Literature*, 14 (August 1979), 59-60.

A letter concerning Waugh's *The Clocks Strike Twice*. See below, F.3: 1949 and 1979.

C32. "Passage from a Diary." *New York Times Book Review*, 85 (25 May 1980), 16.

Pp. 129-141 of *Smile Please* (A10b) which is reviewed in the same issue. See above, A10b: Reviews.

Addenda

Section D
Translations by Jean Rhys

D. Translations by Jean Rhys

PERVERSITY | BY | FRANCIS CARCO | TRANSLATED BY   FORD MADOX
FORD | * | CHICAGO | PASCAL COVICI, PUBLISHER | MCMXXVIII

Pagination: [1-2] blank; [3] half title; [4] blank; [5] title
page; [6] COPYRIGHT 1928 BY PASCAL COVICI, PUBLISHER, INC. |
PRINTED IN THE UNITED STATES OF AMERICA; [7] half title; [8]
blank; 9-249, text; [250] blank; [251] half title: THE KNIFE;
[252] blank; 253-278, text; [279-280] blank.

Contents: *Perversity*, a novel, divided into twenty-two chapters; and *The Knife*, a novella, divided into three chapters.

Binding: Black, textured cloth boards, the front cover
printed in red within a ruled square: PERVERSITY | FRANCIS
CARCO | FORD MADOX FORD. On the spine, in red: PERVERSITY
| * | FRANCIS | CARCO | * | FORD | MADOX | FORD | PASCAL |
COVICI. White end-papers.

Publication: March 1928

Copy examined: Library of Congress copy, call number PZ3.
C1775.Pe.

Notes: Although Jean Rhys's name is not given anywhere in
this volume, there is ample evidence to prove that she made
the translation. The novel was first published in French as
Perversité (Paris: J. Ferenczi et fils, 1925). Francis Carco and the Ford Madox Fords spent the winters of 1924-1925
and 1925-1926 together in Toulon, and Ford was instrumental
in arranging the American publication of the translation.

Covici obviously hoped to increase sales by prominently featuring Ford's name on the cover and title page of the book.
While Ford never publicly acknowledged that Jean Rhys made
the translation, he did write two private letters in which he
gave her credit. That to Edward Naumburg, Jr. is quoted in
David Dow Harvey, *Ford Madox Ford, 1873-1939, A Bibliography
of Works and Criticism* (Princeton: Princeton University Press,
1962, p. 97); his letter to Isabel Patterson is printed in
Letters of Ford Madox Ford, edited by Richard M. Ludwig (Princeton: Princeton University Press, 1965, pp. 176-177). In the
latter Ford wrote: "I could not have done [the translation]
myself half so well if at all because translating is not one
of my gifts and I do not know the particular Parisian *argot*
that Mr. Carco employs."
    In March 1972 Jean Rhys herself wrote to me and told me
that she was the translator of the novel; and of course Diana
Athill repeats this fact in her Foreword to the autobiography
Smile Please. Unfortunately Miss Rhys did not mention to me
the translation of "The Knife." The style of the novella differs so markedly from that of the novel that one questions
whether Rhys actually translated it as well as the novel.
    Harvey notes that the translation was "republished at least
twice in cheap paper-back editions which perpetuate the al-
leged error of naming Ford as translator." He identifies
these editions as being published by Avon Publishing Co. in
1950 and Berkeley Publishing Co. in 1956.

Reviews:

Saturday Review of Literature, 4 (31 March 1928), 725.

    Perversity is listed as having been received by the jour-
    nal; but it does not appear to have been reviewed.

C.P.F. [?Clifton P. Fadiman], "Fiction Shorts." *Nation*,
126 (11 April 1928), 414.

    The reviewer gives a two-sentence summary of the novel,
    the second being: "Despite Ford Madox Ford's generous laud-
    ation, this book is not half as powerful as its author's
    "L'Homme Traque"; but it is distinctly worth reading if
    only for the genuineness of its prostitutes."

Burton Rascoe, "The Seamy Side." *Bookman*, 67 (April 1928),
184.

    Perversity is reviewed with praise alongside of Claude
    McKay's *Home to Harlem*, but there is no mention of either

the translation or of Ford.

"New Books and Reprints." *Times Literary Supplement*, No. 1378 (28 June 1928), p. 448.

The anonymous reviewer gives a fairly long summary of the novel and comments on "The Knife" as well. In conclusion he writes: "Mr. Ford's translation is very good. It reads like a translation--but, with such a book as this, this may not be a bad thing."

T. S. Matthews, "Importations." *New Republic*, 55 (15 August 1928), 337.

The reviewer briefly summarizes the novel and condemns the work on moral grounds without referring to the translation as such.

D2   BARRED   1932

[Title page not available:

Edward de Nève, *Barred*, translated by Jean Rhys. London: Desmond Harmsworth, 1932.]

Format: [ ]$_8$, B$_8$ - I$_8$, K$_8$ - Q$_8$.

Pagination: [incomplete] [3] title page; [4] BARRED BY ED-WARD DE NÈVE WAS FIRST | PUBLISHED IN MCMXXXII BY DESMOND | HARMSWORTH AT 44 GREAT RUSSELL | ST W.C.1 AND WAS MADE AND | PRINTED IN GREAT BRITAIN | BY MORRISON & GIBB LTD. | IN THE CITY OF | EDINBURGH; [5] Dedication: TO | JEAN | [with an eight-paragraph letter beginning DEAR JEAN and ending HERE THEN, MY DEAR JEAN, IS THE BOOK, AND HERE I AM, | EVER YOURS, | EDWARD DE NÈVE. | AMSTERDAM, | 12TH APRIL 1932.; 7-[10] Preface; 13-129, text of Part One; 130-168, text of Part Two; 169-255, text of Part Three.

Contents: Dedicatory letter; Preface; Three parts subdivided into chapters.

Publication: April 1932 at seven shillings and sixpence.

Copy examined: British Library deposit copy, pressmark

12514.tt.2.

Notes: According to the information in the Dedicatory Letter,
Jean Rhys saw the manuscript of this work--the story of her
first husband's arrest and imprisonment in France and of her
deserting him (in other words, the same story that is told in
Quartet)--while she was visiting in Amsterdam. She took the
manuscript and found an English publisher for it. In the same
year the work was published in Holland as *In de Strik* (Amsterdam: Andries Blitz, 1932); it was published in France the next
year as *Sous les Verrous* (Paris: Stock, 1933). A cheap reprint of the English edition was issued by Desmond Harmsworth
in August 1933 at three shillings and sixpence.

In the Dedicatory Letter of the French edition (it is ad-
dressed to Victor E. Van Vriesland who later wrote a Preface
for the Dutch edition of *Voyage in the Dark* [see above, A4.
Translation. 1. Dutch]) de Nève declares of *Sous les Verrous*
that "la version originale ... était française." In his
"Préface" de Nève asserts that the seemingly hostile attitude
to the French republic caused French publishers to reject the
manuscript; and hence the work appeared first in England and
Holland and only later in France. He also suggests that there
are differences between the English, Dutch, and French ver-
sions and that the work in French is "dans sa version et dans
sa forme originales."

According to Diana Athill's Foreword in *Smile Please* Jean
Rhys admitted that she "had given way to the temptation to cut
a few--a very few--sentences about herself which struck her as
'too unfair.'" Comparison of the French and English texts
shows that the English version does not so much suppress or
alter material as that the change in style gives the work a
totally different focus. The narrator in the French version
is an opinionated male who states his mind quite clearly and
without ambiguities; in the English version he is much less
blunt and ultimately less forceful; and overall what in French
is a statement concerning one man's particular situation becomes in English a generalized statement of social protest,
an attack by the have-nots upon the haves. The translation
thus shows Jean Rhys bringing her former husband's view of
the situation into line with the attitudes she herself had
expressed in *Quartet* and *After Leaving Mr Mackenzie*.

Diana Athill calls Jean Rhys's first husband Jean Lenglet.
She writes from her intimate acquaintance with both Jean Rhys
and Mrs. Maryvonne Moermann, the daughter of this first marriage. Yet in 1972 Jean Rhys wrote to me that her husband's
name was Jean Marie Langlet; and in the *Brinkman's Catalogus
van Boeken en Tijdschriften* (Leiden: 1956-1960) the name is
listed as Jean Edouard Langlet de Nève. All of his writings--

those in Dutch include novels, social documentaries, and translations--were published under the name Edouard (or Ed.) de Nève.

The only copy of *Barred* which I have seen is that in the British Library which I examined in 1972 and 1976. Unfortunately, by the summer of 1983 this copy had been "mislaid"-- hence the omissions in the description above.

Reviews:

J. B. Priestley, "Women Put Men in the Pillory." *Evening Standard*, No. 33589 (14 April 1932), p. 9.

A review of six new books including *Barred*. Cited by Edwin Day, *Bibliography of J. B. Priestley* (New York: Garland Publishing, Inc., 1980) and quoted in the publisher's advertisement in the *Sunday Times*, No. 5689 (24 April 1932), p. 8: "J. B. Priestley in *The Evening Standard*. '*Barred* does two things. It casts a light on the inhumanity of the French penal system. It also shows us the ridiculously nationalistic world of to-day.... I do not know whether the book is crude but forceful fiction or a genuine human document, but as either it is worth reading.' (Publisher's note: This IS a genuine human document.)" The rather large advertisement also includes the title *Ferney*, by Donald Stewart.

Compton MacKenzie. *Daily Mail*.

Desmond Harmsworth advertised *Barred* in the *Observer*, No. 7353 (1 May 1932), p. 5, in a large advertisement featuring an abstract drawing of a prison cell [?from the dustjacket] and with the following quotation: "'The agony of recollection has sustained the author from the first page to the last, so that in setting out to produce a piece of autobiography he has achieved a work of art....the reader who can stand horror should not miss "Barred," which as Rosetti [*sic*] wrote, makes a Goblin of the Sun.' Compton Mackenzie in *The Daily Mail*."

Gerald Bullett, "New Novels." *New Statesman*, NS 3 (14 May 1932), 621-622.

After reviewing four other titles, the writer summarizes the contents of *Barred* and comments: "It is written from the heart with a most effective simplicity--a heartrending, an infuriating document, and one which everybody should count it a social duty to read."

"New Books and Reprints." *Times Literary Supplement*, No. 1582
(26 May 1932), p. 392.

The reviewer briefly summarizes the contents without commenting on the language; he praises the documentary aspects
of the work (that is, the prison scenes), and writes: "But
the love-story irritates, for Jan Van Leeuwen puts up with
very much more than a man of his courage, education and
experience would brook for a day. A thoroughly readable
book and, if the prison parts are genuine and in all details true, a valuable social document."

D3 "The Chevalier of the Place Blanche" in Jean Rhys, *Sleep
It Off Lady* (A9), pp. 113-122.

A note on p. [111] points out that "This story is a much-
adapted translation of one written by Edouard de Nève."

In connection with this story it is worth noting that several of the stories in *The Left Bank* parallel incidents or
stories told by de Nève in *Sous les Verrous*. While the
experiences were unquestionably de Nève's (as, for example,
in "The Sidi" in *The Left Bank*--which story reappears in
Sous les Verrous), one cannot say whether the husband or
the wife first wrote the story.

Addenda

Section E
Adaptations

1. Dramatic: Radio, Television, and Cinema
2. Musical
3. Recordings

E.   Adaptations

1. Dramatic: Radio, Television, and Cinema

[Although Jean Rhys very much wanted to adapt her
novels for the stage, she was never successful in
doing so. Although none of the adaptations listed
in this section came from her pen, they are included because of the part they played in enhancing
her reputation and, in the case of the 1949 performance, because of the psychological influence
upon her.]

1949

Theater presentation of *Good Morning, Midnight* (given as a
monologue) by Selma Vaz Dias at the Anglo French Art Centre,
29, Elm Tree Road, St. John's Wood, London, on Thursday, 10
November 1949, 8 p. m. Admission two shillings.

This performance marked the beginning of the relationship
between Vaz Dias and Rhys, as well as the first public recognition of the novelist since 1939. A copy of the pro-
gram is in the University of Tulsa Jean Rhys Collection.
See also below, F. 3: 1949.

1957

Radio presentation (BBC-Third Programme) of Selma Vaz Dias in
Good Morning, Midnight, a dramatic monologue with music by
Roberto Gerhard, on 10 and 11 May 1957. Announced in the
Radio Times, 3 May 1957. See below, F. 3: 1957.

1973

Television presentation (BBC-2 Colour) of "The Lotus"(A7, C10) dramatized by Alan Seymour with Hermione Baddeley on 6 September 1973 in a series of six plays by women entitled "Then and Now." Announced in the *Radio-Television Times*, 6 September 1973, p. 49.

1974

Television presentation (BBC-1) of "The Jean Rhys Woman" on the "Omnibus" programme, 24 November 1974.

Reviews of this presentation were given by Sylvia Clayton in the *Daily Telegraph*, 25 November 1974 (the review included a brief interview with Rhys), and in "TLS Commentary: A Woman's Lot," *Times Literary Supplement*, No. 3795 (29 November 1974), p. 1342.

1976

Radio presentation: Angus Wilson and Milton Shulman discuss *Sleep It Off Lady* on BBC-2 on 28 October 1976 at 8.35 p.m. Announced in the *Observer*, 24 October 1976.

1981

Motion picture presentation: *Quartet*. 101 minutes long, sound, color, 35mm. Director: James Ivory. Screenplay: Ruth Prawer Jhabvala and James Ivory. Director of Photography: Pierre Lhomme. Producers: Ismail Merchant and Jean Pierre Mahot. Distributed in the U.S.A. by New World Pictures. Principal actors: Alan Bates, Maggie Smith, and Isabelle Adjani. American premiere: 25 October 1981.

Reviews and Other Notices:

"Quartet." *Sight and Sound*, 50 (Spring 1981), 108-109.

Seven black-and-white photographs from the film with names of actors and technicians.

New York Times, 28 May 1981, Section C, p. 14.

Announcement that Isabelle Adjani was named best actress at the 34th Cannes Film Festival for her rôle in *Quartet*.

John Coleman, "Postures New," *New Statesman*, 102 (17 July 1981), 24.

Coleman suggests that "it was anyhow inevitable the film of the book would be less (or more) than pure Rhys, given that the book's point-of-view, or pervasive consciousness, is almost exclusively that of its heroine: the old problem of externalising for the screen would guarantee that.... Mrs. Jhabvala has used a lot of the original dialogue, sometimes re-assigning it, and invented more, and more incidents..... What is surprising is that the adjustments rather fail to work as apparently intended." The critic has a very mixed opinion of the film.

Norma McLain Stoop, "Cinema." *After Dark*, 14, No. 5 (October 1981), 63-64.

Unqualified praise.

Judith Crist, "Film." *Saturday Review*, 8 (October 1981), 61.

"The screenplay ... is faithful to Jean Rhys's autobiographical novel." Crist praises the film and gives no negative comments.

Vincent Canby, "Screen: Ivory's 'Quartet,' Based on Rhys Novel." *New York Times*, 25 October 1981, p. 62, col. 3-6.

In this lengthy review Canby studies the relationship of the novel to the film, maintaining that Rhys's technique cannot be translated into visual techniques. "The Marya who is the novel's forlorn, lonely, slightly phlegmatic center is movingly defined by the author's self-obsessed tone, by Marya's seemingly lazy acceptance of fate and by what Marya sees. Though the novel is written in the third person, and though Miss Rhys occasionally darts inside the heads of the other characters, the world is understood entirely through Marya's ... vision of things.... The movie can never go into Marya's mind. We see only what she is doing, and what she is doing seems less mysterious and poignant than foolish. As a result, the movie has no satisfactory center.... 'Quartet' is handsome but, ultimately, weightless."

Joy Gould Bowtum, "Bizarre Bohemia: Was It Really this Boring?" *Wall Street Journal*, 105 (30 October 1981), 31.

The critic acknowledges the biographical origins of the novel and comments that the film suggests "that Rhys was

as boring as Ford was fatuous." While the novel was
"a sensitive literary portrait of bohemia," the film
is a failure.

Bruce Williamson. *Playboy*, 28 (November 1981), 45.

The reviewer stresses the salacious aspects of the
film, describes Rhys as "a famed beauty and former
chorus girl who became the lover of author Ford Madox
Ford," and advises that the film is "Bad (in a moral
sense!) but beautiful, if you have a taste for elegant
trifles."

David Denby, "Movies: Lost Girl." *New York*, 14 (9 November
1981), 67-68.

In this lengthy review Denby shows his knowledge of Rhys,
suggesting that she "is one of the great modern poets of
female melancholy: her precise, dryly lyrical prose rivals
Billie Holiday's voice and phrasing as an expression of
the many shades of unhappiness, confusion, loss." He sees
many faults in the film and comments: "There may be more
masochism and self-pity in Jean Rhys's heroines than her
admirers can easily admit. The masochism is clear enough
in the book, though Rhys's biting elegance gives it a
kind of chic.... [In the film] no amount of classy
'decadence' can make up for Jean Rhys's missing
clarity and force."

[Advertisement] in *New York Times*, 25 November 1981, p. 12d.

Includes quotations from reviews in the *Village Voice,
Life Magazine, Saturday Review, After Dark,* and *Playboy.*

Roger Greenspun. *Penthouse*, 13 (December 1981), 58.

(Not seen)

B. Villien. *Avant Scene: Cinema*, 273 (1981), 4-5.

(Not seen)

2.   Musical

a.   MEMORIES OF MORNING, 1971

GORDON CROSSE | MEMORIES OF MORNING: | NIGHT | A MONODRAMA |
FOR MEZZO-SOPRANO AND ORCHESTRA | TEXT DRAWN FROM JEAN RHYS'S
NOVEL | WIDE SARGASSO SEA | COMMISSIONED BY THE BBC AND GIVEN
ITS FIRST | PERFORMANCE BY THE BBC SYMPHONY ORCHESTRA | CON-
DUCTED BY COLIN DAVIS WITH MERIEL DICKINSON | AS SOLOIST ON
8 DECEMBER 1971, AT THE ROYAL FESTIVAL | HALL, LONDON. | OX-
FORD UNIVERSITY PRESS | MUSIC DEPARTMENT   44 CONDUIT STREET
LONDON W1R ODE

Format: seven gatherings of eight leaves; no signatures

Pagination: [i] title page; [ii] ORCHESTRATION [list of the
instruments and numbers thereof in the WEDDING BAND and OR-
CHESTRA] | This score is a facsimile of the composer's manu-
script. | Large-size scores, orchestral parts, and vocal mate-
rial are on hire. | Duration 33-34 minutes | The text is tak-
en from the novel Wide Sargasso Sea by Jean Rhys. It tells
the | story of the first Mrs. Rochester in Charlotte Brontë's
Jane Eyre--her West | Indian childhood amongst recently freed
slaves; her marriage; the intolerable | pressures of family
and society that lead to her mental breakdown; and finally, |
the story we all know, the burning down of Thornfield. | The
Wedding Band, which should be seated separately from the
strings and | horn, is modelled on the Mexican mariarchi or-
chestras. | G.C.; [iii] text of the lyrics, arranged: PART 1
COULIBRI [three lyrics], INTERLUDE, PART 2 THORNFIELD [five
lyrics]; [iv] TO ERIC AND NANCY CROZIER, | WITH GREAT AFFEC-
TION; 1-107, musical score; at bottom of p. 107: WENHASTON
FEB-JULY 1971 | GORDON CROSSE | REPRODUCED AND PRINTED BY |
HALSTAN & CO. LTD., AMERSHAM, BUCKS., ENGLAND; [108] blank.

Binding: The copy examined has been rebound and the original
binding is not present.

Copies examined: Gorno Music Library, University of Cincin-
natti, call number M1613. C76 M4.

Reviews:

Max Harrison, "BBC Symphony Orchestra. Festival Hall."
Times, No. 58,346 (9 December 1971), p. 13a.

   The critic praises the first performance. The work has subsequently been performed in both America and England.

3.   Recordings

Charlotte H. and David K. Bruner, *First Person Feminine,*
Second Series.   Readings, Interviews, and Commentary on
Literature by Women Writers of the Third World.

Sound recording on fifteen cassettes of a series originally broadcast on WOI-FM, Ames, Iowa, 1981-1982.

Tape 11, Programme 21: Jean Rhys.

(Not heard)

Addenda

Section F
Writings about Jean Rhys:

1. Bibliographies
2. Books
3. Critical and Biographical
   Studies in Books and Periodicals

F.   Writings about Jean Rhys

1.   Bibliographies

Elgin W. Mellown, "A Bibliography of the Writings of Jean
Rhys with a Selected List of Reviews and Other Critical
Writings." *World Literature Written in English*, 16 (April
1977), 179-202.

Robert J. Stanton. *A Bibliography of Modern British Novelists*.
Troy, N.Y.: Whitston Publishing Co., 1978. 2 vols.

   A primary and secondary bibliography of Rhys is given on
   pp. 753-769.

Fred Rue Jacobs. *Jean Rhys--Bibliography*. The Loop Press,
1978.

   (Not seen)

R. C. Reynolds and B. J. Murray, "A Bibliography of Jean
Rhys." *Bulletin of Bibliography*, 36, No. 4 ·(October-December
1979), 177-184.

"Descriptive Bibliography of the University of Tulsa Jean
Rhys Collection." [No date]

   A mimeographed hand-list of the highly important Rhys collection in the Department of Rare Books and Special Collec-

tions, McFarlin Library, University of Tulsa, Tulsa, Okla-
homa. The hand-list has been compiled over a period of
time and has the following pagination: 1-3, 1-13, [1-2],
1-15, 1-4, 1-15, [1-4], [1-9].

Ray A. Roberts, "Jean Rhys: A Bibliographical Checklist."
American Book Collector, 3, No. 6 (November-December 1982),
35-38.

2.   Books

1978

Louis James. *Jean Rhys* (Critical Studies of Caribbean Writers:
Mervyn Morris, General Editor). London: Longman, 1978.
Pp. [vi], 74.

Contents: 1. The Girl from the Island (pp. 1-9); 2. The
European (pp. 10-20); 3. The Making of a Writer (pp. 21-32);
4. The Caribbean in a Cold Place (pp. 33-44); 5. *Wide Sargasso Sea* (pp. 45-65); 6. *Wide Sargasso Sea* and the Caribbean Novel (pp. 66-70); Bibliography (pp. 71-74).

Notes: Although the author received "unfailing and most generous help" from Jean Rhys ("Acknowledgements," p. [iv]), he
makes many errors in reporting biographical details.

Reviews:

Choice, 17 (March 1980), 72.

The anonymous reviewer stresses that the primary value of
this first book on Rhys lies in the author's placing of
the novelist within the tradition of the Caribbean writers.

1979

Thomas F. Staley. *Jean Rhys: A Critical Study*. Austin: University of Texas Press; London: Macmillan, 1979. Pp. [xiv],
140.

Contents: 1. Art and Experience (pp. 1-19);   2. *The Left
Bank* (pp. 20-34);   3. *Quartet* (pp. 35-54);   4. *After Leaving
Mr Mackenzie* and *Voyage in the Dark* (pp. 55-83);   5. *Good Morning, Midnight* (pp. 84-99);   6. *Wide Sargasso Sea* (pp. 100-
120);   7. The Later Writing (pp. 121-131); Postscript (p.
131); Notes (pp. 132-135); Selected Bibliography (pp. 136-
138); Index (pp. 139-140).

Notes: The University of Texas edition is here described.

Reviews:

Hilary Spurling, "Werewolves and Zombies." *Observer*, No.
9821 (18 November 1979), p. 40.

   See above, A10a: Reviews.

Victoria Glendinning, "Maverick." *Times Educational Supplement*, No. 3312 (30 November 1979), p. 23.

   Glendinning, who has her own understanding of Rhys's characters, gives very qualified approval to Staley's study.

Gabriele Annan, "Turned Away by the Tropics." *Times Literary
Supplement*, No. 4005 (21 December 1979), p. 154.

   See above, A10a: Reviews.

British Book News, February 1980, p. 70.

   (Not seen)

Helen McNeil, "Broken Heart." *New Statesman*, 99 (15 February
1980), 253-254.

   See above, A10a: Reviews.

"Literary Studies." *Virginia Quarterly Review*, 56 (Summer
1980), 96.

G. Marcus, "Woman is Losers." *Rolling Stone*, 29 May 1980, p. 32; 12 June 1980, p. 25.

(Not seen)

P.M. [Penelope Mesic]. *Booklist*, 76 (1 July 1980), 1585.

Choice, 18 (September 1980), 96.

The anonymous reviewer advises that the study is "for undergraduate libraries."

Alice Crozier. *Modern Fiction Studies*, 26 (Winter 1980), 712-713.

Crozier praises the study, emphasizing that Staley places Rhys within the modernist tradition. "Staley's book will be an immensely useful and congenial means of approaching this brilliant little *oeuvre* and its elusive author."

Mary Ann Klein, "Autobiography." *World Literature Today*, 55 (Spring 1981), 324-325.

See above, A10b: Reviews.

Karina Williamson. *Notes and Queries*, 28 (August 1981), 367-368.

While Williamson disapproves of the "sociological approach" which Staley sometimes uses, she writes that "The merit of [his] modest but perceptive and well-informed study is that it disentangles the products of Jean Rhys's career as a writer from the now copious evidence of her private life and psychology, salvaging just enough biographical data (drawn largely from personal interviews with Jean Rhys herself and people who knew her, and related with tact and economy) to indicate the social and literary milieu of her formative years and to account for that 'way of looking at the world from the perspective of a displaced person' which he rightly identifies as the peculiar stamp of her writing."

1980

Peter Wolfe. *Jean Rhys* (Twayne's English Authors Series No.
294: Kinley E. Roby, Editor). Boston: Twayne Publishers, G.
K. Hall and Co., 1980. Pp. 186.

Contents: About the Author (p. [8]); Preface (pp. [9]-[11]);
Chronology (p. [13]); 1. Down and Out in London and Paris
(pp. 15-31); 2. The Short Fiction (pp. 32-66); 3. *Quartet*
(pp. 67-83); 4. *After Leaving Mr. Mackenzie* (pp. 84-102);
Voyage in the Dark (pp. 103-120); 6. *Good Morning, Midnight*
(pp. 121-136); 7. *Wide Sargasso Sea* (pp. 137-159); 8. Conclusion (pp. 160-175); Notes and References (pp. 177-181);
Selected Bibliography (pp. 182-183); Index (pp. 184-186).

Reviews:

P.A. Packer. *Durham University Journal*, 74 (1981), 154-156.

The reviewer condemns the study on the grounds of its interpretations and approach and, profiting from the publication of *Smile Please*, offers a number of corrections of
factual errors made by Wolfe.

Choice, 18 (May 1981), 1268.

The anonymous critic writes a very negative review of the
study.

Mary Ann Klein, "Criticism." *World Literature Today*, 56
(Winter 1982), 116-117.

Klein reaches generally negative verdicts about the volume.

1981

Helen Nebeker. *Jean Rhys, Woman in Passage. A Critical Study
of the Novels of Jean Rhys*. Montreal, Canada: Eden Press
Women's Publications, 1981. Pp. [i-viii], i-xii,
1-224.

Contents: Preface (pp. i-xi);   1. Quartet. The Genesis of
Myth (pp. 1-13);   2. After Leaving Mr. Mackenzie. The Emerg-
ing Vision (pp. 14-38);   3. Voyage in the Dark. Apologia.
Awakening from the Dream. The Myths of "Anna" or The Goddess
Lost (pp. 39-84);   4. Good Morning, Midnight. The Labyrinth
of Time (pp. 85-121);   5. Wide Sargasso Sea. The Misty
Isle. Part One--The Island Eden. Part Two--The Snake in the
Garden. Part Three--Far from the Island Home (pp. 122-170);
6. Jane Eyre. Zeitgeist. Rochester. Jane. St.John (pp.
171-194);   7. The Myth of Rhys (pp. 195-199);   8. Conclusion (pp. 200-201);   Footnotes (pp. 202-209);   Selected Bibliography (pp. 210-213);   Index (pp. 214-223);   Picture and
brief description of the author (p. [224]).

Reviews:

Peter Kemp, "Deep Beneath the Cosmetics." Times Literary Supplement, No. 4091 (28 August 1981), p. 972.

Kemp generalizes about the Rhys heroines in the first two-
thirds of this lengthy essay to prove his knowledge of the
Rhys canon, to show the historicity of Rhys's characters
and settings, and to present a composite picture of the
Rhys women. Turning to Nebeker's study he quotes it extensively. Nebeker "opts to travel 'through shadowy mazes
of Freudian symbols and into the Jungian world of mythic
archetype.' Groping her way into the 'dark, almost forgotten racial memory,' she discerns 'the dim outlines of
a female centred myth (long lost in the mists of time).'"
Kemp realizes that Nebeker is concerned with the Rhys women
as "avatars of 'the Great Triple Goddess,'" points to the
"inventive critical procedures" she uses, and quotes some
of her "unusual contentions" about the Rhys novels. He
concludes: "Couched, for the most part, in a style of lurid gush ..., the book finally works itself into a frenzy of
bizarre assertion. Vehemently insisting that Jean Rhys
'created' Jane Eyre ... Nebeker backs this by the dramatic
claim that 'Charlotte Brontë, Jean Rhys and, in a sense,
Helen Nebeker have become inextricable on the immutable
sea of time.' Luckily for the novelists, this isn't so.
As Woman in Passage amply demonstrates Helen Nebeker is
way out on her own, though admittedly all at sea."

Debra Martens. Quill and Quire, 47 (October 1981), 33-34.

Martens points to inadequacies or flaws in the study (for
example, Nebeker "makes no distinction [between] Freudian

symbols and Jungian archetypes") and comes to mainly negative conclusions about it.

3. Critical and Biographical Studies

in Books and Periodicals

1927

Ford Madox Ford, "Preface. Rive Gauche" in Jean Rhys, *The Left Bank and Other Stories*. London: Jonathan Cape; New York: Harper and Brothers [1927]. Pp. 7-27.

Pages 7-23 consist of Ford's idiosyncratic ideas about Paris; in the last five pages he turns to Rhys and, with many ponderous compliments, identifies her as "coming from the Antilles, with a terrifying insight and a terrific--an almost lurid!--passion for stating the case of the underdog...." He stresses her "singular instinct for form" which sets her apart from other English writers and points out that her subject matter has to do with "passion, hardship, emotions," wherever they may be found. Although the "Preface" sounds offensively patronizing in the 1980s, it is actually written in the typical *de haute en bas* tone that Ford and his contemporaries would have considered appropriate for an older writer to use in expressing his sincere interest in a novice.

1928

Herbert Gorman, "Ford Madox Ford: A Portrait in Impressions." *Bookman*, 67 (March 1928), 56-57.

Gorman begins his character sketch by describing a night at the *bal musette* when Ford is the host (the same scene

is described by Rhys in *Quartet* and by Ernest Hemingway
in *The Sun Also Rises)*. Gorman gives the following description of Ford's entourage: "After the music stops [Ford]
will amble over breathing a trifle heavily in memory of
the poisonous gas during the Great War and sit down and
invite us to join his party. And then, at another table
much nearer the dancing floor, we see Stella and Olga and
Jean and Ernest and Bill and realize that this is Ford's
night at the *bal musette*." In 1929 Gorman reviewed *Quartet* for the *New York Herald Tribune* (see above, A2b: Reviews).

1931

Ford Madox Ford. *When the Wicked Man*. New York: Horace
Liveright, Inc., 1931. Pp. [vi], 352.

In October 1928, immediately after the publication of *Postures* in London, Ford began writing this novel about publishers and the book-publishing business in New York. The
work was condemned by contemporary reviewers, and not even
Ford's most biased supporters have been able to say anything good about it. No one seems to have realized, however, that it is closely linked to the Ford-Rhys relationship. The character "Lola Porter" is based on Rhys and in
many instances Ford gives her qualities, traits, or habits
which come from Jean Rhys: Lola Porter even writes a novel
entitled "Triple Sec" (see above, C1). Some of these
allusions are found on pp. 78, 83, 161-165, 182-183, 192-
197, and 286-287.

1932

Edward de Nève. *Barred*. London: Desmond Harmsworth, 1932.
Pp. 225.

While this work is primarily a documentary intended to ex-
pose the brutality of the French penal system, it has a
story that is based on the Ford-Rhys-de Nève relationship.
In effect the novel gives the husband's view of the events
described in *Quartet* (see above, D2).

1935

Victor E. van Vriesland, "Preface" to Jean Rhys. *Melodie in
Mineur*, translated by Edouard de Nève. Amsterdam: Uitgeveriu

de Steenuil, 1935.

Not seen. Vriesland was an art critic in Rotterdam who encouraged de Nève to write a Dutch version of *Barred*; it was
published as *In de Strik*; and in 1933 de Neve dedicated
the French edition of the work, *Sous les Verrous*, to
Vriesland (see above, D2).

1936

Cyril Connolly, "Three Shelves." *New Statesman*, 11 (4 January
1936), 25-26. Reprinted as "The Novel-Addict's Cupboard" in
Cyril Connolly, *The Condemned Playground. Essays: 1927-1944*.
New York: Macmillan, 1946. Pp. 112-118.

In this personal essay Connolly lists the modern novelists
whose work he collects and offers critical remarks that are
designed to encourage readers to sample these novels. Out
of ten paragraphs, one focusses on women writers. Connolly
collects Compton-Burnett, Woolf, Bowen, and Lehmann; he also
has "*Frost in May* by Antonia White, *Orphan Island*, the best
novel of Miss Macauley, *Voyage in the Dark* (Constable) by
Jean Rhys, a short and tragic book--and even shorter,
Mortal Enemy and *A Lost Lady*, the two best books of Willa
Cather, and *Winter Sonata* by Dorothy Edwards." [The personal library of Connolly, now at the University of Tulsa,
contains an edition of *Voyage in the Dark* which may ten-
tatively be identified as the cheap edition of 1936.]

1939

E. de Nève, "Jean Rhys, romancière inconnue." *Les Nouvelles
Littéraires*, No. 880 (26 August 1939), p. 8, columns d-e.

The first essay devoted to Rhys's fiction is by her first
husband and is written in the form of the typical French
"appreciation." It begins with a number of generalizations:
Rhys does not belong to any school or literary group; she
works as the solitary artist whose standard is honesty;
and she takes as her subject matter the outcasts of society.
Her attitude is fatalistic, and she attains levels of profound misery that are comparable only to great classical
tragedies. But it is only the effect which is classical,
for her composition, style, and dialogue are undeniably
modern. The critic describes her childhood in the idyllic
Caribbean, a place of beauty and of dreams, and contrasts
it to the harsh reality of London which she came to know.

From her experiences she gained an understanding of the
disappointed, the fallen, the lost-through-their-frankness,
the rejected, the rebels, the pariahs. In her works she
expresses the cynicism of her generation which rebels against
a hypocritical and cruel world. She writes particularly
about the female victims of the world she opposes, creating
characters who are hard, destined, and actual. Rhys has
avoided contact with her colleagues, preferring to live in
her tiny London flat reading the important works now being
published in England, America, and France. Yet she will
sometimes disappear from London for some weeks, to return
to write the work which she will have composed in her mind.
It will be a truthful account of the unhappiness she has
known, and it will be bearable only because of the artistic
manner in which she presents her material. While she is unknown in France, the literary connoisseurs of Great Britain
and America know and appreciate her work even though they
never see her among themselves. Her principal works are
After Leaving Mr Mackenzie, Voyage in the Dark, and the
novel now being published, *Good Morning, Midnight.* [The
essay is in French and is illustrated by a photograph of
Jean Rhys not reproduced elsewhere.]

1940

Stella Bowen. *Drawn from Life. Reminiscences.* London: Col-
lins Brothers, 1940. Pp. 166-168.

In this autobiography Stella Bowen, Ford Madox Ford's second wife (technically, common-law wife), tells the story
of her and Ford's life in Paris in the 1920s in the chapter entitled "The Rue Notre-Dame-des-Champs." Without
using Jean Rhys's name, Bowen refers to the novelist as
"a very pretty and gifted young woman" and writes of her
having "written an unpublishably sordid novel of great
sensitiveness and persuasiveness [the first version of
Voyage in the Dark]. Bowen's account of the Ford-Bowen-
Rhys relationship confirms in every respect the details of
the story given by Rhys in *Quartet,* while Bowen's tone in
the autobiography is in keeping with the characterization
of her provided by Rhys in the novel.

1946

John Hampson, "Movements in the Underground." *Penguin New
Writing.* 27 (April 1946), 133-151; 28 (July 1946), 122-140.

Examining the characters and situations in novels which deal with life outside the law, Hampson turns to Rhys in the first half of the essay (27: 149-150). She "has written several novels about the lives of prostitutes. Her studies are hard and sharp, she shows the process of deterioration with clarity, her women have intelligence, and usually become drunkards." He summarizes the plots of *Voyage in the Dark* and *After Leaving Mr Mackenzie*. "These novels are unusual, they have a vivid clarity and oddness which recall sharply the sinister and menacing figures encountered in dreams." In the second half of the essay he writes about Graham Greene at considerable length.

1949

Morton Dauwen Zabel, "Ford Madox Ford." *Nation*, 169 (30 July 1949), 110.

Reviewing Douglas Goldring's study of Ford, *Trained for Genius*, Zabel writes: "And beyond these erratic records [Ford's autobiographies] lies a muddle of gossip and legend and what a host of ladies had to say about their parts in it--Violet Hunt's 'I have this to Say: the Story of My Flurried Years,' 'Jean Rhys's 'After Leaving Mr Mackenzie,' Stella Bowen's 'Drawn from Life,' and a cloud of other documents in scandal, defense, and litigation."

Alec Waugh. *The Sugar Islands. A Caribbean Travelogue.* New York: Farrar, Straus and Company, 1949. Pp. 278.

In describing Dominica (which he first visited in the 1920s) Waugh refers to meeting Jean Rhys in London and to "re-reading" *After Leaving Mr Mackenzie*. He "could see how Dominica had colored her temperament and outlook. It was a clue to her, just as she was a clue to it. People who could not fit into life elsewhere found what they were looking for in Dominica. Jean Rhys, who had been born there, chose as her central character one who could not adjust herself to life outside" (pp. 95-96). Waugh included this half-page reference in *The Clock Strikes Twice* (London: 1952) but not in *Where the Clocks Strike Twice* (New York: 1951). Jean Rhys and her husband Max Hamer read *The Clock Strikes Twice* in December 1952 when they were living at 29, Milestone Road, London, S.E. 19. Hamer wrote of their pleasure at the reference to their friend Morchard Bishop (Oliver Stoner) on 29 December, and the next day Rhys wrote to Waugh. Her let-

ter is now in the Boston University Library and has been
published by Elaine Campbell in the *Journal of Commonwealth
Literature* (see below, F.3: 1979). While most of the biographical and bibliographical details given by Campbell
are inaccurate, she quotes a letter by Waugh in which he
states that he "'only met Jean Rhys once in October 1938 in
Berkshire with Carol Brandt and Storm Jameson.'"

[Advertisement in the "Personal" column.] *New Statesman*, 38
(5 November 1949), 533.

Dr. Hans Egli, husband of the actress Selma Vaz Dias who
was then preparing her one-woman performance of *Good Morning, Midnight*, advertised to find Jean Rhys. She saw this
advertisement on the day of publication and immediately responded. From this contact came the lengthy and involved
relationship between the novelist and the actress.

1950

Francis Wyndham, "An Inconvenient Novelist." *Tribune*, No.
721 (15 December 1950), 16, 18.

The first major essay on Jean Rhys appeared in a series en-
title "Neglected Books." Although Wyndham did not know *The
Left Bank* and *Postures* ("it is almost impossible to find
copies of these," he wrote), he was able to deduce from
After Leaving Mr Mackenzie, Voyage in the Dark, and *Good
Morning, Midnight* the novelist's primary themes and attitudes. Questioning the reasons for the neglect of Rhys he
points to the "equivocal position" of the heroines: none
of the terms of literary cliches ("'prostitute,' 'tart,'
'courtesan,' 'kept woman'") fit her for Rhys writes "about
women who are often found in life but seldom in books, and
she describes their experiences from the inside." But she
has done so with such "subtle restraint and artistic integrity" that she has failed to win the attention of the
larger public. Yet she has also been ignored by the "small-
er, more critical public," in spite of the fact that she
has written convincingly about one "sad corner of experience." Her "novels are variations on a theme" and are im-
bued with her personal attitude; while "they complain, ...
they never whine." In them "intellect disciplines emotion;
they are works of art before human documents." Wyndham
summarizes the stories of the three novels, pointing always
to the fact that the heroines form one composite figure and

putting together a reasonably accurate biography of her.
Good Morning, Midnight is the highpoint of Rhys's art: "it
is the tragedy of a distinguished mind and generous nature
which have gone unappreciated in a conventional, unimagin-
ative world." He concludes by hoping that the novels
"will be reprinted."

Wyndham based his subsequent essays of 1960 and 1964 (the
latter being reprinted as the Introduction to *Wide Sargasso Sea*) on this 1950 essay. It has consequently been the
most important influence on the reception of Jean Rhys and
has helped to shape most of the critical attitudes to her
work. Wyndham's intuitive understanding of the novels is
shown by the fact that his still-valid comments were written when he knew only three of the novels.

1956

Francis Wyndham, "Twenty-five Years of the Novel," in *The
Craft of Letters in England, A Symposium,* edited by John Lehmann. London: Cresset Press, 1956. Pp. 44-59.

Considering the important novelists of the time, both those
recognized and those passed over by critics, Wyndham comments on page 57 that Julia Strachey is a writer who "should
be mentioned in any survey of original contemporary writing.
The late Jean Rhys was another, whose bitter and brilliant
Good Morning, Midnight and *Voyage in the Dark* are too little known. Perhaps Stevie Smith, author of the unique and
unrepeatable *Novel on Yellow Paper,* belongs in this exclus-
ive group."

[Advertisement in the "Personal" column.] *New Statesman,* 52
(6 October 1956), 435.

The contact established in 1949 between Jean Rhys and Selma Vaz Dias was maintained with long interruptions until
1953 when Rhys "disappeared" again. After Vaz Dias per-
suaded the BBC to broadcast her *Good Morning, Midnight*
monologue, Rhys's permission was required; and on the suggestion of Vaz Dias, Sasha Moorsom, Features Editor of the
BBC Third Programme, placed this advertisement asking Jean
Rhys to contact her. Again Rhys saw the notice at once
and responded immediately. From this time onward she remained in touch with literary London.

1957

Selma Vaz Dias, "In Quest of a Missing Author." *Radio Times,*
3 May 1957, p. 25.

As part of the publicity for the forthcoming Third Programme broadcast of her rendition of *Good Morning, Midnight,*
Vaz Dias wrote a brief personal essay on her interest in
Rhys's work, her dramatising *Good Morning, Midnight,* and
her long quest to find the author. She does not mention
her contacts in 1949 with Rhys and refers only to the 1956
advertisement by the BBC. Otherwise the essay gives a
truthful account of Rhys's absence from literary circles
between 1939 and 1949 and of the part that Vaz Dias played
in bringing the novelist back to public attention. Vaz
Dias concludes, "[Jean Rhys] is now busy writing a novel
on a most exciting subject. She is full of a new enthus-
iasm, and I hope and pray that the re-emergence of *Good
Morning, Midnight* as a radio monologue will give her sufficient encouragement to write a great deal more and come
out of hiding."

The "romance" of this quest attracted the attention of the
popular press (as Vaz Dias and the BBC obviously hoped it
would), and this essay was commented upon by a number of
newspapers in the week following its publication, among them
being the *Glasgow Herald,* the *Scotsman,* the *Evening Standard,* and the *Hampstead and Highgate Express and the Hampstead Garden Suburb and Golders Green News.*

1960

Francis Wyndham, "Introduction to Jean Rhys." *London Magazine,*
7 (January 1960), 15-18.

This introduction reproduces a somewhat shortened version
of Wyndham's 1950 study with additional comments on *Postures* (which the critic had now read). In the new last paragraph Wyndham acknowledges the 1957 article by Selma Vaz
Dias in the *Radio Times* and the fact that Vaz Dias had located Rhys in Cornwall. He states: "I wrote to her there
and discovered the exciting news that she is at work on a
new novel and that she had some unpublished short stories."
Among these is "Till September Petronella" which follows
Wyndham's Introduction. [Other stories were subsequently
published in the *London Magazine.*]

1962

David Dow Harvey. *Ford Madox Ford, 1873-1939. A Bibliography of Works and Criticism.* Princeton: Princeton University Press, 1962. Pp. [xxiv], 633.

In the standard bibliography of Ford's writings, Harvey provides the first public acknowledgement that Rhys, not Ford, was the translator of *Perversity* (p. 97) and that *Postures* and *After Leaving Mr Mackenzie* were both based on the Ford-Rhys-Bowen relationship (pp. 587-588). Other references to Rhys are on pp. 95, 372, and 440-441.

1963

[Francis Wyndham], "Jean Rhys" in *Concise Encyclopedia of Modern World Literature*, edited by Geoffrey Grigson. New York: Hawthorn Books, Inc., 1963, pp. 369-370.

A survey, with summaries of plots, of the first four novels, written in an enthusiastic tone (Rhys's books "deserve to be far better known than they are, for they are the product of a talent which is dismaying and unique") and presenting the Rhys heroines as "essentially ... the same woman at different stages of her life, although her name alters from novel to novel."

Robert Ruben, "Introduction" and biographical note in *Voices*, edited by Robert Ruben. London: Michael Joseph, 1963. pp. 9-10, 263.

See above, B1.

1964

Francis Wyndham, "Introduction." *Art and Literature, An International Review*, No. 1 (March 1964), pp. 173-177.

Introducing the first part of *Wide Sargasso Sea* which is printed here for the first time, Wyndham reprints most of his 1960 essay, adding to it both critical and biographical comments. For the first time *Postures* is referred to by its American title *Quartet* with the note, "it is the American title that Miss Rhys prefers," and the connection of

the novel to Ford is suggested. The critic analyzes the
reasons for Rhys's long neglect: the five books "were a-
head of their age, both in spirit and in style." In comparison with such contemporaries as Katherine Mansfield,
Aldous Huxley, and Jean Cocteau, Jean Rhys has not "'dated':
the style belongs to today. More important, the novels of
the 1930s are much closer in *feeling* to life as it is lived
and understood in the 1960s than to the accepted attitudes
of their time." Wyndham lists the stories which Rhys has
published since the 1958 Third Programme broadcast (he does
not mention Selma Vaz Dias) and describes the subject matter of *Wide Sargasso Sea*. Although the new novel was inspired by *Jane Eyre*, "it is in no sense a pastiche on Charlotte Brontë and exists in its own right, quite independent
of *Jane Eyre*." The central figure of Antoinette Cosway
"Seems a logical development of Marya, Julia, Anna and
Sasha, who were also alienated, menaced, at odds with life."
As in the earlier works, the novelist's memories of the
West Indies give a sense "of regret for innocent sensual-
ity in a lush, beguiling land" which, seen as "a distant
dream," proves to have been a nightmare. This introduction,
reprinted in all editions of *Wide Sargasso Sea*, provides
most of the attitudes--and even some of the words--used by
later reviewers of the novel.

1966

[Francis Wyndham], [biographical note]. *Art and Literature,
An International Review*, No. 8 (Spring 1966), 212-213.

Diana Athill, "Jean Rhys, and the Writing of "Wide Sargasso
Sea.'" *Bookseller*, No. 3165 (20 August 1966), pp. 1378-1379.

Writing on the eve of the publication of *Wide Sargasso Sea*,
Diana Athill, Director of André Deutsch, provides a brief
account of how Francis Wyndham, then a literary advisor to
Deutsch, introduced Rhys's work to Athill in 1954; how Wyndham learned that Rhys was living in Cornwall through Selma
Vaz Dias after the latter broadcast *Good Morning, Midnight*
in 1957; and how Deutsch learned of the novel Rhys was currently writing and bought an option on it. Athill gives a
brief and not altogether accurate biographical sketch of
the novelist and explains the long delay in the publication
of *Wide Sargasso Sea*: Rhys is a "slow and perfectionist
writer" who faced many physical difficulties in writing the
new novel. It was almost completed in 1964, but Rhys suf-
fered a severe illness and her work on it was delayed until

October 1965. Early in 1966 she put the finishing touches on the novel, and its publication is now scheduled for 27 October. Athill gives a very brief description of *Wide Sargasso Sea*, stressing that "in spite of its romantic story and background, [it] deals with relationships and emotions which are intensely real and modern--or rather, enduring."

Francis Wyndham, "Introduction" to Jean Rhys. *Wide Sargasso Sea*. London: Andre Deutsch, 1966. Pp. 5-13.

A reprint of the essay that first appeared in *Art and Literature*, No. 1 (March 1964) (see above).

1967

"Londoner's Diary," *Evening Standard*, 12 June 1967, p. 6; 21 June 1967, p. 6.

On the occasion of the re-issue of *Voyage in the Dark* (A4d) and *Good Morning, Midnight* (A5b) a personal account of the discovery of Jenn Rhys with some rather catty remarks about Selma Vaz Dias [the author was probably Sally Williams].

[Arts Council Bursary and the W.H. Smith Literary Prize.]

In December 1967 Jean Rhys was given an Arts Council Bursary in the amount of twelve hundred pounds (the other recipients were Kathleen Nott, Christina Stead, and six other writers) and was awarded the W.H. Smith Literary Prize of one thousand pounds by a jury consisting of Lady Huntingdon (Margaret Lane), Sir Rupert Hart-Davis, and Raymond Mortimer. Accounts of the events, including pictures and human-interest stories, were published by many newspapers. Some of them were: *Times*, No. 57121 (11 December 1967), p. 10e; No. 57124 (14 December 1967), pp. 2, 10; No. 57126 (16 December 1967), p. 19; *Times Saturday Review*, 16 December 1967, p. 19; *Sunday Times*, No. 7542 (17 December 1967), p. 26; W. L. Webb, "Lately Prized," *Guardian*, 14 December 1967, p. 6; Charles Greville, "The Late Jean Rhys is About to Live it up a Little," *Daily Mail*, 14 December 1967; Karl Miller, "Views," *Listener*, 78 (21 December 1967), 805.

Wally Look Lai, "The Road to Thornfield Hall. An Analysis of
Jean Rhys' *Wide Sargasso Sea* (Andre Deutsch, 1966)." *New
Beacon Reviews. Collection One*, edited by John La Rose.
London: New Beacon Books Ltd., 1968. Pp. 38-52.

While *Wide Sargasso Sea* has been hailed in England as a
"literary masterpiece," its claims as a West Indian work
of art have been neglected. Although Rhys was born in Dominica, she has spent most of her life in Europe and her
previous novels have concerned "modern urban life in Europe" and, specifically, "the plight of the rejected woman,
tragically isolated in a world in which she is at the complete mercy of men." The same female character appears in
Wide Sargasso Sea, but in this novel the West Indian background is used by the novelist "to convey a totally different reading of experience, one which is much more profound
and ambitious than any she has ever attempted before." Her
main characters symbolize "the theme of the white West Indian's relation to England, the nature and consequences of
his involvement with the world from which his ancestors
came." The title is significant because it refers to the
area dividing England from the West Indies; the Sargasso
Sea is "a symbolic dividing line between two whole worlds"
which can never come together. The white West Indian has
no place in either world, and his lack of identity "can only end in madness." Thus Antoinette's end is "the white
West Indian's historical destiny." The changes which Rhys
made to Brontë's characters, particularly the change of Bertha's name into Antoinette, emphasizes the question of
identity, and Antoinette's final act of self-destruction,
viewed from her perspective--and that of the historical
process--"becomes completely rational and valid." Having
established the validity of the relationship of the novel
to the West Indies, Lai closely analyzes its parts, emphasizing the relationships between the white and the black
West Indians and the English. Historical destiny and personal alienation account for most of the events in the novel, according to the critic. This essay presents the most
convincing argument for considering *Wide Sargasso Sea* as
more than another story about the "Jean Rhys Woman," and
it provides the essential points of view for anyone who
wants to consider Rhys in terms of her West Indian background. (The essay is discussed by Jean D'Costa in the
Caribbean Quarterly, 16 [June 1970], 62.)

Hannah Carter, "Fated to be Sad. Jean Rhys talks to Hannah
Carter." *Guardian*, 8 August 1968, p. 5.

In this interview Jean Rhys speaks quite candidly about her life, her writing, and her aspirations; and it is the source of much of the biographical information in later articles about the novelist.

1969

Marcelle Bernstein, "The Inscrutable Miss Jean Rhys." *Observer Magazine* [color supplement to the *Observer* (London)], 1 June 1969, pp. 40-42, 49-50.

In this interview Bernstein alternately reports Rhys's comments and answers to questions and supplies quotations from the novels which show that the characters in them reflect the novelist's life. Some of the information is repeated from the Carter interview (see above, 1968); but this interview is a major source of biographical information for later writers.

Kenneth Ramchand, "Terrified Consciousness." *Journal of Commonwealth Literature*, No. 7 (July 1969), pp. 8-19. Reprinted in Kenneth Ramchand, *The West Indian Novel and its Background*. New York: Barnes and Noble, Inc., 1970, pp. 230-236.

Through a detailed study of four novels dealing with the West Indies--Rhys's *Wide Sargasso Sea*, Allfrey's *The Orchid House* (1953), Drayton's *Christopher* (1959), and Emtage's *Brown Sugar* (1966)--the essayist proves that Rhys makes use of themes of isolation, alienation, and desire of annihilation that are common in all novels dealing with Europeans in the Caribbean. "In *Wide Sargasso Sea* ... the terrified consciousness of the historical white West Indian is revealed to be a universal heritage."

1970

"Jean Rhys. Interviewed by Peter Burton." *Transatlantic Review*, No. 36 (Summer 1970), pp. 105-109.

The transcript of an interview conducted on a very facile level: the most important aspects are Rhys's comments on Ford and Colette, and the remarks in passing on the writers she was currently reading. She also makes the comment which Burton reports as follows: "'If you experience a thing you know you can write it so much more, but life's one thing, a book's another.'"

Neville Braybrooke, "The Return of Jean Rhys." *Caribbean Quarterly*, 16, No. 4 (December 1970), 43-46.

Writing after the publication of *Tigers Are Better-Looking* Braybrooke summarizes previously published biographical information to give a portrait of Rhys and her literary career before moving chronologically through the stories and novels; for each he gives a brief summary of the story, with many quotations. He suggests that the women in these novels belong "to an in-between world ... they are the flotsam floating between the rich and the poor, just as, in the West Indies, the Creole belongs to neither white nor black." Rhys's "books and stories ... are among the most original and memorable of our time."

1971

"Jean Rhys" in *Contemporary Authors*, edited by Carolyn Riley. Detroit: Gale Research Co., 1971. Vol. 25-28, p. 608.

This half-page entry marks the first time that Rhys was included in a standard library reference work; the information provided comes from previously published sources.

Arthur Mizener, *The Saddest Story. A Biography of Ford Madox Ford*. New York and Cleveland: World Publishing Co., 1971. Pp. xxiv, 616.

On pp. 178 and 343-350 of this standard biography of Ford Mizener tersely describes the Ford-Rhys relationship, drawing his information from the published memoirs and such works of fiction as *Quartet* and *After Leaving Mr Mackenzie* and adding no new facts to those already in print.

1972

Neville Braybrooke, "Jean Rhys" in *Contemporary Novelists*, edited by James Vinson. London: St. James Press; New York: St. Martin's Press, 1972, pp. 1061-1064. [This entry is reprinted in the second edition, 1976, pp. 1162-1165. There is no entry for Rhys in the third edition, 1981.]

After giving a biographical sketch of Rhys, Braybrooke summarizes the plots of the novels, giving particular attention to the references to racial matters. Rhys's writing is highly praised. The only critical study listed is Wyndham's Introduction to *Wide Sargasso Sea*.

Laurence Cole, "Jean Rhys." *Books and Bookmen*, 17 (January 1972), 20-21.

In this detailed, perceptive essay Cole studies the novels in terms of the characters, of the attitudes to life, and of the narrative techniques. He points to the various heroines as manifestations of Rhys herself, asserting that the novels are heavily autobiographical. "Few authors have more instinctively understood how best to distil the essence of their experience and Weltanschauing [*sic*] through the filter of their imagination." The characters in the novels exist to suffer, and their intense sensitivity makes them open "to every nuance of speech and gesture in their fellow men and women...." Though times and situations change from novel to novel, the female character remains the same. Yet while dealing with "sad and sorry themes and personal attitudes," Rhys never bores or depresses her reader because her "technical astuteness" shows her how to provide "the other point of view," and "the heroine represents the author not only as she sees herself ... but as she believes she is seen by others...." Rhys never allows her heroines "to take themselves too seriously," and her "elusive linguistic skills ... flavour even the most spiteful words and gestures with drollery." Writing about and sympathizing with the under-dog, Rhys will always be a neglected writer whose attitudes will make her unacceptable to the larger audience.

John Hall, "Jean Rhys." *Guardian*, 10 January 1972, p. 8.

In a three-quarter page essay Hall reports on an interview with Rhys, relying more upon his impressions than upon attempts to transcribe Rhys's comments. Since he had read the novels, had come to an understanding of their place in literary history (Rhys was "a Hemingway to the Joyces of Mesdames Woolf and Richardson"), and had the ability to understand Rhys as a person, the essay is one of the most important biographical sources for Rhys's later years. Hall conveys the sense of a very conventional, proper lady of an older generation who is concerned to maintain her personal appearance and to say nothing that might be too revealing. Yet at the same time he sees that the author of *The Left Bank* was "a plucky girl, who wrote with great *chic*... and who possessed whatever ladies possess in place of *cojones* ... but she wrote about crooks, midinettes and drifters at

a time when lady novelists were supposed to be knotted up
over internal monologues and the science of psychology.
Slugging the bottle and flopping around were still not nice
scenes for a gal to harp over." Except for skirting the
details of the Jean Rhys-Selma Vaz Dias relationship, Hall
provides important biographical information about Rhys's
personality in her old age.

Elgin W. Mellown, "Character and Themes in the Novels of Jean
Rhys." *Contemporary Literature*, 13 (1972), 458-475. Reprinted in *Contemporary Women Novelists*, edited by Patricia Meyer
Spacks. Englewood Cliffs, N.J.: Prentice Hall, Inc. (Twentieth Century Views: Spectrum Book), 1977, pp. 118-136.

The author summarizes published biographical facts before
turning to the pre-1966 novels; he arranges them in order
of their internal chronology (*Voyage in the Dark, Quartet,
After Leaving Mr Mackenzie*, and *Good Morning, Midnight*) as
a means of recounting their stories as the single story of
a woman who, though appearing with different names, is essentially the same character. Stressing that, although the
character may originate in the author's personal experiences,
Rhys actually makes her into a fictional projection of a
psychological type, the critic sums up the qualities of this
archetypal figure: she is an immature creature who never
forgets her childhood and who constantly seeks the psychic
and physical love which will reassure and comfort her, she
never attains the role of motherhood, and she is always
alienated from everyday society. In economic terms the
character is the epitome of the have-not at the mercy of
the haves. Mellown points to the novelist's increasing
skill in portraying this character and shows through exam-
ples that this skill is a function of the prose technique
which has links to the techniques espoused by Ford and employed by Rhys's contemporaries. Ultimately Rhys found
that "the controlled point of view which holds to the consciousness of the central character is not only a function-
al way of telling her story, but also expresses her solipsistic philosophy." Such a point of view is employed exclusively in *Wide Sargasso Sea* which is "a masterpiece ...
as well as the logical outgrowth of the developments in the
previous four novels." Explaining the details of the story
and its relationships to *Jane Eyre*, Mellown asserts that
Antoinette Cosway, "while a manifestation of the same archetypal figure" that stands behind the other heroines, is more
of an individual and can be understood without reference to
her predecessors. "In *Wide Sargasso Sea* technique, content,
and characterization work together to delineate a mature

artist's view of life." In the conclusion the essayist suggests some of the contemporaries in whose company Rhys might be placed: these include Katherine Mansfield, Djuna Barnes, and Radclyffe Hall. Yet Rhys's links are less to the traditional British novel than to the contemporary European *Zeitgeist*. This essay is the first scholarly treatment of all of Rhys's writings; it is the source of much of the information in later essays; and it anticipates--or provides--the point of view of many subsequent critics, as well as the concepts with which some have violently disagreed.

V. S. Naipaul, "Without a Dog's Chance." *New York Review of Books*, 18 (18 May 1972), 29-31.

Written as a review of *After Leaving Mr Mackenzie*, this essay provides a study of Rhys's entire literary output. See above, A3e: Reviews.

"Jean Rhys" in *Current Biography Yearbook*, edited by Charles Moritz. New York: H.W. Wilson Co., 1972, pp. 364-367 (first published in the December 1972 issue of *Current Biography*).

This survey of Rhys's life and works, complete with summaries of the novels and ample quotations from reviewers, provides generally accurate information. The writer does not attempt criticism of the novels, and indeed the essay is written with one eye on libel laws: there is no identification of Rhys with her heroines or any suggestion of her involvement with Ford. The essay provides only previously published information.

1973

"Jean Rhys" in *Who's Who 1973*. London: Adam and Charles Black, 1973. P. 2711.

The first inclusion of Rhys in this standard reference book.

Katarina Bogataj, "Nekdanja in današnja Jane Eyre. (Ob romanih Charlotte Brontë in Jean Rhys)." *Proster in Čas* (Yugoslavia), 5 (1973), 640-656.

(Not seen)

Arnold de Kerchove, "John Updike, Jean Rhys, André Gide."
Revue Générale Belge, 1970-1973, pp. 91-97.
(Not seen)

Molly Parkin, "Everything makes you want pretty clothes."
Sunday Times, No. 7811 (25 February 1973), p. 33.

Four photographs of Jean Rhys modelling new clothes on the
"Look! Fashion" page, with quotations from the novels and
from an interview.

Nancy Casey, "Study in the Alienation of a Creole Woman: Jean
Rhys's Voyage in the Dark." *Caribbean Quarterly*, 19 (September 1973), 95-102.

Through paraphrase and quotation Casey provides an extended character study of Anna Morgan, emphasizing her immatur-
ity, her lack of sophistication, her sensitivity, her inability to fend for herself, and her need for masculine
support and comfort. Because of her upbringing as a Creole
in Dominica, she has been "taught to do nothing ... being
attractive, well-dressed, and appealing to men is sufficient.
Yet obviously such an attitude is not adequate for England
in 1914 [*sic*], and hence Anna must turn to prostitution
and suffer all the consequent horrors." This essay is based
on a close, though not always accurate reading of the novel,
rather than on biographical or factual information.

1974

A. Alvarez, "The Best Living English Novelist." *New York
Times Book Review*, 17 March 1974, pp. 6-7.

Alvarez begins this essay by surveying the literary reception and biography of Rhys; he acknowledges that she has
at last "got the recognition she ... deserved for so long."
He himself believes "she is, quite simply, the best living
English novelist. Although her range is narrow, sometimes
to the point of obsession, there is no one else now writing
who combines such emotional penetration and formal artistry
or approaches her unemphatic, unblinking truthfulness."
Her first four novels have the same heroine and are written
in the same "utterly personal speaking voice." They all re-
volve around the heroine's need for money, although in *Good*

Morning, Midnight this plot is reversed. Alvarez discusses the novel, focussing on the gigolo's question, why has
this happened to me. Rhys never answers this question, beyond showing that "that's how things are. She is also far
too pure an artist to allow herself the luxury of self-
pity." This detachment is "far more unnerving than any
full-throated howl of anguish could ever be." The novels
present an uncompromising view of the world of vulnerable,
weak women, so much so that Rhys "makes you realize that
almost every other novel, however apparently anarchic, is
rooted finally in the respectable world." She is "particularly expert in the chill hypocrisy of the English," perhaps because of her West Indian origins. *Wide Sargasso Sea*
is linked to the earlier works by the heroine's being a
victim like her predecessors. "It is a hallucinatory novel,
as detailed, abrupt and undeniable as a dream, and with a
dream's weird and irresistible logic. It is also the final
triumph of Miss Rhys's stylistic control, her persistent
search for a minimal senuous [*sic*] notation of distaste."
The pure style of the Rhys novels makes them "peculiarly
timeless;" they are "uniquely concerned in simply telling
the truth." This forthright essay by an eminent critic in
a nationally important publication is generally acknowledged
to be the most important influence upon the American reception of Rhys.

John Hearne, "The Wide Sargasso Sea: A West Indian Reflection."
Cornhill Magazine, No. 1080 (Summer 1974), pp. 323-333.

Wilson Harris and Jean Rhys are the two most important West
Indian novelists, and *Wide Sargasso Sea* is a touchstone
against which all West Indian fiction must be measured.
Its story is a basic, simple myth which derives from yet
another novel (*Jane Eyre*); and in so doing serves as a metaphor for "much of West Indian life" in which there is a
"crisis of personal and historical identity." The Cosway
family and retainers marooned after Emancipation provide a
paradigm for the social situation in general. But Rhys
transcends "the merely political, ultimately banal situation" of oppression "to fashion an enduring symbol of the
horrid malformation that occurs when the purely self-seeking ego uses the inarticulate by so essential offerings of
the instincts as mere energy...." Thus the relationship of
Rochester and Antoinette shows the "sad corruption of the
potential love open to any two human beings...." The freedom to give of herself makes Antoinette a peculiarly West
Indian figure, and Rochester's inability to respond shows

his essentially European attitude. Her West Indian passion and lack of self-consciousness are no match for Rochester's calculating nature and the qualities caused by his
"lack of fulfilled instinct." He is literally the "nothing"
for which the peasant boy weeps as he rides away. But the
most essential quality in *Wide Sargasso Sea* is the "quest
for love," and Rhys's most important contribution is her
ability to see it taking "the form of mirror reflections,
of duplicated experiences." These images--parallels and
duplications--are found throughout the novel; and the answer to the quest is given by Rhys "with courage and an
obstinate honesty of vision:" in the words of Forster,
"'No, not yet ... No, not there.'"

Nancy J. Casey, "The 'Liberated' Woman in Jean Rhys's Later
Short Fiction." *Revista Interamericana Review*, 4 (Summer
1974), 264-272.

In this close study of "I Spy a Stranger" and "Temps Perdi"
Casey stresses the fact that the heroines represent a development of the passive female who figures in the first
four novels: she now "rejects love, men, and most all other
human beings as well." Casey compares this new woman to
the character in the novels to show that Rhys is now expos-
ing both male domination and the female desire to be sup-
pressed, as well as the complicity of women in suppressing
other women. The two stories show that Rhys has a place
within the women's liberation movement.

Alice K. Turner, "Paperbacks in the News: Jean Rhys Rediscovered: How it Happened." *Publishers Weekly*, 206 (1 July 1974),
56, 58.

Writing for the professional audience of booksellers and
librarians, the author gives a succinct account of the reception of Rhys's novels in America as indicated by the
printing and sales records of the paperback editions. The
sudden popularity of Rhys in 1974 was due to the Alvarez
essay which Alvarez wrote on his own initiative and the
Broyard review of *Good Morning, Midnight* (A5e). This critical approval led to the reprinting of the early novels.
Turner gives the number of copies in different printings
and quotes a telephone conversation she had with Alvarez,
as well as a letter written by Rhys in response to an enquiry from *Publishers Weekly*.

Nancy J. Casey Fulton, "Jean Rhys's *Wide Sargasso Sea*: Exterminating the White Cockroach." *Revista Interamericana Review*, 4 (Fall 1974), 340-349.

A detailed study of *Wide Sargasso Sea*, this essay uses Wally Look Lai's 1968 declaration that *Wide Sargasso Sea* is a Caribbean novel as a point of departure for examining the characters of Antoinette, and of Tia, Josephine, and Amelie, in terms of the conflict between the dispossessed white colonial society and the newly enfranchised blacks. Antoinette represents not only the Creole alienated from her native society, but also the West Indian who cannot find an identity in European society. Rochester, in addition to standing for "English frustration and hostility when confronted with the West Indies," is yet another of Rhys's dominant, "faceless" men who oppress women.

Mary Cantwell, "A Conversation with Jean Rhys, 'the best living English novelist.'" *Mademoiselle*, 79 (October 1974), 170-171, 206, 208, 210, 213.

A sympathetic reader of the Rhys novels who identified herself with their heroines, the writer interviewed Rhys in Devon in the summer 1974 and here reports the conversation in detail. The resulting essay gives one of the most balanced pictures of the novelist in her old age and provides the most unequivocal evidence that the Rhys women are to be identified with their creator--with certain, specified differences. In addition to providing important biographical facts and identifications of the characters in the novels, the essay also contains Rhys's statements about her literary and aesthetic intentions in her writing.

Gini Stevens, "Every Day is a New Day." *Radio Times* [BBC], 23-29 November 1974.

(Not seen)

Robert Leiter. *New Republic*, 171 (7 December 1974), 22-24.

An essay occasioned by the publication of *Tigers Are Better-Looking* but treating all of Rhys's work: see above, A7c: Reviews.

Howard Moss, "Books. Going to Pieces." *New Yorker*, 50 (16
December 1974), 161-162, 165-166.

Writing on the occasion of the publication of *Tigers Are
Better-Looking*, Moss introduces Rhys and her work to readers of the *New Yorker* in this complex and sophisticated
essay. He stresses the individuality of the Rhys women as
shown by their antagonism toward "the bourgeoisie and the
authorities" and analyzes the love-hate relationships between characters in the novels. From their behavior he de-
duces the ethos behind Rhys's attitudes to and understanding of life, seeing that "the connection between love and
money may be Miss Rhys's most original contribution to the
history of emotional exploitation." She has shown over and
over how a woman is "smashed" by the world, even though her
characters are usually victims of their own personalities.
In telling these tales Rhys has "carefully measured out ...
every centimetre of torture ... with an exactness and a
lack of sentimentality all the more painful for being tem-
peramentally unavoidable." *Good Morning, Midnight* is the
"culmination" of the Rhys story, although *Voyage in the
Dark* is the "most harrowing." In *Wide Sargasso Sea* Rhys
brings together the two landscapes of the West Indies and
of England, although there is a bookish quality to the novel which limits its achievement. Too, while it is "the
most dramatic of the novels," it shows a heroine who actually goes mad and who "commits a final demonic act--the burn-
ing of Thornfield Hall;" such action makes the novel different from "the genuine Rhys article." Comparisons of Rhys
to other writers are not very helpful, for her novels have
a timeless quality; they seem "to have written themselves,
and, after reading them, one flinches at truth after truth."

                                  1975

Hanne Nielsen and Flemming Brahms, "Retrieval of a Monster:
Jean Rhys's *Wide Sargasso Sea*" in *Enigma of Values*, edited
by Anna Rutherford and Kirsten Holst Petersen. Aarhus: Dan-
geroo Press, 1975. Pp. 139-162.

(Not seen)

"Jean Rhys" in *World Authors, 1950-1970*, edited by John Wake-
man. New York: H.W. Wilson Co., 1975. Pp. 1206-1207.

A generally accurate account of Rhys's life and writings

with many quotations from contemporary reviews, a list of the primary titles, and a short secondary bibliography.

Ralph Tyler, "Luckless Heroines, Swinish Men." *Atlantic*, 235 (January 1975), 81-84.

An essay occasioned by the publication of *Tigers Are Better-Looking*: see above, A7c: Reviews.

Jonathan Raban, "Opinion: Living with Loose Ends. *New Review*, 2, No. 19 (October 1975), 51-56.

Within the context of an essay on the family as a theme in literature Raban comments briefly on *After Leaving Mr Mackenzie* and *Voyage in the Dark*, pointing out that the Rhys heroines are exiles from "the family, that safe, conclusive institution.... They learn to regard the texture of their own lives as being temporary and freakish; the result of an accidental warp in the social order."

1976

Judith Thurman, "The Mistress and the Mask: Jean Rhys's Fiction." *MS*, 4 (January 1976), 50-52, 91.

This "appreciation" of Rhys's life and writings is based on previously published material and is written from the point of view of the feminist. Thus Thurman finds the "fragility" of the Rhys woman to be "a carefully observed symptom of advanced loneliness in modern woman, the woman on her own, the woman who has renounced 'respectability'-- the protection of a father or husband--and who is, in society's eyes, without a place, illegitimate and therefore fair game for the presumptions of men and the vindictive- ness of other women." The writer suggests that the beauty of these women prevents their being accepted as individuals: they are trapped within a disguise. The essay gives sum- maries of *Quartet, After Leaving Mr Mackenzie,* and *Good Morning, Midnight;* and *Wide Sargasso Sea* is dismissed as "a regression" after the accomplishments of *Good Morning, Midnight.*

Anthony E. Luengo, "*Wide Sargasso Sea* and the Gothic Mode." *World Literature Written in English*, 15 (April 1976), 229-245.

Luengo argues that *Wide Sargasso Sea* can best be understood by seeing it within "the Gothic mode of fiction." He
examines the novel and the well-known Gothic predecessors,
both English and American, in terms of such topics as the
use of landscape description, of ruins, of moonlight, of
the supernatural machinery, and of the stereotyped character (the villain and the innocent). While the specific
arguments are straightforward and convincing, the essay as
a whole is an example of seeing the trees and ignoring the
forest.

Ned Thomas, "Meeting Jean Rhys." *Planet* (Llangeitho, Tregaron,
Wales), No. 33 (August 1976), pp. 29-31.

(Not seen)

Angela Williams, "The Flamboyant Tree: The World of the Jean
Rhys Heroine." *Planet* (Llangeitho, Tregaron, Wales), No. 33
(August 1976), pp. 35-41.

(Not seen)

Dennis Porter, "Of Heroines and Victims: Jean Rhys and *Jane
Eyre.*" *Massachusetts Review*, 17 (Autumn 1976), 540-552.

While the heroines of the first four novels are the alienated woman in a modern setting who never reaches the antic-
ipated complete breakdown, in *Wide Sargasso Sea* Rhys deals
with a heroine who is "the most hideous example of the power exercised by men over women" and who reaches the ultim-
ate breakdown. *Wide Sargasso Sea* thus gives "fresh significance" to the earlier works and provides "a provocatively
new critical reading" of *Jane Eyre*. The continuity between
the novels is that the women are brought to their condition
by men, but in *Wide Sargasso Sea* Rhys brings in "the realities of colonial society," considering "the relations between the sexes in the age of colonialism, of the multiple
hidden connections among class, race, and sex." Rhys's
success is due to her use of different types of language
for the different classes of characters, including a lyric-
ism for Antoinette and Rochester that she had not used before and a "Creole speech" for the non-English characters.
These new practices allow the novelist to show in language
the human problems fostered by a colonial system that had
institutionalized not only slavery but "a complicated caste

system," particularly the awareness of difference and isolation. Rochester provides "a paradigm of male cruelty
towards women" and an example of how colonialism and male
sexuality are inextricably linked: his cruelty to Antoinette is largely based on his fear of her inferior racial
position. Turning back to *Jane Eyre* Porter suggests that
Rhys's novel brings "to consciousness some of the hidden
implications of *Jane Eyre*, which it both develops and chal-
lenges." Among these are Brontë's awareness that Rochester's wealth and position have been built upon human suffering, and hence he must be stripped of "his baronial
dwelling, the symbol of a power rooted in sex and class
arrogance." In addition, while Brontë sees redemption possible for Rochester, Rhys does not; Jane Eyre is also a
stronger character with a more accurate understanding of
male sexuality than Antoinette Cosway possesses. Both the
fire and the ensuing blindness are direct references to
Rochester's sexuality being chastised, and the death of
Bertha in the fire is a sacrifice of one woman to allow the
happiness of another. Although *Wide Sargasso Sea* appears
to be at some distance from Rhys's earlier works, it actually supplies both the beginning and the end of the itinerary
of the Rhys heroine. Like the women of nineteenth-century
colonial society, the twentieth-century heroines "carry
within them a sense of hopelessness and of worthlessness
that is socio-economic, racial and even political before it
is existential." They are "victims" and therefore "sisters
of ... Antoinette Cosway...."

Barry Pree, "Meet ... Sargasso Lady." *The Observer Magazine*
[color supplement of the *Observer*, London], 3 October 1976,
pp. 8-9.

As part of the pre-publication advertisement for *Sleep It
Off Lady* Pree interviewed Rhys in Devon; he quotes her opinions on returning to Dominica, on her life in Paris, and on
Hemingway; and he gives a not altogether accurate account
of her life and literary career.

1977

Eunice de Souza, "Four Expatriate Writers." *Journal of the
School of Languages* (Jawaharlal Nehru University), 4, No. 2
(Winter 1976-1977), 54-60.

Within the context of an essay in which Third World writers

are criticized for assuming European rather than native
standards and values (Dom Moraes is unfavorably contrasted
by Farrukh Dhondy), the author puts Rhys forward as a writer who "though English herself ... has not bent backwards
to find favour with the English establishment by caricatur-
ing the 'natives.' ... Characters black, white, or coloured
are recognizable human beings." Rhys's practice is contrasted by that of Ruth Prawer Jhabvala in her novels.

Michael Thorpe, "'The Other Side': Wide Sargasso Sea and Jane
Eyre." Ariel, 8, No. 3 (July 1977), 99-110.

The critic, who considers Wide Sargasso Sea to be Rhys's
"most balanced novel in its even-handed treatment of the
sexes," examines the textual and thematic links between it
and Jane Eyre on the assumption that readers of both novels
are enriched by such comparisons. He notes as well that
"the plight of Antoinette" is prefigured in the passage in
Good Morning, Midnight in which Serge tells the story of
the mulatto woman and her "very Angliche" lover in London.
Thorpe's scholarly treatment of the two texts allows important insights into Rhys's and Brontë's characters; and the
critic sees that Rochester's "relationship with Antoinette
has been developed into a many-sided and complete study of
tragic incompatibilities retrieved from Charlotte Brontë's
workshop floor."

Louis James, "Sun Fire--Painted Fire: Jean Rhys as a Caribbean
Novelist." Ariel, 8, No. 3 (July 1977), 111-127.

James surveys the critical literature which treats Rhys as
a Caribbean author, provides biographical details about her
life in Dominica and points to her use of Caribbean material
in certain stories and novels. The larger part of the essay
concerns Voyage in the Dark and Anna Morgan's memories of
her childhood, and James treats both the content and the attitudes as taken from the author's Caribbean heritage. He
examines Wide Sargasso Sea in less detail but provides important historical details in order to show "the imaginative
interfusion of the Caribbean context with the personal
themes which are the content of Jean Rhys's books." This
essay is reprinted in James's Jean Rhys; see above, F.2:
1978.

Nancy Pell, "Resistance, Rebellion, and Marriage: The Economics of *Jane Eyre*. *Nineteenth-Century Fiction*, 31 (1977), 397-420.

A long essay on *Jane Eyre* with one reference to *Wide Sargasso Sea* and to Rhys's perception of Brontë's novel (p. 411).

"Sir Douglas Allen and Equal Opportunities Chairman among five Life Peers in New Years Honours. Mr. Jack Jones and Dr. Leavis become Companions of Honour." *Times*, No. 60, 199 (31 December 1977), p. 1.

"Those created CBE include ... Miss Jean Rhys, the writer."

"New Years Honours. List of Awards in Full." *Times*, No. 60,199 (31 December 1977), p. 10.

Rhys--identified as "Miss Jean Rhys (Mrs. E. G. Hamer), writer"--is listed among those receiving the CBE [Companion of the British Empire].

1978

Eunice de Souza, "The Blinds Drawn and the Air Conditioner On: The Novels of Ruth Prawer Jhabvala." *World Literature Written in English*, 17 (April 1978), 219-224.

The critic refers in passing to *Wide Sargasso Sea* (p. 223).

Elaine Campbell, "A Report from Dominica, BWI." *World Literature Written in English*, 17 (April 1978), 305-316.

Campbell studies the Caribbean elements in the novels of Phyllis Shand Allfrey and Jean Rhys, pointing to the similarities which exist "in spite of the great time difference in the periods represented in" *Wide Sargasso Sea* and *The Orchid House*.

Helen Tiffin, "Mirror and Mask: Colonial Motifs in the Novels of Jean Rhys." *World Literature Written in English*, 17 (April 1978), 328-341.

Tiffin examines the Jean Rhys heroine as she appears in
the novels as exemplifying psychological attitudes which
derive from the colonial awareness of master-slave relationships. The women almost always display a "slave" men-
tality toward their (invariably) English masters. "The
parallel between destructive male/female relationships and
between imperial nation and colonial underdog is obvious."

Clara Thomas, "Mr. Rochester's First Marriage: *Wide Sargasso
Sea* by Jean Rhys." *World Literature Written in English*, 17
(April 1978), 342-357.

An appreciation of the novel structured around a paraphrase
of its dramatic action and with detailed comments on the
characters.

Thomas F. Staley, "The Emergence of a Form: Style and Consciousness in Jean Rhys's *Quartet*." *Twentieth Century Literature*, 24 (Summer 1978), 202-224.

The critic studies *Quartet* as it reveals Rhys's "own self-
discovery as a writer" and the novelist's "distinctive
style." He considers the novel "a product of the modernist movement--its sparse style, the author's gift for un-
derstatement and irony, the careful rendering of the heroine's preoccupations in a hostile, alienating urban envir-
onment." Yet Rhys was not concerned with "the technical
innovations of modernism" for "her art developed out of an
intensely private world." *Quartet* marks "the discovery and
initial development of that original voice and tone" of the
Rhys fiction of the 1930s, and Staley proceeds to give a
detailed paraphrase with quotations from the novel. He
concludes: "The economy of language and directness of style
can lead us to underestimate the range, depth, and quality
of feeling in her work, but her narrative focus and technique relieve the intense subjectivity in *Quartet* and offer
a dramatic, human portrait of the female consciousness in
the modern world." This essay is reprinted in Staley's
Jean Rhys; see above, F.2: 1979.

Theodore Colson, "The Theme of Home in the Fiction of Canada,
the United States, and the West Indies." *English Studies in
Canada*, 4 (Fall 1978), 351-361.

There are references in passing to Rhys (pp. 353 and 359)

within this descriptively titled, wide-ranging essay.

Todd K. Bender, "Jean Rhys and the Genius of Impressionism."
Studies in the Literary Imagination, 11, No. 2 ("The Female
Novelist in Twentieth-Century Britain") (Fall 1978), 43-53.

Bender gives the outlines of the Rhys-Ford relationship
and a summary of *Wide Sargasso Sea* before arguing that the
novel originates in "the theory of literary impressionism
as practiced by Ford and Conrad in their best work." He
uses Ford's *Joseph Conrad* (1924) as a source for the standards of such fiction--the use of "an 'affair' as plot, limited 'unreliable' narration, and 'psychological' structures
of time and space, so as to require a constructive activity
from each reader"--and demonstrates that *Wide Sargasso Sea*
is written according to this "formula." The situation of
the alien woman occurs in all of Rhys's fiction, for the
novelist "tells the same tale over and over, a powerful feminist plea. All of her stories are about the indignity, the
personal damage, which flows from a woman's financial and
emotional dependence on men in an alien world." Such concerns are present in *The Left Bank* in which Rhys uses Brown-
ing's "formula" of creating "a tension between the reader's
sympathy and his judgment of a character." This practice
helps to create "split figures" who in turn force the reader to question normative behavior patterns as they are
used in the novels.

Frank Baldanza, "Jean Rhys on Insult and Injury." *Studies in
the Literary Imagination*, 11, No. 2 ("The Female Novelist in
Twentieth-Century Britain") (Fall 1978), 55-65.

Following in the footsteps of earlier critics, Baldanza
sketches the character of the Rhys heroine as she appears
in the novels and stories (he omits *Wide Sargasso Sea*),
stressing the obvious themes.

Minda Rae Amiran, "What Women's Literature?" *College English*,
39 (1978), 653-661.

Arguing that "women's literature' is not a valid literary
category, the author quotes two paragraphs from *After Leaving Mr Mackenzie* and comments upon them (pp. 655-656).

Pamela Law, "*Letty Fox, Her Luck.*" *Southerly*, 38 (December
1978), 448-453.

A review-article on Christina Stead's novel (and on *Miss Herbert*) with a comparison in passing to Rhys on pp. 451-452.

1979

Cheryl M. L. Dash, "Jean Rhys" in *West Indian Literature*, edited by Bruce King. London: Macmillan; Hamden, Conn.: Archon Books, 1979, pp. 196-209.

In her pre-1966 novels Rhys makes "an overwhelming and cohesive statement on the situation of women in regard to society in general and men in particular." In *Wide Sargasso Sea* she uses all the themes of her previous work while making "a wider and more comprehensive statement on the intricacy of human relationships that does not focus on the plight of the woman alone." Thus the entrance to *Wide Sargasso Sea* is through the themes of the earlier novels--the vulnerable woman who is a victim; the withdrawn, alienated woman who lives solely in the present moment; the woman whose life would be the same no matter where she is. But in *Wide Sargasso Sea* both physical setting and historical events are integral parts of the novel. Dash outlines the historical events which determined the status of the white creoles in Dominica and convincingly demonstrates that Rhys accurately portrays both individuals--white creoles, English, and blacks--and their society at a certain historical moment. *Wide Sargasso Sea, Voyage in the Dark,* and certain stories in *Sleep It Off Lady* stand out in West Indian fiction as studies of the white, rather than the black, West Indian.

Other references to Rhys in this collection of essays are made by the editor (p. 6), by Rhonda Cobham ("The Background," pp. 11, 12), and by Anthony Boxill ("The Beginnings to 1929," pp. 42, 44).

Helen E. Nebeker, "Jean Rhys's *Quartet*: The Genesis of Myth." *International Journal of Women's Studies*, 2 (1979), 257-267.

(Not seen)

Elizabeth Abel, "Women and Schizophrenia: The Fiction of Jean Rhys." *Contemporary Literature*, 20 (Spring 1979), 155-177.

Dismissing previous critical studies as "unsympathetic" and "misguided," or "descriptive and biographical rather than analytical," Abel studies the Rhys heroines in terms of the psychological theories of R. D. Laing (as stated in *The Divided Self* [1960] and in *Sanity, Madness, and the Family* [1970] with A. Esterson), while making unacknowledged use of the information in the earlier critical studies. She selects from the symptoms of schizophrenia those which allow her to categorize the Rhys heroines as displaying the characteristics of "ambulatory schizophrenia" or "the schizoid (as opposed to the schizophrenic) state." Abel analyzes *Voyage in the Dark* as it reveals "the conflict between Anna's two halves and the gradual loss of her more authentic self." This reading makes Abel decide that "the tone is curiously flat and dry" and that *Voyage in the Dark* is "one of [Rhys's] least engaging novels." The critic continues with *Good Morning, Midnight,* paying particular attention to Sasha's use of various languages and evidently forgetting that Sasha's European life has forced her to use languages other than her native English. Both *Good Morning, Midnight* and *Wide Sargasso Sea* indicate to Abel a connection between the world of the schizoid and the world of the oppressed female. This essay is an interesting example of the selective use of a non-literary discipline as a critical tool: this practice brings Abel to the conclusion that within the novelist's "apparent determinism lie some subtle variations that a psychological framework can illuminate and clarify. Rhys's microscopic vision ... may be small, but her perceptions are deep, and her pessimism not as final as it seems to be.... Rhys's unremitting vision ... will illuminate us if we persevere."

A.C. Morrell, "The World of Jean Rhys's Short Stories." *World Literature Written in English,* 18 (April 1979), 235-244.

A close reading of "In a Café" (*The Left Bank*), "Goodbye Marcus, Goodbye Rose" and "I Used to Live Here Once" (*Sleep It Off Lady*), and "Till September Petronella" (*Tigers Are Better-Looking*) to show Rhys's "coherent world-view."

Herbert Mitgang, "Jean Rhys, British Novelist, Dies: Known for 'Wide Sargasso Sea.'" *New York Times,* 128 (17 May 1979), p. B12, cols. c and d.

In this notice of Rhys's death on Monday, 14 May 1979, Mit-

gang provides biographical details and comments that Rhys
was "widely admired by writers and critics, but ... was
not widely read by the general public."

[Obituary]. *Newsweek*, 93 (28 May 1979), 103.

A brief notice pointing out that the "early works ... are
enjoying new popularity."

"Obituary Notes." *Publishers Weekly*, 215 (28 May 1979), 26.

A notice of Rhys's death at the age of 84, accompanied by
a brief survey of her literary career.

"Milestones." *Time*, 113 (28 May 1979), 71.

A brief notice of Rhys's death.

P.A. Packer, "The Four Early Novels of Jean Rhys." *Durham
University Journal*, 71 (June 1979), 252-265.

A reading of the four novels.

Elaine Campbell, "From Dominica to Devonshire: A Memento of
Jean Rhys." *Kunapipi*, 1, No. 2 (1979), 6-22.

(Not seen)

Phyllis Shand Allfrey, "Jean Rhys: A Tribute." *Kunapipi*, 1,
No. 2 (1979), 23-25.

(Not seen)

Anne Sarraute, "Une Femme à la dérive." *La Quinzaine Lit-
téraire*, 296 (1979), 11-12.

(Not seen)

Louis James, "Obituary. Jean Rhys." *Journal of Commonwealth
Literature*, 14 (August 1979), 5-6.

In this graceful, appreciative account of the author's
life and work James stresses that the first five books
give "what were basically [Rhys's] own experiences," that
"in writing of Europe, she never lost her Caribbean sensibility," that *Wide Sargasso Sea*, in addition to "describing her grandmother's near-death facing a plantation riot
in nineteenth-century Dominica, ... reflects aspects of her
own childhood experience of racial division in the Caribbean," and that "Jean Rhys occupies an important place in
the Caribbean novel."

Elaine Campbell, "Jean Rhys, Alec Waugh, and the Imperial
Road." *Journal of Commonwealth Literature*, 14 (August 1979),
58-63.

Campbell prints a letter by Jean Rhys to Alec Waugh [see
above, C31, and F.3: 1949] and gives not-completely-accur-
ate information in this nevertheless important biographical essay.

John Thieme, "'Apparitions of Disaster': Brontëan Parallels
in *Wide Sargasso Sea* and *Guerillas*." *Journal of Commonwealth
Literature*, 14 (August 1979), 116-132.

Within the framework of a symposium on V.S.Naipaul's *Guerillas* Thieme examines "the remarkable similarity ... in
both form and theme"--particularly in the use of the Brontë sisters' novels--between Rhys's 1966 novel and Naipaul's
1976 novel. He summarizes the critical views of *Wide Sargasso Sea* which see it on a continuum from completely dependent upon, to completely independent of, *Jane Eyre*, and
proceeds to discuss its general relationship and indebted-
ness to both nineteenth and twentieth-century novels in
terms of form and of theme. The analysis of these elements
leads to the conclusion that *Wide Sargasso Sea* "is, then,
a very carefully constructed, detailed response to *Jane
Eyre* and nowhere more so than in its detailed reworking of
the earlier novel's most important patterns of organic imagery." The second half of the essay is given over to
Naipaul's *Guerillas*.

Shusha Guppy, "Novel Choice: Wide Sargasso Sea by Jean Rhys."
Observer Magazine, 4 November 1979, p. 130.

This appreciation of Rhys as a feminist writer includes a
summary of *Wide Sargasso Sea*--and a number of factual
errors.

David Plante, "Big Tree, Falling. A Conversation with Jean
Rhys." *Guardian*, 10 November 1979, p. 11.

A full-page extract from the memoir by Plante in the *Paris
Review* (see below). This article and that by Guppy (above)
were arranged as pre-publication advertisements for *Smile
Please*, published on 15 November 1979.

Elizabeth Vreeland, "Jean Rhys. The Art of Fiction LXIV."
Paris Review, No. 76 (1979), pp. 219-237.

A transcript of Vreeland's interview with Rhys in which the
novelist comments on many topics including her attitudes to
writing and to matters occasioned by her writing her autobiography. The interview includes a photograph of a manuscript page of *Smile Please* and concludes with a notice of
Rhys's death.

David Plante, "Jean Rhys: A Remembrance." *Paris Review*, No.
76 (1979), pp. 238-284. Reprinted in David Plante. *Difficult
Women: A Memoir of Three.* New York: Atheneum, 1983 (Not seen).

The American novelist David Plante (b. 1940), long resident
in England, became a friend of Rhys in her later years and
was closely associated with her as she compiled and wrote
Smile Please. This memoir presents a distressing picture
of Rhys in her last years, the physical problems of aging
exacerbated by her sense of frustration at not being able
to complete her autobiography and by her dependence upon
alcohol. While there is no reason to doubt the truth of
this account of the novelist's last years, Plante has been
criticized for publishing details which a less sensation-
seeking generation would have passed over. Among his critics is Gail Pool, "Jean Rhys: Life's Unfinished Form,"
Chicago Review, 32, No. 4 (Spring 1981), 73, who declares
that the reminiscence "is excessive, tasteless, and finally pointless...." Plante "reveals but this one useful
fact: that Rhys was in no shape to write anything, let a-
lone give form to the material that had been her life."
See above, A10b: Reviews, 1981, Pool; and the review of

Difficult Women in *Publishers Weekly*, 19 November 1982, p. 68.

1980

Marie-José Codaccioni, "L'Erreur chez Jean Rhys" in *L'Erreur dans la littérature et la pensée anglaises.* Actes du Centre Aixois de Recherches Anglaises. Aix-en-Provence: University of Provence, 1980. Pp. 127-141.

(Not seen)

Wilson Harris, "Carnival of Psyche: Jean Rhys's *Wide Sargasso Sea.*" *Kunapipi*, 2, No. 2 (1980), 142-150.

(Not seen)

Elaine Campbell, "Apropos of Jean Rhys." *Kunapipi*, 2, No. 2 (1980), 152-157.

(Not seen)

Alan Shelston, "Recent Studies in Nineteenth-Century Fiction." *Critical Quarterly*, 22 (Summer 1980), 47-51.

The critic refers in passing to *Wide Sargasso Sea* on p. 49.

John Updike, "An Armful of Field Flowers." *New Yorker*, 56 (29 December 1980), 69-72.

While reviewing Colette's *Letters* Updike refers to Rhys on p. 72.

1981

Margaret Crosland, *Beyond the Lighthouse: English Women Novelists in the Twentieth Century.* New York and London: Taplinger, 1981. Pp. 260.

Within the context of a feminist survey of the modern English women novelists, the author gives a short introduction,

not without factual errors, to the life and writings of
Rhys (pp. 172-177). She names only *The Left Bank, Quartet,
Good Morning, Midnight,* and *Wide Sargasso Sea* as she discusses, always in general terms, the forces that shape the
lives of the Rhys women.

Andrew Gurr, *Writers in Exile: The Creative Use of Home in
Modern Literature.* Atlantic Highlands, N.J.: Humanities Press;
Brighton: Harvester Press (Harvester Studies in Contemporary
Literature and Culture, No. 4), 1981. Pp. 160.

(Not seen)

Irene Thompson, "The Left Bank Apéritifs of Jean Rhys and
Ernest Hemingway." *Georgia Review,* 35, No. 1 (Spring 1981),
94-106.

Writing from the point-of-view of the militant feminist
critic, Thompson examines the careers of Hemingway and Rhys
in order to show that Rhys's long silence and neglect were
caused by prejudiced attitudes to female writers. She
calls attention to the parallels in their lives, noting
their relationships to Ford Madox Ford, and she refers at
length to *The Sun Also Rises* and *Good Morning, Midnight,*
contrasting the attitudes of Jake Barnes and Sasha Jansen.
The essay makes use of well-known facts about Rhys and is
written more to express a political-feminist point-of-view
than to comment on Jean Rhys.

[Letter]. *New Statesman,* 101 (29 May 1981), 16.

An announcement that Francis Wyndham and Diana Melly will
edit the collected letters of Rhys and a request for the
loan of Rhys's letters.

Harriet Blodgett, "Enduring Ties: Daughters and Mothers in
Contemporary English Fiction by Women." *South Atlantic
Quarterly,* 80 (Autumn 1981), 441-453.

Within the context of an essay on the mother-daughter theme,
Blodgett gives three psychologically oriented paragraphs to
Wide Sargasso Sea (pp. 443-444), finally deciding that
"Rhys resents not only men's victimization of women, but

the psychic injuries mother-women, under male influence,
inflict on children of their own sex."

Louis Simpson, "Realists." *Hudson Review*, 34 (Winter 1981),
511-522.

The critic makes various observations on realism within
the context of an impressionistic essay structured upon his
reading of Trollope, Rhys, Balzac, and Galdós. He deals
with Rhys on pp. 513-515, finding that the "motif" of her
work is "man's inhumanity to man."

Henrik Mossin, "The Existentialist Dimension in the Novels of
Jean Rhys." *Kunapipi*, 3, No. 1 (1981), 143-150.

(Not seen)

Ronnie Scharfman, "Mirroring and Mothering in Simone Schwarz-
Bart's *Pluie et vent sur Télumée Miracle* and Jean Rhys's *Wide
Sargasso Sea*. *Yale French Studies*, No. 62 (1981), 88-106.'

(Not seen)

Joe Jackson and Kim Connell, "Gigolos: The Last of the Courtly
Lovers." *Journal of Popular Culture*, 15, No. 2 (Fall 1981),
130-141.

The "Appendix. Bibliography of Gigolo Prose and English-
Lanugage Translations" includes "Le [*sic*] Grosse Fifi" in
Tigers Are Better-Looking.

1982

Linda Bamber, "Jean Rhys." *Partisan Review*, 49 (1982), 92-100.

Distinguished by its factual errors, this essay presents
Bamber's hostile view of Rhys whose "role" as "Establishment Victim" annoys the critic. She accepts without argument the idea that there is a single, autobiographical
Rhys "heroine" who "is a natural victim, not a victim of
sexual politics or class oppression," and she is annoyed
by "the continuous retreat that is the form and content of

Rhys's work: and by the "helplessness" that becomes "a
kind of 'weapon' in her fiction just as it was in her
life." Bamber also dislikes the fact that "Rhys seems to
equate her femininity with her pathos, the one reinforcing
the other." In the last part of the essay Bamber deals
specifically with *Smile Please*, disapprovingly noting that
the book "treats Rhys as a classic author. There is something incongruous between the featherweight text and the
solemn superstructure that surrounds it." Bamber is particularly offended by Rhys's treatment of race relations
in Dominica; and here and elsewhere the writer reveals her
ignorance of Rhys and her inability to bridge the historical and cultural gap between herself and her subject.

                             Addenda

INDEX